Praise for *The Business of Happiness*

———

"A happy team can be a winning team—that's why you see me with such a wide smile on my face. I love my teammates and our fans and our coaching staff. Our owners believe in creating a place where we all care about each other. It is all about following Ted's belief in happiness and success. I buy into it completely, and it really works; I believe Ted's book can help you become MVP in your life, at work, and at home."

—**Alex Ovechkin,** *two-time NHL Most Valuable Player—Washington Capitals*

"Ted Leonsis is one of the most creative minds in business. For more than twenty-five years he has been shaping the digital world that is now such an important part of our lives. In *The Business of Happiness*, he offers a personal guide to navigating the traditional boundaries between work and life. His insights on business, career planning, and how to succeed in today's 24/7 environment reflect the wisdom of a renaissance man whose interests range far beyond the realm of technology or commerce."

—**Ken Chenault,** *CEO and Chairman, American Express Company*

"Ted's successful path to happiness in life, from the mean streets of Brooklyn, NY, to AOL executive to philanthropist, moved him to share his story and his way. Do yourself a favor: read it and be inspired."

—**Mitch Kapor,** *founder of Lotus Development Corporation and the Mozilla Foundation, which created the Firefox browser*

"This wonderful book is as bouncy, ebullient, energetic, and likeable as its author. It contains much sage advice, dozens of great stories, and guest appearances by everyone from Allen Ginsberg to Alex

Ovechkin. You can decide whether it contains the secret of happiness; it definitely holds several hours' very pleasant reading."

—Don Graham, *CEO and Chairman of the board, The Washington Post Company*

"With today's economic downturn, this inspiring and essential read couldn't have come at a better moment. This is an important American business visionary's take on an age-old question: How can we achieve true happiness? Ted Leonsis has done a remarkable job."

—David M. Smick, *author of the international bestseller* The World Is Curved

"If happiness is your goal, Ted Leonsis puts the stick in your hand, gives you the puck and tells you how and where to shoot!"

-Gary Bettman, *NHL Commissioner*

"Ted Leonsis is absolutely correct that money can't buy you happiness, but it can buy you Ted's book, which will bring you happiness—and success."

—Lebron James, *Cleveland Cavaliers*

"This book makes so clear why Ted Leonsis has succeeded at everything he has touched—a first-class mind and a first-class appreciation of life's true values. That is a rare combination."

—David Rubenstein, *co-founder and Managing Director, The Carlyle Group*

"Ted Leonsis should be an easy guy to hate: wonderful family, fabulously and repeatedly successful in business. But people in Washington root for Ted, not resent him, because he seems to be genuinely happy. Read this book. You may not end up with his life. But there's a good chance you'll get something even more valuable—— his outlook on life."

—Chris Wallace, *FOX News*

"Buying Ted Leonsis's company was one of my best moves. Buying Ted's book could be one of yours."

    –Steve Case, *co-founder of America Online, Chairman and CEO, Revolution*

"*The Business of Happiness* is a primer for finding success, real success, in life. Ted Leonsis, the consummate gentleman businessman, has walked the road to spiritual fulfillment. His words are valuable and they ring true."

    –George Pelecanos, *novelist and screenwriter*

"Being successful enough in business to own a sports team isn't easy, and being successful in business, sports, and most of all, this business of happiness is even harder. Ted Leonsis has pulled it off, and written a really terrific book that tells the tale. Anyone who aspires to being both successful and happy would do well to read *The Business of Happiness*."'

    –David Stern, *Commissioner of the National Basketball Association*

"Few successful businesspeople have truly embraced the notion that you can and SHOULD be happy pursuing your financial and business goals. Ted Leonsis not only embraces the notion, he lives by it. Ted's list of 101 things to do is not only legendary among entrepreneurs around the world, it has served as a source of motivation for me many, many times. *The Business of Happiness* reminds all of us that you can enjoy every minute of every day as you work hard to achieve your goals."

    –Mark Cuban, *Internet pioneer and owner of the Dallas Mavericks*

"Ted Leonsis has graced us with the gift of his determined journey to find happiness. In *The Business of Happiness*, Ted gives us a remarkable roadmap toward what for so many people is desperately elusive, and that is achieving a truly fulfilled and happy life. As a proven entrepreneur with a zest for living, Ted Leonsis reveals the 6 tenets of happiness that have emerged from his thought-provoking experience in pursuing a life that truly integrates business, passion, faith, and purpose. Ted speaks to our hearts as he gives wise instruction on how to attain a 'life without regret,' a life that is imbued with the secret sauce of happiness, an amazing elixir with the power of providing financial success as well as deep satisfaction for the human spirit."

—John S. Hendricks, *Founder and Chairman, Discovery Communications, Inc.*

"Ted and I shared a part of our journey to self-actualization together as students at Georgetown University—under the wise tutelage of Father Joseph Durkin, S.J. He was a wise man and emphasized to us living a life in balance where head, heart, body, and soul needed to be nourished. He gave us both permission to seek happiness in our lives and careers. Applying this Jesuit ideal to business and to public service is at the heart of this book. We have been given permission to be happy—and as Ted shows, the happier the company, the more successful it can become."

—Maria Shriver, *author, journalist, First Lady of California*

"In *The Business of Happiness*, Ted shares insights about designing a 'business plan' for personal growth and success. Ted's life story by itself would be a compelling read. But by sharing these valuable insights, he has drawn a road map for readers who share his commitment to personal development."

—Senator Mark Warner, *(D-VA)*

"Ted Leonsis is the happiest person I know and one of our most successful entrepreneurs and business leaders. He is a founding father of the information age. Follow his personal journey; learn from his life lessons and deepen your own pursuit of happiness."

—Jack DeGioia, *President, Georgetown University*

The Business of
Happiness

The Business of
Happiness

---

6 SECRETS TO EXTRAORDINARY
SUCCESS IN WORK AND LIFE

TED LEONSIS
with JOHN BUCKLEY

Since 1947
REGNERY
PUBLISHING, INC.
An Eagle Publishing Company • Washington, DC

Cataloging-in-Publication data on file with the Library of Congress

ISBN 978-1-59698-114-0

Published in the United States by
Regnery Publishing, Inc.
One Massachusetts Avenue, NW
Washington, DC 20001

www.regnery.com

Manufactured in the United States of America

10 9 8 7 6 5 4 3 2 1

Books are available in quantity for promotional or premium use. Write to Director of Special Sales, Regnery Publishing, Inc., One Massachusetts Avenue NW, Washington, DC 20001, for information on discounts and terms or call (202) 216-0600.

Distributed to the trade by:
Perseus Distribution
387 Park Avenue South
New York, NY 10016

To Lynn, Zach, and Elle, and in memory of
Father Joseph Durkin, S.J., and Mr. Abe Pollin

Contents

PART TWO: YOUR JOURNEY TO HAPPINESS

Introduction

I t is my hope that your journey to happiness has begun by reading this first sentence.

My journey to happiness began by drawing up a list.

It was 1984. I was twenty-eight years old and had recently sold for $60 million an early New Media company that I'd built. And then in fulfillment of the randomness of life, I got on the wrong plane. A routine flight from Melbourne, Florida, to Atlanta, Georgia, ended with an emergency landing. No one was hurt, but in the thirty-five minutes that we spent unsure of whether the landing gear was going to work, circling the airport, burning off fuel, and learning how to brace for a crash-landing, I had to face up to something I really didn't like: if that plane crashed, I wouldn't die happy. It was a reckoning, a wake-up call. I had all the toys money could buy. At a ridiculously young age I had achieved what we all believe is the American Dream, and for a poor kid from Brooklyn, New York, it had all seemed to come easy. But I wasn't happy.

It was the most important discovery of my life. The moment I got off that plane, with shaking knees and a queasy stomach, I resolved to pursue happiness and live my life without regret. I was given the world's all-time great Mulligan, the gift of a second chance to live my life properly. I determined that when my time to die really did arrive, I would die happy.

The only problem was, like many people, I didn't really know how to become happy. I'd figured out how to make money and grow a business by that time in my life. I'd figured out that the future lay in computers and what could be done with them, and I was already playing a role among that first generation of entrepreneurs who shaped the personal computing industry. But when it came to figuring out something so basic—so human—as knowing what steps one takes first on the journey to happiness, I was amazingly clueless.

So I treated my pursuit of happiness as if it were a business plan. I drew up a list of 101 things I wanted to achieve before I died. At the time, I thought that ticking items off my list would make me happy, and that if only I were diligent in working my way through my list, when my time to die really did come, I would have achieved the big goal: to be happy. More than twenty-five years later, with many of the items I initially put down on my list having long since been checked off, I now understand that making the list was just my first step on a long journey.

For more than twenty-five years, I've been on a quest, trying to determine what makes people happy, so that I can be happy. I'm now far enough along on my quest that I can properly share what I've learned. In the last twenty years, I've given more than 1000 speeches, and each speech has included a section on happiness. I have been encouraged to put this thinking into a book and, well, here it is.

This is a book about personal happiness, written by someone who's been blessed to achieve it. As you will see, the very act of writing this book is in furtherance of my goal of being a happy and fulfilled human being.

The strangest thing that has happened is that by systematically attempting to achieve happiness, I have actually increased my prospects to be successful in business and life. It didn't start out that way; as a 28-year-old who'd made millions of dollars selling his first business, as far as I was concerned, I already had made it. But as I studied friends and acquaintances whom I believed to be happy—some of them people you've never heard of, some of them household names—it became clear to me that the people I knew who were actively pursuing the path to happiness also seemed to put themselves in a better position to achieve their goals. To be clear: I'm a businessman and a relatively happy guy, not a social scientist. So take this next sentence as a layman's attempt to explain in scientific language what he's learned along the way. From my observation, the connection between happiness and success doesn't merely correlate—they don't just come together in random order. I've found that actively pursuing happiness seems to be a *driver* of success.

That's why I call this book *The Business of Happiness.* I believe that happiness can be achieved by approaching it with the same degree of discipline and rigor that's needed to build a successful business. I'm also convinced that people who approach happiness in this manner increase the odds that they'll be successful. Money buys happiness? Not necessarily, as we shall see. Working toward happiness makes you more successful in achieving your business and career goals? Yes! I truly believe that.

Along the way, I've learned that there aren't only happy people; there are happy businesses and companies. Some of the same rules seem to apply to institutions as individuals. An enterprise that actively seeks to create happiness for the customers it serves, as well as its employees, partners, and yes, of course, its shareholders—a business that in its multidimensional ambitions for fulfillment has an outlook similar to many of the happy people I have known and studied—is more likely to be successful than one that doesn't care about the happiness it creates, or over-indexes entirely in favor of shareholders at the expense of everyone else. There is, I believe, a "double bottom line" that is made up of fiscal results and positive impact on people and society. I believe that by pursuing happiness, people and businesses alike increase the odds that they will be successful in achieving their broadest goals. This concept of the "double bottom line" is now the overriding pursuit of all my business interests.

I know that pursuing happiness probably isn't what is taught in business school. It's only exotic countries like Bhutan, a remote Buddhist kingdom nestled in the Himalayas, that measure output in terms of Gross National Happiness, as opposed to the Gross National Product. So I can understand that for some people, thinking about happy people and happy businesses is a stretch.

I can also understand how easy it might be at the outset to resist what I have to say. Yes, I'm a guy who at a young age built and sold a successful business, bought much of that business back, and ended up parlaying it even more profitably into a big stake in America Online, just as AOL was poised for liftoff. I helped build AOL into a global phenomenon. I also ended up becoming the principal owner of the NHL's Washington Capitals, among other sports properties. I've now made award-winning movies, and since leaving AOL, I've launched new businesses that are predicated on my "double bottom line" and seem to be on fast paths to success. In fact, just as this book was being wrapped up, Revolution Money, a business of which I am chairman, sold to American Express for $312 million. So perhaps you're thinking: "Yeah, sure, it's easy for Ted Leonsis to be happy; he made a bundle off AOL, and now he makes movies and owns sports teams; how could he not be happy?"

But as you read on, remember: I was already wealthy and successful as a young man, but I wasn't happy. I'm so much happier—and I believe I'm more successful—now than I was then. Money didn't make me happy. I believe with all my heart that my pursuit of happiness has made me a better businessman than I would have been otherwise. And if you follow the tenets outlined in this book, you too can increase the probability that you will achieve both happiness and success.

===

Becoming a happy and successful person was not foreordained. There was nothing inevitable about it. It was a long learning process; a process of discovery.

I became happy in the same way I became successful in business: by developing a plan based on information gleaned from books, research, personal observation, listening to consumers, and learning from my mistakes. I became happy by paying attention on a continual basis to how I was tracking against my plan. Early on in my business career, I would impress upon colleagues the importance of continually monitoring whether we were on the right course. A good day leads to a good week, which becomes a good month, then a good quarter. Four good quarters make for a good fiscal year. Multiple good fiscal years make for a great company that has earned trust and value and . . . you get the point. Well, I believe the same principles are true in approaching happiness. Getting on, and staying on the path to happiness, is a matter of understanding the items you need to focus on daily, weekly, and monthly to ensure that you're on track.

This book is a compilation of what I've learned about the business of happiness—how to live without regret and die with a smile on your face. I'll tell you the common beliefs and practices of happy people I know and how emulating their approach can offer the same rewards they have found: happiness and, not incidentally, success in whatever they're pursuing.

I am a family man and businessman, so consider this book the kind of advice I would offer a young man or woman who is entering the work force after college and wants to know the best approach to finding his or her way in life. The only way I really know how to do this is to tell something of my own story, about how a child of first-generation immigrants who grew up in Brooklyn, New York, and Lowell, Massachusetts, learned to connect the dots and become happy and successful. Maybe I can offer some inspiration and a way of looking at the world that, even if your life and circumstances are completely different from mine, can help you get on the right path. Maybe if I tell you about mistakes I made along the way, you won't have to make the same ones. Maybe if I explain to you how I faced a reckoning and learned from it, you can learn the same lessons without suffering the trauma I did.

So *The Business of Happiness* flows in two parts. The first half concerns my journey to happiness, and is meant to explain how I've come to the beliefs I hold. The second part is about your journey to happiness, and offers prescriptions based on the things I've learned along the way.

I've read enough books written by business leaders to take them with a grain of salt. So many of them seem to center on how tough-minded the businessman was when he faced his key decisions. (And it's usually businessmen, not women, unfortunately, who get in a position to write these books.) There's usually a palpable surge of testosterone in the prose. "You have to be tough, and make the tough decisions!" they all seem to say. But that's not what this book is about. Yes, I'm a businessman who's learned most of what he wants to impart to an audience from having lived in the world of business. And in order to tell you what I know, I have to tell you how I know it, so there's an autobiographical element to what I'm up to here. But my purpose in telling you about my life isn't to show off how smart I am, or what a good businessman I am, or how tough I am. My purpose in telling you about my life is to share the quest I've been on.

When I was a student at Georgetown University in the 1970s, I read Chaucer's *The Canterbury Tales*, and I still remember the Knight, who had high ideals and championed the concept of achieving happiness. As he listened to the pilgrims telling stories in an effort to get a free dinner at the roadside tavern at which they stopped, the tales he wished to hear were the ones that would "gladden all hearts." My quest for happiness is a little bit like that. As an optimist, I'm attracted to positive people. I also believe, as the Dalai Lama teaches, that our real role in life is to manage our personal journey to becoming a happy human being. From reading *The Canterbury Tales* to scores of books and studies on happiness and personal development, I've pursued the question: what makes us happy? I believe that by pursuing happiness as I have done—and as some of the most successful people I know have done—it will be clear that happiness is attainable by everyone, and so is success.

The Business of Happiness relies on three concepts.

First, you should treat the attainment of happiness in the same way an entrepreneur would approach building a business—with a vision, plan, goals, and a systematic approach and metrics to measure your progress. If you do this, you will increase the odds of becoming happy, and success will follow.

Second, enterprises—like companies, businesses, charities, sports teams, and political campaigns—that consider themselves in "the happiness business" will do better than those that pay no attention to the tenets outlined here.

Third, happiness is a driver of success, not the other way around.

People who are happy tend to have had some reckoning in their life that forces them to take stock of their situation and commit to attaining happiness. It is my observation that the happiest and most successful people live by six common practices, or tenets.

1. **Goal-Setting:** I believe that the path to happiness begins by identifying the life goals you have and actively pursuing them. It may seem basic, but it's surprising to me how the happy adults I know, like the happy teenagers I know, are the ones who pay attention to whether or not they are on track to achieve their goals. Many of the unhappy adults I know are the ones who aren't steering their way to a firm point on the horizon. Goal-setting is a *sine qua non* for business success, and as may already be clear, I believe individuals and enterprises achieve success in very similar ways. I made my list, and you should too.

2. **Communities of Interest:** The more communities in which you are an active participant, the more likely it is that you'll be happy. Following this principle can make you more successful, even as it offers personal happiness. When someone is referred to as "an excellent networker," they are usually con-

sidered to be successful. It's my experience that they are also likely to be happy, social people who enjoy the connection they have to others and get great benefits from their sociability.

3. **Personal Expression:** Having an outlet to express yourself is vital to your wellbeing. Moreover, finding a means to express and communicate your authentic, unique, and individual outlook increases the prospects that you will be successful. This is true, in my observation, whether your vehicle for personal expression exists within your work, or is completely separate from it. Whether you are an artist, a blogger, or just sing in the shower, happiness flows from having such an outlet.

4. **Gratitude:** I believe that a critical ingredient in finding happiness is being able to express gratitude. No matter what the circumstances one faces in life—whether life is good on a given day, or absolutely daunting—being able to show gratitude for what one has to be thankful for keeps us humble and grounds us. Being able to show gratitude is also one way of arresting the harmful domino effect of a bad day becoming a bad week, which becomes a bad month, and then a bad quarter. Being able to step back from any situation and connect with what you are grateful for—from a beautiful sunset to the love of your children—will center you and create the potential for happiness.

5. **Empathy Expressed by Giving Back:** Giving back to society out of what you have been given is an investment, the returns on which will enrich your emotional life and sense of wellbeing. Some of the happiest people I know are also the most

generous. Or maybe it would be better to say that there's a
clear reason why the most generous people I know are happy.

6. **Higher Calling:** Finally, it is my conviction that to be happy, all
of us must find a higher calling of some sort. No doubt, many
people find it in their religious faith, but as you will see,
regardless of whether religion or spirituality play a role in
your life, I believe happy people live their three score and ten
years on this planet as if they are on a mission. The happiest
among us are the ones who find that mission, whether it is
finding a cure for cancer or teaching children the practice of
virtue.

It took me a quarter of a century to connect these dots and understand how they amount to a formula for achieving happiness. It all
began with my facing a reckoning—a moment when I was forced to
look at my life, and I realized that on the course I was on, I would not
die happy. I wanted to change the outcome and committed to working
toward a happier ending.

On my list of 101 goals I wanted to achieve before I died, there was
no entry for writing a book that would help others become happy,
because I didn't fully appreciate then that finding an outlet for personal expression was an ingredient in success. I couldn't have anticipated that giving something back—in this case, sharing with others
the things that I've learned—would make me happy. I didn't know that
leaving to others more than I took in life would be an aspect of my
higher calling. I was clueless about nearly everything other than the
need to get started.

Welcome to *The Business of Happiness*. Your reading this book
makes me happy. I hope to repay the favor.

PART ONE:
My Journey to Happiness

Chapter One

Once in a Lifetime (How Did I Get Here?)

I'm a big fan of David Byrne, and I loved the Talking Heads. Of all the songs they recorded over a career that was way too short, my favorite has always been "Once in a Lifetime."

You know the song. It's the one made famous in the 1984 film *Stop Making Sense*, and the lyrics include these words:

> And you may find yourself in a beautiful house
> with a beautiful wife
> and you may ask yourself
> well, how did I get here?

How did I get here?

How I got from Bay Ridge in Brooklyn to living in multiple homes with my beautiful wife Lynn is a story in itself. While there's no question that Horatio Alger would smile on my story of how a young man, with a little "luck, pluck, and determination" became successful, it's not the journey from my immigrant household to owning sports teams and big houses that really matters. It's the journey from cluelessness on happiness to being able to share with you the things I've learned that matters most to me. There were pivotal moments in my life that prepared me for writing this book.

I was born in a happy era, during America's post-World War II economic surge. It was January 1956, the peak of the Baby Boom, and Ike was president. My mother and father were Greek Orthodox, and their childhood was emblematic of immigrant America. Their families, like millions of others, passed through Ellis Island as they fled Greece in search of a better life in America. It's said that the most optimistic act one can perform is to pack up and sail to a country thousands of miles away, seeking a new life. So all of us who were the sons and daughters of immigrants had a sense of limitless possibility imprinted on our personalities.

We also had, from our earliest memories, a sense of community, because most of us had large extended families, and for a host of reasons, immigrant communities tended to settle in certain neighborhoods. So let's establish at the outset that I was born into an optimistic household, amidst a broad, well-defined community, in an optimistic age.

My father, who never finished high school, was a waiter in a restaurant. My mother, who never went to college, was a secretary at the Topps Company, which made baseball cards. Later she went to work at G.H. Walker & Company as an administrative assistant to Jonathan Bush, the brother and uncle of two United States presidents, and the father of *Access Hollywood*'s Billy Bush. Isn't America a great place?

In their best year, my parents never earned more than $30,000 between them.

My mother met my father after the war. They got married and moved from Lowell, Massachusetts, where her family had settled, to New York City, in search of work. My father was forty-two when I was born, and my mother was thirty-two. I grew up in the Sunset Park area of Bay Ridge, Brooklyn, which was made famous in the movie *Saturday Night Fever*.

You remember John Travolta in his white suit? The movie was made in the late 1970s, not long after my family had moved from Brooklyn back to Lowell, and when I saw it, it brought back really awkward memories. It captured the neighborhood pretty well. If I'd stayed in Bay Ridge, would that have been me wearing a white suit at discos? (Probably not, because by the time that movie came out, I much preferred bands like the Talking Heads to the Bee Gees.)

From where I grew up, we saw the Twin Towers being built. Manhattan was a few miles away, but just like Tony Manero, the John Travolta character in *Saturday Night Fever,* I knew Manhattan was a different world. I grew up in what was a quintessential melting pot community—Italians, Puerto Ricans, Swedes, African-Americans. It was socially cohesive, but it was lower middle class at best.

My parents always told me that I was gifted. My mother insisted that someday I'd be president of the United States. On a certain level, I have no idea where this confidence came from, because if you looked at my parents and their families from a financial or class perspective, they were pretty close to the bottom rung of the ladder. However, the economy was producing enormous opportunities for people who were willing to try, which my parents certainly were. They created an environment that was very positive. While I personally had no sense I would be president of the United States—I had no idea where I'd end up in life—I was not really aware of limitations to my prospects. I knew that the bright lights of Manhattan signified a more glamorous world, but I really didn't know that we were poor, or that someone might characterize the apartment building I lived in as a tenement. The graffiti on the outside walls of my building should have been a clue, don't you think?

Though optimistic, my parents were also realists about the struggle to be successful in America. But they also believed that every generation would do better than the last one and that education was the key that unlocked doors. I consider my childhood happy, because our house was filled with love, and I felt supported and cared for. I realize now that my childhood was also, by the standards of today—or even maybe then—quite disciplined. I always had a book that I would read in my bedroom after doing homework. I didn't spend much time watching television, though I'd listen to Knicks or Rangers games on a transistor radio in my room. Those are very fond memories, and my love of sports started really early on.

Because I tested well and learned to read at an early age, I was put into an experimental program the New York City public schools ran called SP, for Special Progress. It was a pretty extraordinary program. We stayed with the same teacher, and mostly the same kids, from kindergarten through 7th grade, and at the end, if you did well, you skipped 8th grade. I never attended 8th grade, which, given the fact that I started school early, meant that by the time I went to high school, I was very young for my class.

My mother and father both worked, so when school let out, I'd go across the street to a big park where there were baseball fields and basketball courts, and I would literally play sports every day with the same group of kids that I'd been going to school with since kindergarten.

By the time I was twelve or thirteen, I was hanging out with kids who were older, and some of them started to get into trouble. Real trouble. Many of the kids I knew didn't have the same sense I had that getting into trouble might keep you from your dreams. The thought of someday going to college mattered to only a very few of us. Many of the kids I knew either believed college wasn't an option or just didn't take the prospect of going to college seriously, so it's fair to say there weren't a lot of kids I knew who were goal-oriented. Add to this that by the late 1960s, drug use had spread throughout our neighborhood, and you could see paths diverging pretty sharply, some kids heading toward college and maybe success outside the neighborhood, some kids not. I watched one of my closest friends and next-door neighbors go from being a child I had sleepovers with to becoming a teenage drug addict who ended up getting shot and killed while robbing a drugstore. The tension between my neighborhood being a good place and it being a dangerous place became clearer with each passing year. I could identify kids who I knew would make it, and kids who would not, and there wasn't a clear difference between them. I wanted to be one of the kids who made it; at this point in life, I didn't have a set of goals, but there was something innate in my personality, in addition to the environment my parents created, that made me strive for something other than a life sitting in the park watching the world go by. Sometimes I felt it was as simple as 100 more steps from the park bench, where guys would sit drinking wine and smoking pot, to the youth center where you could play basketball. You just had to walk a little farther.

I was thirteen years old when my childhood friend was shot trying to rob that store. But the most pivotal event in my early life wasn't his death. It was the decision my parents made to leave Brooklyn and move to Lowell, Massachusetts, where my mother's family lived. This decision was very traumatic. My mother went on a vacation to visit her family, and when she got back, she announced to my dad that we needed to move, and apparently the reason was me. "We have to save our son," she said.

It was very painful because I was just ripped out of school and the neighborhood and community I'd lived in my whole life. While I sort of understood, it still seemed like a radical solution to a problem I didn't fully appreciate.

It's not like my arrival at high school in Lowell was an automatic continuation of the positive environment I'd known in school since kindergarten. I went in the blink of an eye from having been part of an accelerated class that had all gone on to Brooklyn Tech after being together our entire lives, to a new school in a new town that frankly seemed pretty dull. I've stayed close to a lot of my Brooklyn friends, many of whom went on to real success. However, there's no question that a great many others went down an unfortunate path and ended up dying young. My mother's push to get me to a safer environment where we would be surrounded by family and friends was instinctive, and in hindsight, it's helped me to understand that family and friends, neighborhoods and communities, help drive your destiny. But at the time, I lost my mooring, my context, and because I was no longer in a special academic program, I lost my grip on the goals I had, even if I couldn't have articulated it that way at the time.

But it wasn't all bad. My extended family—cousins, aunts, uncles, and the Greek friends I met in church or school—became my world, especially since I arrived in Lowell as a teenager without other friends or connections. Having this community of interest was a very strong base for going out into the world. Throughout the Greek community in Lowell, people focused on working hard to make life better for the next generation, rather than on material things.

Even though I was an only child, I felt like part of a larger family, and it gave me strength. It also helped to have a social outlook, to genuinely enjoy other people, and to have a connection with them. But I shouldn't minimize how hard the transition was for me to go from Brooklyn to Lowell.

I was the new kid, and I didn't really fit in. For the first time in my life, I was pretty unhappy, and my unhappiness was reflected in my performance in school. In retrospect, it seems likely that by being less happy, I was less successful (not the other way around). There was no sense anymore that I was gifted. The expectations for me began to be defined down. I got a job at the local supermarket after school and suddenly it seemed that my horizon had narrowed from someday being president of the United States to being a manager of a supermarket. And then came the kicker.

My guidance counselor at Lowell High School, whose name was Beatrice Hoar, told my mom and dad, "Ted is really not college material. When he graduates, he should consider a vocational school."

This was not my wonderful life; how did I get there?

I remember thinking, how did I go from being "rescued" from Brooklyn to find myself working at a grocery store with the notion that I was no longer college material?

On a certain level it was clear. I'd gone from having gotten As and Bs my whole life to getting Cs, though I still got As in English and History, the classes I really liked. I had drifted. I didn't have goals. I was unhappy. Part of what I was going through, no doubt, was an understandable byproduct of being a teenager: brooding, living in my head, withdrawing. But I knew at some level that if I didn't fix things, it could very easily turn into a life trend. I knew the difference between sitting on a park bench drinking wine and smoking pot and walking 100 feet to the youth center. In Brooklyn, I'd always walked the extra 100 feet. I had to recapture that motivation, and it was hard.

This was my first moment of reckoning. It was a pivotal moment in which I told myself I had to adjust my course and get on a better path. In those days, the length of your hair was a statement of sorts, and my hair was pretty long. I decided I wanted to make a different statement, so I went to the barber and told him to cut my hair really short. When I came home, I remember my mother and father looking at me, and my mother actually got teary-eyed. Neither one of them had ever said, "Cut your hair." I'd grown my hair long partly because I wanted to fit in as one of the cool kids, but it didn't really help. On some level, letting my hair grow long was symbolic of the way I was drifting, and I didn't want to drift anymore.

Being told by a guidance counselor that I wasn't college material was one of those moments in which I slapped my forehead and said, "Aha, I get it. I'm on the wrong track. Time to change course, or else."

Only a short time afterwards I walked in the door at my house and announced to my parents, "I am going to get really good grades, and I am going to go to a great college."

Within weeks, I had started to set goals that I articulated and committed to. And it's pretty incredible how quickly things seemed to turn around for me. I became happier. I no longer felt adrift. I stopped brooding. The irony of this moment, of course, is that neither of my parents had gone to college, so although they wished the best for me, their own feelings might have been a little closer to those of my guidance counselor, in that they certainly understood the utility of my going to a vocational school, while college was the great unknown. This was maybe the last time in American life when going to college seemed like just one of the options to choose in pursuit of a good life; it wasn't the necessity we know it to be today—the dividing line between prospects for middle class success and falling behind. While they were surprised at my quick turnaround, my parents didn't believe I would excel in college.

I was able to pivot from mediocre grades to at least get into the local branch of the University of Massachusetts. While my parents might have viewed UMASS Lowell as a good option, from the start of my freshman year there, I viewed it as a launching pad for getting into a better school.

As luck would have it, I also had a job in those days mowing lawns, and one of the people whose lawn I mowed was a wealthy stockbroker named Jim Shannon. Jim had gone to Georgetown, and after talking with him about the advantages of going to a Jesuit institution in the nation's capitol, I set a goal of going there. And somehow I pulled it off. I worked hard to get good grades, and after Jim wrote me a strong letter of recommendation, I eventually got in. (Years later, when I was in a position to make my first serious charitable gift to Georgetown, I handed a $1 million dollar check to Jim, who was a trustee of the endowment fund.)

Getting accepted to Georgetown was an achievement, and it made me really happy. I look back at the process I went through in getting accepted, and it makes me realize I caught myself before my trajectory went further downward. At some level, I said to myself, I can go down this road that will not have a happy ending, or I can take control and make my own path.

As I connect the dots of my life, it's clear that my community, starting with my family, provided a platform to stand on. I consciously worked toward a goal, in this case not just to get into Georgetown, but maybe also to show my guidance counselor that she was wrong about whether I was college material. By being so deliberate in pursuing my goal, rather than having a bad day lead to a bad week, which would lead to a bad semester and a bad school year, I put things together, step by step. For example, I became more careful about the people I hung out with and made sure I was surrounded by peers with a more positive outlook. I intuited that the company you keep and the goals you set will drive the way your life turns out. For a kid from Brooklyn, Georgetown seemed like the proverbial shining city on a hill—and getting accepted there made me feel like I was back on the track I'd been on when as a young kid I'd been chosen to be in the Special Progress class.

On so many levels, going away to college changed the trajectory of my life for the better. I'm sure I didn't realize then that by setting a goal of going to an elite private college in a city far away from home, I'd organized my life around a large and specific purpose. Moreover, while my life seemed to brighten as I sought a slot at Georgetown University, I know I was unaware that setting and attaining goals was contributing to my prospects for happiness. I just knew the way my behavior changed. I stopped brooding in my room and was much more social with my classmates. I expressed myself through my schoolwork, and put more effort into writing and all my other school projects. I was animated by the gratitude I felt because someone (Jim Shannon) was helping me to get into a really good school. And I had, for the first time, a higher calling: to get a college education at one of the best universities in the world.

Going to Georgetown was a critical step in getting from a tenement apartment in Bay Ridge, Brooklyn, to a beautiful house with a loving wife. Whether I truly appreciated it at the time, setting such a goal and working hard to achieve it was a critical step in becoming happy. Going to a really good school was the biggest step I could possibly take in becoming successful in business.

Chapter Two

In Dreams Begin Responsibilities

When I arrived at Georgetown, the first thing I learned was that my family was poor. The kids I met all seemed to have gone to the best private schools. Their mothers and fathers had gone to college and apparently didn't have jobs; they had careers. My classmates would identify their parents' vocation by citing their title. "My father's the CEO of..." I was reminded that my father was a waiter and had not finished high school.

My classmates had cars; I arrived at Washington's Greyhound bus terminal on New York Avenue with a single duffle bag containing all of my stuff. My parents had given me a small sack filled with little bars of soap and shampoo that they'd collected from motels they'd stayed in as they traveled. In contrast to me, the kids I now met had gone all over the world, and they used the word "summer" as a verb, as in, "We summered in Nantucket; how about you?" Um, I summered in Lowell—fifty miles from Nantucket as the crow flies, but in practical terms, a million miles away.

It was the first time I realized that my happy childhood seemed maybe a little bit deprived. My life in Brooklyn and Lowell turned out not to be emblematic of the American experience. It represented, rather, a lower middle class immigrant experience that was very different from even the more middle class kids who arrived from the suburbs. I wasn't, as I'd also assumed, from the middle of the middle class. I'd have to work just to get there.

My new friends had big houses—sometimes more than one. They could concentrate on the university experience without having to work to get spending money. I had a job at a shoe store on Wisconsin Avenue.

At Georgetown, there were different ways of keeping score. I couldn't compete on the basis of the clothes I wore, the things I owned, or where I "summered." And c'mon, while athletics had always been important to me, and I'd grown up a pretty fair outdoor-court basketball player, it counted for nothing there. Georgetown's basketball team, which the legendary coach John Thompson had just then taken over, was on the verge of becoming one of the nation's elite programs.

There was only one way I knew to compete, and that was through applying myself. So I worked hard—on my studies, as well as in other endeavors I soon became involved with.

———

Many of the kids I knew at Georgetown were interested in politics and public service, and this was perhaps the one area where I had a competitive advantage.

While I was still in Lowell, the summer before going to college, I volunteered to help a member of our extended Greek family, Paul Tsongas, who was preparing to run for Congress. Paul wasn't literally a

relative, but such was the environment in Lowell that we all felt kin-
ship when one of our own was involved in something as momentous
as a political campaign.

While working on Paul's campaigns, I began to feel part of something larger for the first time. It helped forge a belief system, not in any
way ideological, that politicians wanted to help people, and that they
had a higher calling. I know that today people are pretty cynical about
politics and politicians, but I was idealistic, and Paul Tsongas was one
of those figures who could inspire a young man to believe in what I
later came to think of as my double bottom line: that you could do
good while doing well. That what might help your bottom line—in his
case, getting elected—was tied to doing good things for others. I
hadn't yet figured out that this concept could apply to business, too.

Paul and his wife Nikki lived half a mile from our house, and I found
it inspiring that someone from our community could be as well educated and ambitious as he was. It was also something of a revelation
that he could so clearly have a higher calling to serve his community
and ultimately his country. I knew people who'd volunteered for the
military, and even some young men who'd heard a calling to the
priesthood. Paul's calling was different, though—I could relate to it a
little more directly. Paul had gone to college and then served in the
Peace Corps before getting elected to the Lowell City Council, and
eventually becoming a county commissioner. He was elected to
Congress in 1974, when I was a sophomore at Georgetown, as part of
the large class of post-Watergate Democrats, and got elected to the
U.S. Senate four years later. Ultimately, he ran for president in 1992,
and although he won the New Hampshire primary, he lost the
Democratic nomination to Bill Clinton. It was a very sad day when he
died of cancer in 1997.

When Paul was elected to the Congress, I was able to work as an intern in his office. Aside from having the kind of extracurricular activity that many of my ambitious and better-off classmates really wanted—which provided me more of a sense of being equal to them—being a Congressional intern had one great advantage for a kid who didn't have a lot of money. Working in Congressman Tsongas' office meant I could make long-distance calls to my parents in Lowell. To a student scraping by on his wages from a shoe store, this was a big deal.

I also worked at the Georgetown Library, earning the grand sum of one thousand dollars per academic year. Between my internship, my work at the library and the shoe store, as well as all the typical activities of a student, I was very involved, very busy, but I found I had pretty high bandwidth. I matured a lot and explored a new capacity for really hard work. When other kids went home for Christmas, they'd go skiing with their families, or off to St. Barts. I worked two jobs and tried to make as much money as I could in the limited time I had before classes resumed.

It was clear that I was going to graduate from college with debt. Georgetown was not in those days a "need-blind—full-need" institution, and I had to take out student loans to pay my way. It used to really bother me to see affluent kids whose parents were paying their way screw around and not apply themselves the way I had to. It's possible that I worked as hard as I did, and fully appreciated what Georgetown offered, because I knew I was paying for it.

The Brooklyn poet and author Delmore Schwartz famously entitled his first collection *In Dreams Begin Responsibilities*. From my exile in Lowell, I had dreamed of going to Georgetown. When I achieved my dream, I took it very seriously.

When a student arrives at Georgetown, he's assigned a mentor, and mine was a 75-year-old Jesuit priest named Father Joseph Durkin. I have to admit that when I met him, I was a little disappointed. I wondered what I could possibly have in common with this old man who'd lived a comparatively cloistered life within an academic institution. Little did I realize that he was a legendary figure, and a great institution in his own right, and that being assigned as one of Father Durkin's mentees was one of the luckiest breaks of my life.

When Father Durkin died at 100, he was writing his 25th book. He was the single greatest person I have ever known, and one of the reasons I say that is he was such an authentic human being. There was nothing about him that was not as advertised. He never had a hidden agenda or an ounce of negativity. He never made an inauthentic statement in pursuit of laughs at someone else's expense. He didn't have a cynical bone in his body. His was as genuinely pure a soul as I have ever met. He was a serious, but very happy man whose diction was filled with words such as "mission," "purpose," and "higher love." He was so earnest it wasn't corny, even to a wisecracking teenager.

Father Durkin was the embodiment of the Jesuit ideal. He was someone who could find God in all things, and in fulfillment of the Jesuit ideal, his quiet attentiveness was remarkable, especially when it came to the students he mentored. He would ask simple questions and get me to open up to him, and from these conversations, he suggested books I should read and topics I should study. They became part of my Georgetown education regardless of my curriculum at the time.

Father Durkin was a happy man whose happiness flowed from his higher calling. His life was not merely in service to the Lord; his mission was to help spark a higher calling among the young adults he mentored. He believed the way to do it was through keen and vigorous development of head and heart. We were urged to cultivate our minds and spirits in a joyful way, because the ultimate goal was to die in peace, with prospects for the Afterlife. He passed on to me the desire to live a life in which you have given more than you have taken. He taught me that the way you function should also balance with all other aspects of your life, which should include work, sports, the arts—all of the pleasures of life that enhance our humanity. Father Durkin tried to instill the desire to live an engaged and fulfilling life with all the pieces in balance.

Intellectually, Father Durkin was a man ahead of his time. In our Web 2.0 world, we talk about mash-ups, which combine the data or functionality from two or more sources into a single integrated application. In the mid-1970s, Father Durkin already thought that way, and it was his guidance on a project that led to perhaps the most pivotal event in my education and, ultimately, my career.

In Georgetown, you had to write a thesis in both your junior and senior years. Because I had done well in English and History in high school and loved to read, it was clear by the end of my sophomore year that I should concentrate in English, and perhaps major in a new integrated discipline called American Studies. Father Durkin told me before the end of the school year that I should read Hemingway's *The Old Man and the Sea*. It was the kind of book that he really loved to talk about, because you could explore elements of the spiritualism within the book at whatever depth you wanted. It was like peeling an onion, and that appealed to Father Durkin; he had a mind that could delve into a topic one tissue-thin layer at a time. Over the course of the summer, I read *The Old Man and the Sea*, not once, but twice. From there, I immediately read Hemingway's *Across the River and into the Trees*.

Across the River and into the Trees was written in 1950, and *The Old Man and the Sea* was written in 1952. To me, it just didn't add up that two, so profoundly different books, each written in such a different style from the other, could have been created back-to-back. I knew that Hemingway was a great artist, but I also knew that he was a journalist who churned out reams of material in a career that had started thirty years before the publication of *The Old Man and the Sea*. There was something about the difference between that book and the one that preceded it that made me suspect that some elements of *The Old Man and the Sea* might have been written by Hemingway earlier in his career. Curious, I went to the library, got every book by Hemingway I could find, read as many as I could, and it seemed to me that my hunch was correct. *The Old Man and the Sea* seemed to have far more in common—in terms of style and the word choices Hemingway used—with his earlier novels and articles than his later work. I couldn't wait to tell Father Durkin about it.

So I arrived back at Georgetown at the end of the summer, and I went to see my mentor. "How was your summer?" Father Durkin asked. "Did you read the book?"

I told him everything I'd done: the hours in the library, the comparisons I'd made between *The Old Man and the Sea* and works from earlier in Hemingway's career. I told him I thought that Hemingway had written, if not all of *The Old Man and the Sea*, at least portions of it earlier in his career. I told Father Durkin I thought it was possible that perhaps because Hemingway lacked inspiration for a new book, or because he needed to get a book published to pay his bills, he'd pulled an older story out of a drawer and given it to his publisher.

I remember Father Durkin getting very emotional. He hadn't been certain that I was even going to read the book he'd recommended, and here I'd gone and studied it intently enough to have developed an original theory about it. We talked about it for weeks, and at one point, I told him I really wanted to prove my theory; I just didn't know how.

This was the autumn of 1975—about the time that Bruce Springsteen's *Born to Run* came out, Patty Hearst was arrested, and President Gerald Ford was being imitated on a new television show called *Saturday Night Live*. In the scale of time, it wasn't that long ago, though in the world of technology, it might as well have been Ancient Egypt. It was not a time when computers were widely used outside of big corporations, or NASA. In fact, if I'd been asked at the time to tell you everything I knew about computers, I probably would have started and finished with Hal from *2001: A Space Odyssey.* Computers, and technology in general, just didn't figure much in my consciousness.

But Father Durkin, who really thought in terms of interdisciplinary mash-ups, knew some of the people in Georgetown's graduate program in linguistics. And when we went to talk to a professor there about how we might prove that *The Old Man and the Sea* had been written earlier than the 1950s, she told us that we could examine his writing, sentence by sentence and word by word, and see what patterns could be divined. How did he use pronouns in *For Whom the Bell Tolls* as compared to *Across the River and into the Trees,* and then in both as compared to *The Old Man and the Sea*? Was there a way he used adjectives in sentences that might date one work conclusively as having come earlier or later than another? She was very helpful conceptually, but she made it clear that it was going to be really difficult, not to mention labor-intensive, to prove my theory. That was when my septuagenarian Jesuit priest mentor, approximately six years before the introduction of the IBM PC, said, "Well, maybe we could use a computer?"

I think there was one computer on the Georgetown campus, an IBM 360 mainframe with a terminal in the Registrar's office. So, together with Father Durkin, the linguistics professor, and a technical assistant from the Registrar's office, I went on a journey to use a computer to explore whether Ernest Hemingway wrote *The Old Man and the Sea* not in 1951, but in the 1930s or 1940s. The massive, "big iron" IBM 360 had about the same level of computing power as a present-day iPhone, and it literally used punch cards to process data. But it was thrilling to harness it to my project. It was like being a scientist, a detective, and an historian all at the same time. I never would have expected that using computing power to solve a riddle would fill me with excitement. That I was embarked on this journey with an aged Jesuit priest beside me is something I never would have predicted in a million years. Boy, was I happy!

I would tell my friends about the project, and they thought I was nuts. I think they liked it more when I talked about how the New York Rangers were going to crush the recently formed Washington Capitals, or when I talked about politics or rock 'n' roll. My trying to explain how I was using a mainframe computer to pursue an English project must have seemed too odd for words to all the future doctors and corporate lawyers who were a part of my community.

I remember telling my parents about it over Christmas vacation that year, and they really couldn't understand what I was doing. Using computers was just so foreign to their experience. For me, it was like conquering a new world. I felt like I was in control of my destiny, even as I was relying on the expertise of others, and without a precise sense of what we were going to find. Later on, when I was creating a new business, I would recognize that feeling of camaraderie in service to a goal with an unknown outcome. It was a genuinely entrepreneurial moment.

I had to type the first 5,000 words of Hemingway's book into the computer, and thousands of words from earlier books and articles. Our technical assistant was able to write a program to search through word patterns using punch cards containing the sentences I'd laboriously inputted, and lo and behold, one day the computer "told us" that, at the very least, some elements of *The Old Man and the Sea* had been written prior to the 1950s.

It was a Eureka moment. I'm not sure that Father Durkin high-fived me, but I know he was as thrilled as I was. Our discovery blew everyone's mind, and maybe mine most of all. Georgetown is constructed around the concept of interdisciplinary studies, and the fact that my junior-year thesis was a mash-up of literature and history, as well as computer science and linguistics, was a very big deal.

Though Hemingway biographers have never warmed to our theory, the paper I wrote was published in an academic newsletter dedicated to computing and the humanities. Most important to me in the short run was that I won an award for having written the best junior thesis at Georgetown that year. In the long run, what was most important was that the journey I'd gone on with Father Durkin—using a computer to prove an original thesis—created a life-long interest in the power and practical application of computers. Everything I was to achieve in the first part of my career stemmed from an unwritten playbook we made up as we went along, infused with the belief that computers would change the world. I'd witnessed firsthand how you could use computers to make something happen. I can't tell you that there was a flash of light, or a divine inspiration. That actually came later, as we shall see. All I can tell you is that a Jesuit priest insisted that I read *The Old Man and the Sea*, and through that, I had landed something awesome.

By the time I went back to school for my senior year, I'd already decided my senior thesis was going to be on Jack Kerouac. While *On the Road* had become one of the great post-war literary phenomena, my interest was local and personal. Jack Kerouac grew up in Lowell, was very good friends with my uncle Bill Koumantzelis, and after the surge of fame from *On the Road* had made his life unmanageable, he'd married Stella Sampas, a Greek-American woman from Lowell, and moved back to his hometown.

Jean Louis Kerouac was the son of French-Canadian immigrants to the United States, but in Lowell, my Uncle Bill and other members of my family thought of him as sort of an honorary Greek. I met him only once, when I was a young child, but as a senior at Georgetown, I found I could relate to him in many ways. He was a member of an immigrant community and had escaped from Lowell to attend a first-rate college, Columbia University. That wasn't too far from my experience.

For my senior thesis, I started interviewing people who had known Kerouac at various stages of his life. I realized I might be able to offer a different perspective on Kerouac than any other English major might have. I had access to original material: the oral history of people who'd known him. And I didn't have to imagine what it was like to grow up in a tenement in Lowell.

One day I saw that Allen Ginsburg and William Burroughs, Kerouac's fellow Beat writers, were staging a reading at the Folger

Library. So I went to see them, and afterward got in position to introduce myself. I told them I was a Greek kid from Lowell whose relatives were close to Kerouac and his family, and that I was writing my thesis on him. I asked if, while they were in Washington, we might be able to talk so I could include their remembrances in my thesis.

To my surprise and delight, these two legendary writers—Burroughs tall and thin as a beanpole, Ginsburg like an R. Crumb conception of what a hirsute and intellectual Beat writer might look like—agreed on the spot. They told me that they were a little estranged from Kerouac's family, and maybe because my relatives were still close to a number of them, we might be able to help repair relationships.

The next day, Allen Ginsburg and William Burroughs came to my apartment. You can't imagine what a thrill it was—and what an opportunity for a college student writing about a Beat writer. Having two living legends sitting in my apartment, offering up their memories of their friend Jack Kerouac, was a lucky break of the first order, though maybe not entirely lucky, since I did have a connection. Just as having Paul Tsongas get elected to the Congress was a way for a poor kid from Lowell to land one of the coveted congressional internships sought after by seemingly better connected Georgetown kids, my Uncle Bill's connection to Jack Kerouac had led Burroughs and Ginsburg to my apartment. But soon I had a problem. I had to get to class, and they seemed perfectly comfortable staying there talking to me the whole day. So I cleared my throat, and interrupting Allen Ginsburg midway through a long remembrance, I said, "Excuse me, and I really hate to break this up, but I have to go to class."

"What class?"

"English class," I said.

"Can we come?" Burroughs asked.

So we walked together across the Georgetown campus to my English class. Dr. Hugh Cloke, my English professor, looked at me slightly askance as I walked in late. "Dr. Cloke, I am so sorry to be late," I said, "but I brought along a couple of friends." Needless to say, my professor was more than accommodating. Even though you probably couldn't imagine a gulf wider than that between William Burroughs—heir to the adding-machine company, a unique stylist who'd deconstructed the English language and once been arrested for murdering his wife; Allen Ginsburg—a gay poet who had famously converted from Judaism to Buddhism; and a professor at a Jesuit institution, it was the nature of Georgetown to foster this kind of an opportunity for students with tolerance and respect.

Later, I took my new pals to the Georgetown campus radio station, where Ginsburg read from *Howl* and started chanting, "Ohmmmm." We had a late lunch, and they headed on their merry way, leaving me with original research for my thesis, not to mention an instantaneous campus legend.

The material I got for my thesis on Kerouac and Lowell was incredibly helpful. It certainly didn't hurt my chances for a good grade that my English professor had incontrovertible proof that I really had been able to conduct interviews with Burroughs and Ginsburg, and wasn't either making it up or only relying on visits to the library.

On a profoundly personal level, delving into the story of Kerouac and Lowell, and examining the Greek community of which he was an ex officio participant, I was able to embrace the community—the locality—that in many ways I'd rejected. This Massachusetts mill town that my parents had grown up in had been where Jack Kerouac had returned after achieving immense fame and fortune. If he could re-embrace it, maybe I could too. Even as I was approaching my graduation from Georgetown, an eminently more sophisticated young man than the boy who had arrived three years earlier, I was going to leave college reconciled with what, by now, was my hometown. I hadn't quite run away from Lowell while at college, but even with my parents there, even with my extended family there, I felt no real affinity for it. Now, because of my Kerouac thesis, it was like I had permission to accept this part of my personality, without embarrassment or regret. (Many years later, I was a bidder on the original holograph of *On the Road*, but dropped out when the bidding crossed the $2 million mark. I would love to own the long scroll of paper that Kerouac typed continuously, but not for $2 million.)

I got an A on my senior thesis. In fact, I got As in everything my junior and senior years. Georgetown had just started awarding the most outstanding senior with a prize named after my mentor, Father Joseph Durkin. I finished my career as a college student as the winner of The Durkin Prize for Georgetown's class of 1977. It was an emotional and touching moment, not just because the prize was a validation of everything I'd achieved in college, and not just because fewer than five years before, I'd been deemed "not college material." It was touching because the prize was named for Father Joe Durkin, who for the past three years had been an incredible influence on my life, my success, and my future happiness.

Going to Georgetown had a profoundly positive effect on me. From having arrived with a bit of a chip on my shoulder, and no small inferiority complex, to graduating as the winner of The Durkin Prize, it had been quite a journey. I learned how to become fulfilled through hard work and through a really high-bandwidth engagement with the world around me. I'd learned about computers through my junior thesis, and politics through both academics and the internship with Paul Tsongas. I learned to think critically and have confidence that I could succeed in big and different endeavors, even though I'd arrived on campus without knowing that "to summer" was apparently a legitimate verb form for upper-middle class kids from the Eastern seaboard. Most important, under the tutelage of Fr. Joseph Durkin, S.J., I'd embraced the Georgetown ethos of developing my head and heart, and tending to the whole person, with a nascent orientation toward service to others. At what was a cynical and pretty depressing moment in American life—the late 1970s—I left college as an ambitious, idealistic young man.

And I was happy. I had not yet figured out the component pieces of happiness. I'm pretty certain that I thought happiness was binary: you either were or you weren't. I had no sense that by paying attention to certain things, and by emphasizing certain behaviors, you might increase your odds of being a happy person. If you'd asked me then, I would probably have told you that success drove happiness, not the other way around. In hindsight, however, as I look at my 21-year-old self, graduating from Georgetown at the top of his class, a few things are clear.

By nature an extrovert, I was a social being who had become comfortable with circulating among multiple communities. Far from being estranged from the Georgetown student community whose affluence and experiences had intimidated me upon arrival, I thrived in its midst. I had made lifelong friends. At the same time, I was still in touch with some friends I'd left behind in Brooklyn and Lowell. In no small part because of the way my Kerouac thesis had opened up my mind about Lowell, my sense of estrangement from what was now my hometown was over. I derived happiness from the way I was able to flow among these communities, with different aspects of my identity being reinforced through contact with others.

I had found outlets for personal expression. My two theses had opened up possibilities. I was deeply intrigued with the possibilities for personal computing. (It's not like I was writing computer code in FORTRAN or other programming languages in use at the time. But at some important level, I graduated from college in 1977 viewing computers as a means to achieving an end. On a purely practical basis, this was the equivalent to the Dustin Hoffman character graduating from UCLA in *The Graduate* with a tip that the future lay in plastics. Being an English major hip to the potential for computers at the dawn of the personal computing era was an incredible stroke of luck.)

I felt, and could express, my gratitude—to Georgetown, to Father Durkin, to Congressman (soon to be Senator) Paul Tsongas. I was grateful to Jim Shannon who'd made it possible for me to be accepted at Georgetown. I was especially grateful to my parents. I was not the kind of young man who can only accept adulthood by rejecting his parents. I knew my mother and father had made sacrifices so that I could get on the right track.

But my happiness was incomplete. I wasn't yet an actualized, fulfilled happy person. While I understood obligations to one's community, and had been touched by the Jesuit ethos of a life devoted to service, my ambition at that moment was for myself. I was empathetic to others—I believe that empathy, like extroversion, is an aspect of my nature. And yet my higher calling at that moment of graduation related principally to...me. I don't want to say my higher calling was money, because it wasn't, fully. It's undeniable that on the threshold of adulthood, I'd been shaped, in part, by pressing my face against the glass and looking in at the incredible ease with which my wealthy classmates approached life. I'd visited their homes and seen the good life. I remember going to a classmate's ranch at a beautiful place called Pierce Farms, which had a massive red gate and a mile-long drive to the main house, and I thought to myself that someday I'd have a spread that impressive. Measuring myself against my classmates, it seemed every bit as likely that I would be successful as they, if given a fair shot. I was determined to get a good job and be financially successful. It's probably understandable that graduating with something like $27,000 in college loan debt, financial success meant getting out of debt, and not necessarily being charitable. This clearly was a moment in my life where I was geared toward the pursuit of financial success. I wasn't mature enough to realize that once I found it, it wouldn't be sufficient to make me truly happy.

As I look back on this exciting time in my life, I was successful and happy, up to a point. However, my happiness wasn't sustainable because the elements supporting it were incomplete. I was no longer an undergraduate. I was clearly on a path to success of some kind. But I had a long way to go as a student of happiness.

———

At Georgetown I met many great and lifelong friends. Maria Shriver was a classmate who also had Father Durkin as a mentor, and we've stayed in close touch for more than thirty-five years. My roommate Michael Jacobs was one of the producers of my film, *Nanking*. Laurence Armour and I have remained in contact over the years, and it was Jon Howard who took me to my first Caps game.

I was a hard worker, but I really enjoyed and capitalized on the college benefit of having all my friends available on a single campus.

There was one incident that took place while at Georgetown that in retrospect reveals to me that I was struggling, even in those years, to define the components to happiness. I'm thinking of a funny exchange I had with one of my roommates who, in part because he had certain advantages, seemed to have figured out a shortcut to happiness. Remembering this conversation, maybe I wasn't completely clueless.

I had a roommate named Bill Macdonald, who has since gone on to be a very successful Hollywood producer. One Friday night—I think it was probably during my junior year—Bill and I had gone to the library to get some of our weekend studying out of the way. We studied hard, and afterward went off in search of campus parties, eventually getting home around midnight. I went upstairs to go straight to bed. I set the alarm clock for 8:00, because I had to get to my job at the shoe store on Wisconsin Avenue. That was the way my life worked at college.

I woke up, showered, and got ready to go to my job. I walked downstairs, and there was Bill, a handsome prep school graduate, sitting on a couch with an absolutely beautiful blonde girl in his lap, laughing and talking. Now this was something of a surprise to me, because the previous night, Bill and I had returned to our apartment together, and somehow between when I'd gone upstairs to bed and the next morning, Bill had met up with this gorgeous girl.

"What are you doing, man?" Bill asked.

So I said, "Well, I've showered. I'm going to go get some breakfast, and then I'm going to the shoe store to work for four hours. And when I've finished my shift, I'm going to go to the library to study for a few more hours."

Bill looked at me and said, "And why are you going to study some more? I thought we studied last night."

"We did. But I need to study more so I can get good grades."

So Bill goes, "And why do you want to get good grades?"

So I thought about it for a moment and I said, "So I can graduate and get a good job."

"And why do you want a good job?" Bill asked.

I said, "Well, Bill, I need to make a lot of money."

And he said, "Why do you need to make a lot of money?"

So I answered, "I need to pay off my college loans, and besides, I think it will make me happy."

"How do you define happiness?" he asked.

And I said, "I guess looking at you, I'd say sleeping late and having a beautiful girl sit in my lap, and being able to laugh and giggle without a care in the world."

Bill went, "Exactly the point. I'm just cutting out all of the intermediate steps."

I remember thinking to myself that what Bill said contained an element of genius, and that he was a really fortunate guy. He could lead me through a Socratic dialogue on happiness because he'd already figured it out. Or at least what would work for him.

Even then, I viewed achieving happiness as a step-by-step process. Bill, born into maybe a cushier berth in life, went straight to the finish line.

I respected that, and acknowledge that my handsome, Hollywood-producer friend and former roommate has a certain genius for living. He comes to it naturally. He was born with it.

Maybe I'm a little more of a plodder, someone for whom A leads to B which leads to C. It's clear to me from this memory that before I ever left Georgetown, I believed that achieving happiness was a methodical journey. Bill went directly to the end point, and God bless him for it.

I'm betting that for most people, constructing your journey to happiness, just like constructing your journey to success, involves the kind of systematic approach I've learned over the years. Few are the people who have the genius, charm, and luck to vault from a standing start to the sofa with a beautiful girl in their lap.

Chapter Three

The Leonsis Index of Software Technology

When people think about the center of technology development in the United States, the first place that comes to mind is probably Silicon Valley. But in the late 1970s, the center of the developing computing industry was as much on the East Coast as the West Coast, specifically Massachusetts' Route 128 Corridor. In fact, the so-called Massachusetts Miracle that helped propel Michael Dukakis from being governor of a comparatively small state to being the 1988 Democratic presidential nominee was an outgrowth of high tech companies, like DEC and Data General, that sprang up in the exurban region north and west of Boston. Fortuitously, one of the companies hitting its stride just as I was graduating from Georgetown was Wang Labs, which one year previously had moved its headquarters from Tewksbury to Lowell.

In the summer of 1977, I had a BA degree and a huge bill to show for it. My parents offered to let me move home and live rent-free while I found a job and paid off my student loans. This made sense, and one of the first places I thought of to apply for a job was at Wang.

Wang Laboratories was founded in the early 1950s by Dr. An Wang, a Chinese-born, Harvard-educated computer engineer. The business was primarily built around the manufacturing of desktop calculators. In 1976, Wang had introduced one of the first so-called word processors, which was a bridge between typewriters and the personal computers that would soon be on every office desktop. Word processing held the potential to liberate clerical staff from the tyranny of typing every document practically from scratch, and it thus enabled a typist to be much more productive. The year I applied for a job, the company was, as they say in Massachusetts, wicked hot, and Wang was a really happy company. It stood in great contrast to IBM, which in those days was still working its way out of its antitrust problems and was notable for the rigidity of its unhappy culture. Wang Labs was innovative, both in the products it developed and in how it treated all of its constituents, from employees to customers. The year I arrived, the company's Office Information System, which was an early effort at creating a corporate-wide network, was being snapped up by smart enterprise customers wanting to automate their offices, thereby increasing their office productivity.

I was a fairly unique job applicant. I wasn't an engineer, but I was a local boy who had graduated from a good college with knowledge of computers and an English degree. I could talk, write, and I wasn't allergic to technology. I could bridge the gap between the graduating MIT students who knew electrical engineering but couldn't write to save their lives, and the English majors from Boston College or UMass, who could write but grew flummoxed trying to explain just what an Office Information System was.

For the first six months, I worked in Wang's technical support group, which gave me a chance to learn a lot more about computers and technology. It was also a pretty good window into how the company operated, and working within what was essentially an inbound telemarketing operation for Wang's customers, I grew increasingly knowledgeable about the products and services we sold. Because I was sociable and interested in different communities within the larger Wang Labs community, I began to circulate around the company, as my curiosity led me to explore everything I could learn about the business, its products, and the office productivity market. Because I could express myself and tended to translate what the engineers told me into language a human could understand, I ended up going to work in the in-house advertising department, writing copy for ads, manuals, and brochures. I found myself absolutely in the right place at the right time.

With the introduction of a word-processing solution that could enable a big company to shed its typewriters and connect its by-now happier clerical staff to terminals, Wang Labs became for a time the fastest-growing company in the Fortune 500. However, like many companies started by introverted engineers, it had trouble managing the external world's interest. It was somewhat ill at ease communicating with non-technical audiences. It seemed to me that the company needed to take the practice of public relations seriously. So I expressed myself in a memo suggesting that the company create what would these days be called a corporate communications department, handling media inquiries for the corporate entity, and offering marketing communications support for the company's product line. I used a remarkable innovation that Wang Labs had pioneered—email—to circulate my memo around the company. Such was the pace at which

Wang was operating, it took about two days for the word to come from on high: "That sounds good. You do it."

And so I did. By now I was about twenty-two, and I was the head of the PR department for the fastest-growing company in the Fortune 500. I was making good money—my salary had gone from $10,500 per annum to a munificent $36,000 per year—and was able to make progress working off my college debt. As soon as I was able to, I moved out of my parents' home and into my own apartment.

One day, I was in a line at a supermarket, and I saw *TV Guide* in the rack by the cashier. Emblazoned across the cover were the words, "The Number One Selling Magazine in America." I was curious, because I'd never actually read it—my parents weren't big television watchers—so I bought a copy. I brought it home and opened it up, and saw the front of the book was comprised of interviews with directors and television stars, and some reviews of shows. But the bulk of the magazine was just a directory of what program was on which of the three networks at what time. I could not believe that this was the best-selling magazine in America. So I tossed it out.

This very night, I went into what was my home office and turned on my brand new Apple II computer. Some months before, when I was out on the West Coast visiting a computer fair, I'd bought it for something like $2,600. Wang was working on a product called the Wang Writer, which was to be our early entry in the personal computer space, but Apple was already selling computers, mostly to hobbyists, and by 1978 I had to get my hands on one, out of a combination of curiosity, passion, and professional need. Out of the box, the Apple II came as a series of components pretty haphazardly wrapped in a plastic bag, and reading the instructions from the Xeroxed sheets that came with it, I had to get someone to solder it together. It used a very simple operating system called CP/M, but it didn't have many programs that worked with it. There were some games, and by Wang's standards, a pretty crude word processing program, and a spreadsheet program called VisiCalc. You couldn't do much, but at least I had a computer on my desk at home. I knew that more and more programs were going to be released that would enable someone like me, an enthusiast, to make practical use of my personal computer, and that it was only a matter of time before companies like Wang Labs would exponentially increase the number of people who, comfortable with computers at work, would want to use them at home. It just seemed blindingly obvious to a young man running the PR operation for one of the country's hottest technology companies.

On this particular evening, fresh from having looked at *TV Guide*, I now stared at the monitor of my Apple computer, and it hit me: this computer was really no different from the television that sat in the next room. It just had different programming. In the case of the TV, shows were broadcast from Los Angeles or New York, and they arrived in your television via over-the-air transmission. In the case of the computer, programs like VisiCalc were loaded on your computer via floppy disks. Same stuff, different process.

Because I worked at Wang, I knew what a computer network was. And so it seemed there were television networks, and there were computer networks. There were television programs, and computer programs. Televisions. Computers. Networks. Programs. I remember thinking: someone is going to figure out that computers and televisions operate on the same essential model, and that as more and more programs are developed for computers, it would be as helpful to the user to have a guide to those programs as it was to the couch potato to have a *TV Guide*. Which, as the cover reminded me, was The Number One Selling Magazine in America.

At some point that evening, I turned off my computer. But long after the monitor went dark, that insight stayed aglow in my mind.

———————

It was some weeks later that I got a completely unexpected offer. I was recruited to run the corporate communications operation of a big electronics company in Melbourne, Florida. Harris Corporation made instruments used by the military and NASA, and they had their eye on the office systems business, which they would enter in 1983 when they bought the Lanier Corporation. Given the business they were in and where they were going strategically, it made sense that their head-hunter would find me. I was happy at Wang, maybe not entirely ful-filled, but things were going well. Yet when the Harris Corporation dangled before me a salary of $98,000, I jumped, even though it meant having to move to Florida.

It was a mistake from the outset, and it made me unhappy. I quit a job I'd created within a corporate community in which I'd thrived. Lowell had become a home I really appreciated, and I had spread my wings—volunteering to work in political campaigns, dating lots of girls, hanging out with friends. I had to leave my parents, and my fam-ily, and what was by now a pretty enriching social community. What I did not own up to until I got down to Florida was that I had made a decision almost entirely because of the money involved. What a clas-sic mistake, one made all the time by people struggling to understand the components and drivers of happiness.

Harris Corporation was a really big company, a conglomerate, not a founder-driven institution like Wang Labs. Within three months of my arrival, all I could think about was how I could get out of the company and fix the mistake I'd made. The thing I really wanted to do was start my own business.

My mind had been mulling over the same big idea ever since I'd tossed the *TV Guide* in the circular filing cabinet and chanced upon the insight about the links between the television and the computer. The more I thought about it, the more obvious it seemed that as software companies produced ever more programming for computers, there should be some way for a computer enthusiast to keep track of what was available. If there was a weekly publication that told you what your programming options were on TV, why couldn't there be some kind of regular publication that tracked the software available? In fact, I already had a name for the company that would publish it: LIST. The Leonsis Index of Software Technology.

Ever since being appointed head of PR for Wang, I'd been a regular attendee of the personal computer trade shows and fairs that were springing up around the country. I started to ask questions of the various software vendors whose businesses were represented by folding chairs set up behind cheap card-table displays. The computer business was just beginning to come to a boil. Various early-stage personal computers such as the Commodore PET and the Atari were now being launched, and there was even a rumor that IBM was going to introduce its own model. An IBM PC. Wow.

As I talked to software vendors at these fairs, I'd ask them if there was anywhere I could find a comprehensive guide to which programs were available to run on which machines. I was assured that there weren't any such guides. It was also clear that software vendors would

really benefit if such a publication existed, because their natural customer base would have a sense of what options were available.

I kept hearing that in Boca Raton, IBM had a small skunk works
devoted to building a personal computer using off-the-shelf components. Having worked at Wang Labs, I had immense respect for the
power of the IBM brand and its marketing machinery, and I knew that
if the rumor was true, the market entrance of the IBM PC would be a
pivotal event.

By that time I'd been at Harris for about a year, and I knew it wasn't
going to work. I'd taken the job primarily because the money offered
was so fantastic that I just couldn't resist it. I had money, but it wasn't
leading me to happiness. By then it was late 1980, and I was almost
twenty-five years old, prosperous, but miserable at work. Success had
not brought me happiness. I liked Florida well enough, and I was
meeting lots of women and making friends, and there were some very
nice people at the company, but Harris Corporation wasn't really the
kind of community in which I could feel at home. At that point in time,
it was really a big government contractor. Compared to Wang Labs, it
wasn't a happy company. It didn't really have a higher calling, or if it
did, it was to provide technology and services to the military, and thus
win more government contracts. I had no real problem with that, but
it didn't align with what my higher calling seemed to be. What
intrigued me at this moment in my life was what was happening in the
personal computing space.

I was serious enough about creating the Leonsis Index of Software
Technology that I contacted a friend I'd met while at Wang Labs
named Vincent Pica. Vin was head of information systems at E.F.
Hutton in New York, and as a big customer of Wang's, I'd interviewed

him for some PR materials we produced showcasing our happy clientele. Vin and I hit it off, and we were still in touch even after I left Wang. (We're still in constant touch today, and I consider him one of my best friends. I'm really proud that his daughter recently graduated from Georgetown.) I told Vin my idea: that as personal computers became even more of a phenomenon—we were both certain this was just a matter of time—producing a guide to the software available to run the hardware might make for an interesting business. Vin didn't take much persuading. In fact, as a corporate MIS chief whose job depended on using state-of-the-art technology, he told me that E.F. Hutton would buy the first copy of whatever I produced. But of course, that was the rub. I had to produce the index, and that would involve having to hire people to amass the data, and not only did I not have funding to start a company, running a company wasn't a part-time endeavor. I'd have to quit my job and get serious about it. So Vin offered to introduce me to people at E.F. Hutton who might help me raise the venture capital I needed to get things rolling.

I wrote a 15-page business plan and flew to New York. It turned out Vin wasn't just connecting a 24-year-old would-be entrepreneur (me) with some 26-year old MBA in the E.F. Hutton's business development unit. No, Vin believed enough in the idea—and believed enough in me—to set me up with the CEO, Robert Foman, and the company's president, George Ball. These were the days when the company's tag line was, "When E.F. Hutton talks, people listen." And now the two most important corporate officers were poised to listen to my pitch.

I remember walking into a conference room on some very high floor of their building, and seeing a number of executives sitting around a table. I was probably the youngest person in the room by twenty years. But I knew what I was going to say. I walked through my analysis of what was happening in technology and the opportunities that were out there.

I told them that in a short period of time, consumers would have computers in both their offices and their homes. I said that computers were going to be just like television sets, and that media would be available via software. I explained that *TV Guide* was the largest circulating publication in America, and that surely there was an opening for a computer analog, a guide to the software programming available on personal computers.

I then expanded the concept from a mere directory to something more. I told them that the publication I had in mind would be more than a magazine; it would be a software database itself, which you could put in your computer and use to get even more information about the programs then-available. I even told them that I believed someday, software would be available to download into your computer from other computers to which you were connected. This conversation took place in 1980, but it all made sense to me, and I must have made my case with both authority and passion.

I talked for thirty minutes without interruption. Maybe without even breathing. Someone once told that when you've made the sale, stop selling, but I didn't know whether I'd made the sale. When I finished, I was pretty happy because whether I got the funding or not, I really felt I'd connected the dots: television, computers, software, the need for compiling a dictionary of available software, and even the part about my publication existing in both magazine form and as a database. I'd come a long way in five years from inputting lines from Hemingway into an IBM 360, through my experience as a young communications and marketing executive at Wang, to be proposing to one of the most admired Wall Street firms that they support my venture in publishing a magazine and software database. They were very polite when I wrapped up and asked if I wouldn't mind stepping outside so they could discuss my proposal.

I sat outside in the lobby wondering if I'd blown it. About twenty minutes later, Mr. Foman asked me to come back into the room. In short order, he told me, "None of us understands a single word you said, but we think you can sell snow to the Eskimos, and we are going to back your business." And they did, with a check for $1 million to get me going. Within weeks I'd quit my job. The Leonsis Index of Software Technology was born. I was ready to create my LIST.

I left the Harris Corporation in March of 1981, just a few days after a would-be assassin shot President Ronald Reagan. I was twenty-five. But I was so focused on getting LIST off the ground, I was barely aware of the outside world. There was a recession, apparently, but all I knew was I needed to hire young people to help me amass the database necessary to get the Leonsis Index of Software Technology up and running. Modern American business lore is filled with the stories of the startup: young people binging on caffeine and pizza, working late to bring a product to market. In my own experience, it's all true. A small group of us worked night and day for the next fifteen months in order to bring our product to the market.

In August 1981, the IBM PC launched, and it was the instantaneous phenomenon the computer industry had needed. The Apple II had sold to hobbyists—early adopters, people who actually knew how use a soldering iron. Other computers were basically toys for the guys who had their own slide rule and had competed for prizes at their high school science fairs. Once IBM launched a PC, the category went mainstream.

For me, what was phenomenal was that LIST ended up becoming an integrated part of IBM's marketing campaign. If you are of a certain age, you might even remember the ad campaign IBM launched in the fall of 1981 to build awareness of the PC, showing a silent-movie Charlie Chaplin character learning how to use this new invention. The implication was that if the Little Tramp could use a PC, anyone could: moms and dads, clerks and even CEOs.

After the IBM PC came to market, I paid a sales call to Don Estridge, the executive who was running the skunk works in nearby Boca Raton.

It's 107 miles from Vero Beach, where my home was, to Boca Raton, but when I wangled an appointment to meet the executive IBM had entrusted to create its PC, I think I drove there without stopping. He was a busy man who'd just launched a hit product, yet he was willing to take the time to meet with a young entrepreneur who hadn't even gotten his product out the door. (Don Estridge was a wonderful human being who tragically died in a plane crash in 1983. In 1988, I wrote *Blue Magic*, an account of Don and his team in Boca Raton throwing out the IBM rulebook to create the PC—and thereby changing the world. I wanted to honor someone I consider one of the most influential businessmen of the twentieth century.)

When I sat down with him, I said, "Mr. Estridge, I really want to thank you for having built your PC as an open system." An open system meant that it wouldn't just accept IBM's proprietary software, but would run software created by others. In fact, the operating system they first used was called BASIC, licensed to IBM by a couple of young men who'd grown up together in Seattle, namely Bill Gates and Paul

Allen. From that one transaction, Gates and Allen were able to tie a little company called Microsoft to a rocket that shot higher in the sky than anything fired off at nearby Cape Canaveral.

I told Don, who was a good listener, that I was working on a database of all the software currently available, and that perhaps when I brought my publication to market, I could help IBM in the marketing of their new product. I even asked him if, prior to my publishing the first LIST in magazine form, he might want to pay me, upfront, to get it going.

When Don Estridge had built the PC as an open system, he took a really radical step for a company like IBM. IBM's business model was to be a vertically integrated organization that sold businesses mainframe computers, the software to run them, and contracts to maintain this "Big Iron." But Don took almost the opposite approach with the PC. He did so because he knew that by opening up the PC to use non-IBM software and peripherals—printers and other hardware—it would jumpstart the PC industry, and IBM would sell even more PCs. But he also knew that his customers had a problem in not knowing what software was on the market to use with the PC. He instantly grasped that LIST could be a tool that would help bring order to the marketplace, and to the ecosystem that IBM was helping to create. This would help them sell more PCs, because consumers would have a better grasp of what you could do with them.

On the spot, Don committed to purchase access to the database I was compiling. Because of Don, IBM committed to buy full-page, inside cover spread ads not only in the first issue of the magazine we were going to call *LIST*, but for each of our quarterly issues for the next two years. They were our first advertiser, and in so many ways, our most important one. The support from IBM didn't end there. IBM used our database in creating a subsequent ad with the Little Tramp, which showed boxes of software all over the floor. The database from which the names of all those software titles was compiled was the Leonsis Index of Software Technology.

For months, we hustled to complete our database of all the software compatible with the IBM PC, as well as other computers on the market, so that we could publish our first magazine before anyone else did, and harness the full flush of energy that the IBM PC had created. We were in a continual game of catch-up, because new software was proliferating like crazy.

When the first issue of *LIST*, the magazine, was published in the fall of 1982, it sent ripples throughout the software industry. We were providing an essential service to both buyers and sellers of hardware and software. First the Apple, and now the PC had created a vibrant ecosystem, and I found myself standing near its center. My staff and I would go to a trade show, and software publishers who saw *LIST* as their vehicle for getting their new product seen by customers swarmed us.

Just like *TV Guide*, *LIST* had a front of the book with interviews, stories, and reviews (in our case, reviews of products). It was published on slick, heavy stock paper. The back of the book was a series of directories printed on a much rougher stock, with every piece of software then available listed in separate categories: for example, games, or office productivity applications (word processing programs and spreadsheets). We would indicate which software was compatible with which operating system that worked with which hardware device. (It was clear from the outset that the key was compatibility with the IBM PC, which used Microsoft's operating system, by now called MS-DOS.) Just like *TV Guide*, I'd list the "programming" (software) in the directory for free, but if software vendors wanted to communicate in their own words, they could buy advertising, on the Yellow Pages model, paying by the column inch. We had display advertising at the front of the book, classified advertising at the back of the book, and we sold the magazine for the unheard of price of $19.95. Unlike just about every magazine since the dawn of time, we were profitable in the very first issue.

The first issue of *LIST* sold 50,000 copies. We sold it at bookstores, newsstands, and we sold subscriptions. Many of the first computer stores had stacks of *LIST* piled near the cash registers. Amazingly, hardware manufacturers started buying copies to give away with their products. The entrepreneur's fondest desire is to seize an opening with tremendous demand for a service that only he offers. With *LIST*, I'd hit that perfect crease: the nanosecond between when the cognoscenti are aware of the Next New Thing and the moment when the mass market discovers it. And the mass market had surely discovered the world of personal computers. Between August 1981, when the IBM was introduced to the market, and January 1983, when *TIME* put the personal computer on its cover as "Machine of the Year"—personal computing seemed to accelerate.

I don't need to overstate the effect this would have on the economy, and on society. In August 1981, America was in a recession. Sixteen months later, when *TIME* anointed the PC as the first non-human stand-in for its "Man of the Year" designation, the longest bull market in history had begun.

The effect on American society went way beyond just the economic benefit. From productivity gains to the creation of whole new industries, I believe the moment when computers came to the masses was as important a pivot as the end of World War II, and as important an invention as the automobile or the telephone. At the time, those of us in the maelstrom could barely get perspective on it, because things just moved too fast.

We had competitors almost instantly: *PC Magazine* launched around the same time as *LIST*, and it too was a hit. But where *PC* was more of a traditional consumer publication, selling for a few bucks and with feature articles and profiles and lifestyle segments in between display advertising, *LIST* was closer to its inspiration, *TV Guide*, and provided more of a functional service to potential buyers. We were part catalogue, part consumer guide. We had developed relationships with advertisers, but as important were our relationships with software publishers and hardware manufacturers, both of whom found it in their interest to treat us almost like a partner whose output was integral to their success. When I met Mitch Kapor, whose Lotus 1-2-3 spreadsheet software was to become the first "killer app" of the PC era, he liked what we were doing so much he invited me to sell *LIST* in the back of the room at his launch event. (Many years later, I would somewhat repay the favor by having AOL cede to Mitch's Mozilla Foundation the intellectual property for what became the Firefox browser. Under my prodding, AOL also invested $2 million in the Mozilla Foundation to help stimulate the Open Source software movement.)

I'd launched LIST, the company, and *LIST*, the magazine, with no thought of selling the business, but it didn't take long—just a few months after our publication hit the stands—for buyers to begin pursuing us. Right around the time that *Time* made the PC its "Machine of the Year," a publishing industry trade magazine wrote an article on how, practically overnight, the IBM PC had created a new publishing category: the computer magazine. With a tone not far from amazement, the piece stated that one of the publications that had sprung up from seemingly nowhere was a little venture called *LIST*, run by some kids in Vero Beach, Florida. The story mentioned that with our very first issue, we'd sold 50,000 copies and were in the black.

Within a few days of the article coming out, I was contacted by people from American Express Publishing, and Ziff Davis (who went on to buy *PC* several months later), all of them gauging whether I had any interest in selling them my company. I also was contacted by the head of American operations for International Thomson, the publishing arm of the Thomson Corporation. As it turned out, he had a second home in Vero Beach, and within just a few weeks of our magazine hitting the stand, I was sitting across a table from a potential buyer.

The Thomson Corporation had its roots in publishing newspapers in Canada, but by the early 1980s, it was an international conglomerate that had branched out into everything from oil and gas to airlines, as well as magazines, textbooks, and what was referred to as specialized information. Today, Thomson Reuters is one of the world's most successful information companies, with Thomson having merged nine years ago with the venerable British financial news service. As it was explained to me then, Thomson wanted to use the profits from its travel and oil and gas businesses to fund further penetration into niche publishing, and *LIST* seemed to perfectly fit their ideal acquisition target.

At first, Thomson offered to invest in the company, but I explained that we really didn't need more venture capital, as we were profitable already. I also mentioned that American Express and Ziff Davis were soon going to visit. In short order, they made an offer to buy the company, successfully preempting any potential bidding war. And we hadn't even published our second issue of the magazine.

When Thomson offered $60 million to buy the company I'd created less than two years earlier, it didn't take long for me to say yes. This wasn't what I'd had in mind, but this was victory. I still had student loans to pay off. My parents in Lowell were still paying down a $29,000 mortgage on the home they bought, with my father referring to his monthly payment as "the sword of Damocles" above his head.

Even after all of the investors in my company were paid off, even after all of the partners who I worked with had taken their share, even after the IRS had taken the hindquarters, I would walk away with $20 million. I was twenty-seven years old.

Back in the relatively carefree days when I was a college graduate starting out at Wang Labs, a neighbor in Lowell named Bob Hatem had declared his candidacy for the seat Paul Tsongas was vacating in order to run for the U.S. Senate. Bob was a wealthy executive at Raytheon, and he lived in a big house not far from my parents. Even though I was working pretty hard at Wang Labs, I loved politics, and I liked what I heard Bob say, so I volunteered for his campaign. I've always had sufficient bandwidth to juggle multiple responsibilities, and in those days, I also had the young man's ability to work without rest. I worked on Bob's campaign on weekends, and at night after my real job ended, and I gave him as much time as I could possibly squeeze in while still holding down my day job. When the campaign was over, and my candidate narrowly lost, I was pretty disappointed. I remember Bob said to me, "You shouldn't be disappointed. You did a really good job, and I'm grateful. And I just have to say, if you work as hard building your own business as you worked for me, you'll be a millionaire by the time you're twenty-five."

Bob was right, even though his timetable was off by approximately two years. The purchase of LIST by International Thomson was completed in 1983, and I'd turned twenty-seven in January. They gave us a great deal of money upfront, but I also had to sign a five-year employment contract, paying me $1 million per year. The good news was I was wealthy. The bad news was that I went back to being the employee of a big conglomerate.

At the time we sold the business, I was like someone who worked out with barbells with only one arm. If being hardworking, driven, and focused was the symbolic province of one arm, and being conscious of my obligations to society, in touch with my spiritual side, and a multi-dimensional young man was the other, I was one-half Popeye, one-half Wimpy. I can still remember the Argentine tennis player Guillermo Villas who was so formidable in the 1970s. His tennis arm looked like he could pick up a car with it, while his other arm was comparatively so skinny it seemed deformed. That was me at the moment I sold my business. The worst thing about being so one-dimensional was that it was the opposite of what I'd learned at Georgetown—almost a total refutation of the teachings of Father Joe. My head and my heart were not in balance. I was rich and successful, but I wasn't happy.

I do not mean to imply that I did not have fun as a twenty-seven-year-old healthy young man who, after just a few years of hard work, woke up and found he'd been sleeping on a big pile of money. When the check from International Thomson cleared, I paid off my student loan, and an immense burden lifted. I paid off my parents' mortgage and bought them a brand new car—and that really felt good; they'd never had one. All of a sudden I had all of this *stuff.* I built a house by the ocean. Now I really started making up for lost time with women. As many professional athletes discover, it is amazing how popular you become when you are young, single, and rich.

At first I liked it. The sale of my company was covered in the *Boston Globe*, and I knew that my friends in Lowell had followed the story. I went home and visited my old pals, and I was like a conquering hero. I'd made it. Ten years earlier, my guidance counselor at Lowell High had said I wasn't college material, and here I was visiting high school friends after I'd struck it rich. There is no question I was full of myself. I was probably really arrogant. And in fairness, I'm not sure how many people could have processed success like that without at least some of it going to their head.

But even with the toys, even with the brand new BMW I bought, and the Mercedes, and even with the million-dollar annual salary and the employment contract, I was an employee again. My financial freedom was paradoxically massive and conditional—I had obligations to run my company, which had become a small profitable cog in a big profitable machine. I went from being a boss to having a boss. I didn't like that so much.

It didn't take long for a sort of ennui to settle in. Is this all there is? It was like having a hangover; like I'd anticipated how much fun I was going to have with my buddies going out drinking. Maybe the evening really was fun, but it passed quickly, and there I was after the event with a hangover and a really uncomfortable feeling. I had been so programmed to be successful, and now I had that success. It seemed to create more challenges, not a perfect state of bliss.

My college roommate Bill Macdonald had skipped all the intermediate steps—good job, making money—to achieve happiness with a beautiful blonde girl in his lap. Now I had everything, but it didn't feel the way I thought it would. I thought I'd be happy, but I wasn't. I shrugged it off and continued working really hard, and in some ways my life was similar to the way it had been before. The big difference was that I'd drive to work in a fancier car, and after work I'd maybe go out to dinner with a beautiful young woman who, two years earlier, might not have returned my phone call. And after that I'd return to my beautiful house at the edge of a golf course. What was there not to like about that? Why wasn't I happy?

I continued to work, and the business was still going great, but it was clear that International Thomson was a traditional publisher, and my vision of *LIST* being available as a software database itself was far less interesting to them than just cranking out magazines. They moved quickly from the quarterly publishing schedule that we were on to making *LIST* a monthly magazine. They were the pros from Dover, with their own way of doing things. They started telling me who I should hire and who I must fire. I found myself reporting to a division chief who reported to a group president, who reported to . . . somebody up the food chain. Their version of casual Friday was to loosen their ties.

On the surface, everything was good for me. By any definition other than one that perhaps Joe Durkin would have recognized, I'd made it. But I'd lost my higher calling. My dream of publishing the Leonsis Index of Software Technology as a software database was of little interest to my corporate masters. But how could I complain about anything? If I didn't like things, I had enough money to spend the rest of my life sitting on the beach in Bora Bora, if that's what I wanted to do.

Perhaps the worst thing going on was I was being defined by the sale of my company. My friends had long since ceased introducing me to people as their friend, a nice and interesting guy. Instead it was,

"This is my friend Ted, he just sold his company for $60 million." Or, when introducing me to a pretty young woman, they would say, "This is my friend Ted. He's the youngest guy living on John's Island. People think he's living in his father's home." I wasn't a fun guy, a smart guy, or even a nice guy. I wasn't even a name: I was a number with eight zeros.

And then one day I had to go to New York for a business meeting, and I rushed from my big new home in a fancy new car to get to the airport. You see, I had a plane to catch.

Chapter Four

A Crisis Is a Terrible Thing to Waste

Reckonings come in all shapes and sizes—small, medium, and large. The reckoning I faced when I got on a plane that seemed like it might not ever land wasn't a big one, at least not by the standard of people who've stared down cancer, or overcome addiction, or seen their lives crumble around them. At the end of the day, I was still alive and in one piece. I think of it as a medium-sized reckoning because everything turned out okay, and I was open to learning from it. It was almost as if I was looking for a whack on the side of the head—an opportunity to stop and assess what had become of my life, my dreams, and my sense of happiness.

The old joke among people who live in the South is that before you go to Heaven, you have to switch planes in Atlanta. And so it was in 1984, in order to go from Melbourne, Florida to just about anyplace north or west, you first had to fly to Atlanta's Hartsfield Airport.

On this particular morning, not twenty minutes into the flight, the pilot came on over the intercom and said in that calm, Chuck Yeager voice they all seem to acquire in flight school, "Can I have the chief flight attendant up front, please?" I was in the front of the plane, First Class, and I didn't think much of it. But then the chief flight attendant came out of the cabin, and she looked a little grim. I watched her get on the intercom and announce, "Can I have all the flight attendants up front, please?" Okay, that's unusual, I said to myself. This can't be good.

She briefed her colleagues in the little kitchen, and when she was finished, stepped back into the cabin. Within a minute, the pilot was back on the intercom, and this time, Chuck Yeager seemed just the slightest bit freaked. He told us that there was a light on in the instrument panel, and that it might be nothing, but on the other hand it was of sufficient concern that he was asking the flight attendants to take some precautions while he put the plane in a holding pattern and tried to figure out what was wrong.

Well, this was a little disconcerting. Within ten minutes, the flight attendants were going up and down the aisle trying to get us all ready for an emergency landing. All the times I'd gotten on a plane, I'd sort of tuned out the flight-safety instructions, and now I regretted it. It was the first of many regrets I would review during the course of this flight.

In order to better balance the load, the attendants started to check what was in overhead compartments, and began moving people from one side of the plane to the other. They started to connect people who were traveling alone with other lone passengers to create safety buddies. They told us to read the card enumerating instructions for an emergency landing, and taught us to brace ourselves properly. I remember thinking that this couldn't be happening to me; I had a business meeting to get to!

The pilot came back on and told us we had too much fuel to land, so we were going to fly in a big circle around the Atlanta airport until it was burned off. He didn't give us any more information than that; just that we had to prepare for an emergency landing, and that, in the meantime, he was going to try making the plane lighter. The subsequent absence of communication was the most sobering aspect of our predicament, because I instinctively understood that, in this case, no news was not good news.

I remember that while they wouldn't tell us exactly what was wrong—it was only after we landed that we learned the instrument panel had indicated a problem with the plane's flaps, and there were signs that the landing gear might not properly deploy—we were told we had approximately thirty-five minutes before we would attempt our landing.

It was the longest thirty-five minutes of my life. Some people were crying, and others were audibly praying. Couples clung to one another. I'd never been particularly religious, but I knew how to pray, and I remember that even as I found myself negotiating with God, I was surprised at the track my mind took.

"Please, God," I said silently, "I don't want to die. I promise that if I live, I'll give back more than I take. If I die now, I'll miss the opportunity to do good for others. I'll miss finding and achieving my true higher calling. If You allow me to live, I promise that I will live my life so that when my time really does come, I'll be satisfied with what I've achieved and the way I've lived my life. I am not satisfied now with how I've lived. I want to change."

Thinking as clearly as I ever had, I realized that I wasn't happy. I had everything a person could want; I was the most successful young person I knew. I was also maybe twenty minutes away from dying, and I wasn't going to die happy. I was so far from being at peace with myself—I wasn't even in the same *time zone*. I had so many regrets—about the way I'd lived my life, and what I'd taken for granted, and how I'd thought that becoming a rich man at a young age was an end in itself.

It is not in retrospect that I had these thoughts. I really do remember assessing where my life had brought me at that moment, and it was clear that in the time since I'd left Georgetown, I'd jettisoned the wonderful lessons taught me by Father Durkin—that head and heart needed to be in balance in order for the whole person to be developed. I was that guy with the one strong arm, listing to one side.

The plane began to turn toward the airport, and the pilot announced we were going in, and needed to brace ourselves. I felt panic, and not simply because the plane might crash. I felt panicked because I wasn't at all the person I wanted to be. At that moment, all of the clichés were true. I didn't have a single thought that I wished I had owned something I didn't have. Instead, my thoughts were flooded by the desire for being at peace with myself, at having contentment and true happiness, the attainment of which would have made the immediate prospect of death so much less frightening.

In the end, the wheels came down. The flaps worked fine. We went whizzing by the emergency vehicles, and the plane, intact, came to a stop at the end of the runway. Cheers went up, and now we all had a story to tell. I don't know whether any of my fellow passengers felt the same thing I felt. I sat there in my seat knowing that I'd come incredibly close to dying, but I'd made it. But the most important thing was that I now had a second chance to live my life right.

Some people negotiate with God for survival, and then quickly forget the promises they made. For me, a deal's a deal. I'd promised God that if I got down on the ground in one piece, and that if my end were delayed for another day, by the time my death finally came, I'd be a different person. At my life's end, I wouldn't have anything to regret.

I still made it to New York for that business meeting, a shaken man. Outwardly, I was normal, my usual self. But the reality was I'd been rocked to my roots.

I tried to break everything down into components and analyze what had happened, and what it meant. What could I learn from it? How could I live the rest of my life with greater reflection, humility, and a focus on what mattered? I knew that I wasn't at a place of peace, happiness, and contentment. How could I get there?

It was the proverbial wake up call, and I immediately recognized it as such, which on some level was a sign of new maturity. I'd negotiated with God, and my prayers were answered. Now it was time to follow through on my end of the bargain.

I spent the next couple of weeks working hard, because there was an issue of *LIST* to produce, and things were very busy. In addition to the regular magazine, which now was on its monthly schedule, we had a custom-publishing assignment. A few months earlier when the Macintosh launched, Steve Jobs had asked us to produce the Macintosh Buyers Guide, so as to provide the same benefit to the successor to the Apple II that we'd provided the PC market, and we had a July deadline staring us in the face.

But staring a deadline in the face—even one from Steve Jobs—is not the same as going eyeball to eyeball with Death. And so on a Saturday afternoon a couple of weeks after the incident on the flight to Atlanta, I found myself sitting alone by the pool, thinking about what had happened, and what I needed to do to get my life on track.

I've always organized my thoughts by drawing up lists. The company I'd founded was called LIST. I'm an inveterate list-maker, and I carry little notebooks in which to scrawl enumerated instructions to myself. Every day since I was a student, I've drawn up my list of what I needed to get done that day. Microsoft PowerPoint notwithstanding, I believe lists are the central organizing tool of business, and all you really need is a pen and a pad of paper.

Since the *question* was what would it take for me to become happy, fulfilled, and keep my promise to God so that, in the event I found myself once again on a plane going down, I'd be able to smile in contentment, the *answer* was to write down a list of things I wanted to accomplish, and then get to work. I ended up that day with a list of 101 things that I wanted to do, or own, or see before I died—a sort of Life List. I remember going into the office that Monday and handing the list to my assistant, saying, "Here, don't ask any questions, but could you just input this list, please?" I couldn't have explained it to her at the moment, but in retrospect, I know that from the moment I had put pen to paper, my journey to happiness had begun.

My Life List was random and reflective of my maturity at the time. As sobered as I was by my brush with death, as serious as I was as a successful businessman, at twenty-eight years of age, I hadn't fully grown up, and as I look back on the list I wrote at the time, I'm not proud of everything on it. But by writing a list of things I wanted to accomplish in life, I created a scorecard—a means of tracking my progress on the road to fulfillment. Businesses measure progress at intervals as narrow as counting what's in the till at the end of the day, and more broadly track what they've earned over the course of a quarter or year. Not for nothing did some businessman create the adage, "You are what you track." In the parlance of business, we track metrics of success. Making a list to track my progress was what I knew how to do.

(The complete list is reprinted on page 287 in Appendix A.)

Even after having had a brush with my mortality in which I knew, beyond any doubt, that attaining possessions wasn't the ticket to happiness, I put down on my list such items as "own a Ferrari," and "own a great personal collection of watches." (In fact, there was a whole section entitled "Possessions.")

Some of the items I put down were the equivalent of eating empty calories; there was no real benefit derived from them. But I also put down things like, "Change someone's life via a charity." And I'm proud that the first item was, "Fall in love and get married." At least I got those things right. And in retrospect, many of the aspirations I wrote down do speak to my seeking some kind of higher calling.

There are elements of whimsy: "Go into outer space." "Swim with dolphins." "Catch a fly ball." Whether or not I hit a hole-in-one in golf (#59) is almost completely dependent on kismet, not skill. But a goal such as making a movie (check) was an ambition that upon fulfilling it (and by so doing, also achieving a second goal—winning an Emmy Award), as we shall see later when I talk about SnagFilms, opened an entirely new avenue for happiness and success.

A little later in this book (item #85 was "write a book," something I first achieved not long after completing my list and circulating it to friends and acquaintances), I'll go through the process of list-making as a practical first step for embarking on the path to happiness, and explain the impact trying to tick items off my list has had on my life. For now, I'd like to explain the way I was thinking at the time I wrote my list, to offer perspective on how and why this became so essential to my efforts to live my life on offense, and without regret.

========

Coming up with a list of things I wanted to accomplish so as to not "waste a crisis" was a logical outgrowth of the way my mind worked, and the way I was trained at Georgetown. As an intellectual process, it was almost as important to think through what wouldn't be on my list as what would. I mean, keeping up my end of the bargain and doing good in the world didn't mean I was going to be a priest. And this wasn't St. Augustine's plea to God, "Give me chastity and continence, but not yet." Instead, I wanted to come up with a more or less practical list of things to accomplish, goals to meet, and aspirations to fulfill, in order to become a more balanced individual. And I knew it was important to start right away.

While items #24 and 25—"own a jet" and "own a yacht"—likely weren't goals that Father Joseph Durkin, S.J. would have smiled upon, there was much to be said for the list's breadth—its multiple dimensions. To this end, "have grandchildren," "give away one hundred million dollars in my lifetime," "meet Mickey Mantle," "go to Tahiti," and "see the Rolling Stones" were all elements in constructing a life in which my full personality would be developed and fulfilled beyond simply making a killing in business and having lots of toys. As I wrote my list, I was conscious of the desire to be self-actualized as a three-dimensional human, and notwithstanding the tilt toward the material ("make ten million dollars on an outside investment," "own a convertible, Porsche, or Mercedes Benz"), at that moment I was conscious of the need to have both arms become equally muscular. I had to get into better balance both the hypertrophied moneymaking/business-directed side of my personality—the ambitious side that had helped make me wealthy at a young age—and the side that showed appreciation for the richness of life itself. I clearly remember that when writing my list, I was conscious of the need to put my life in better balance, and even if I didn't completely hit the mark, the reckoning I had just gone through had, to use an expression from a prior era, raised my consciousness.

All I really wanted to do was become happy. My Life List was a crude way of measuring the progress I might make in achieving that end. It also became something of a blueprint for a level of success that went way beyond what I'd already achieved. I had actively begun the journey toward happiness. Greater success would come along for the ride.

From the start, my list became the new mountain that I needed to climb. I'd sold my business and made a lot of money, but at the end of the day, my life seemed purposeless. Now I had drawn up 101 goals to achieve, and I figured I better get on with it. The theory was that by ticking off items, I'd make myself happy, and when I completed my project, I would have fulfilled my end of the bargain I'd negotiated at 33,000 feet.

The thing that's remarkable is how right this turned out to be. At that moment, all I knew was that I had created a set of aspirations. I finally had a means of focusing on the ultimate goal of happiness. My list was flawed, because I didn't have the proper tools to prioritize the central elements ("Have children become individuals and self-actualized while staying loving and within the family") from what at best were ephemeral, tertiary desires ("Catch a foul ball").

My Life List was insufficient, in and of itself, to create the happiness I desired. But I know for certain that attempting to achieve my 101 goals has made me happy and more successful than I would otherwise have been. And as I close in on goal #72, or maybe it's 73, I can see the progress I've made since 1984.

In the end, no one sits on a burning plane and says, "Well, Lord, I'm 7/10ths happy." My instincts as a college student were correct: happiness *is* closer to being binary—you either are or you aren't—than measurable by a CFO or financial analyst. The process of getting there, however, can follow the same steps as successfully managing a business. And by following the six tenants I discovered while pursuing my happiness, you will increase your happiness as well.

When I sat down and tried to determine the things I wanted to accomplish, in the belief that this would create a life in which I would be happy and fulfilled, I was no longer adrift. My compass had a target. Now I had direction. And this was infinitely more valuable than $20 million in the bank.

Chapter Five

New Rules, New Media

My Life List of 101 things that I wanted to do before I die did not include getting out from under International Thomson, but it probably should have. I'd gone from being a pioneer to being a professional manager within a big company, and it was not making me happy. I learned then that you can be very well-compensated, but if you do not feel like what you are doing fulfills your higher calling and you don't have an adequate outlet for personal expression, it is difficult to feel fulfilled and, ultimately, happy.

For the next year and a half, I dutifully tried making things work, but it was clear that International Thomson was a traditional publisher with both feet in the camp of physical media, and I was increasingly convinced that the future lay in electronic distribution of content. I had that same restless feeling that I'd had working at the Harris Corporation—that same need to pursue my vision of what ultimately would be called New Media. This time, rather than taking my ideas elsewhere and seeking funding for a new company, by late 1985, I sat down with the brass at Thomson and had a very productive conversation.

Since it was clear their interest in electronic publishing was minimal at best, I offered to buy back all but the magazine publishing elements of what had been my company, and to my relief and delight they said yes. Having sold LIST for $60 million, I now bought back the parts of it I really wanted for less than $3 million. In the same month as my 30th birthday, I once again became master of my own fate, cleaving Redgate Communications out of International Thomson.

The name of my new company was telling. As a student at Georgetown, I'd visited that ranch with the big red gate, owned by the parents of a wealthy classmate, and the image of those beautiful gates had stuck with me. I jumped into Redgate with urgency, because it offered me a new chance to fulfill the vision I'd had of publishing content electronically—databases, interactive catalogues, and entertainment available through your computer. Being able to once again build my own company, answering to myself while pursuing my higher calling—turning the computer into as robust a media platform as a television set—made me happy. Once again, I was working long hours, but in pursuit of something I believed in. My identity wasn't tied up in the tight knot of just being a wealthy young man, because I was back in my preferred role as a hardworking entrepreneur. Besides, while I was far from poor, my wealth now was principally tied up in funding my new business.

There was, of course, the danger that I would go back to being the unbalanced individual with the overly muscular right arm: all work, all ambition, and once again one-dimensional. I was at the very beginning of my campaign to achieve 101 goals on the list I'd set down, and at this point, some goals were easier to accomplish than others (like "go to the U.S. Open golf tournament.") Within a matter of weeks of Redgate Communications being formally constituted, however, my life took a dramatic turn for the better.

Even with the work involved in starting up Redgate, I stayed active on the golf course and on tennis courts in and around Vero Beach. One day, some friends introduced me to a woman playing doubles in tennis, and I was thunderstruck. Lynn Peterson was the most beautiful woman—the most beautiful human being—I had ever seen. I soon came to find out, as we dated and fell in love, that she was also the smartest and toughest person I had ever met, and that our goals were very similar. We both were single and dating, and yet we both really wanted to have a family. (Goal #1: "Fall in love and get married.")

We were married in August 1987, and that period between meeting Lynn and getting married was a time of great happiness. The central building block for participating in multiple communities is to find your soul mate, and in Lynn, I'd found mine. I actually couldn't be one-dimensional anymore, because by being so deeply in love with one another, each of us had taken on a new dimension. When our son Zach was born in October 1988, our lives expanded further, and the birth of a healthy child created even more happiness. By 1992, when our daughter Elle was born, our family was complete, and the relationship between the four of us became the central element of my life. My family is the primary platform for everything I do. When I over-index toward work, or some project, Lynn, Zach, and Elle bring me back to center. Even if you have everything—money, success, an interesting life, fulfillment in your career, and accomplishments galore—your family is the most important factor in making your life add up to a meaningful sum.

At the same time that, as a husband and father, I was becoming a more complete human being, Redgate Communications became the first New Media company. (LIST had contained the seed, and I consider it a New Media company, but the concept really flourished as Redgate.) In 1988, I wrote a white paper entitled, "New Rules, New Media," which is often credited with coining the term. In that paper, and in every conversation I had with potential customers, partners, and investors—in fact, with just about anyone I met—I proselytized on behalf of the idea I had first had almost a decade earlier, when I sat down in front of a little Apple II. My epiphany about the future of computers and televisions had become a higher calling. More than ever, I envisioned a day when computers and televisions would be largely interchangeable: computers connected to media in a fashion similar to what was currently the province of television, and television being hooked up to programming and data, with interactive features then available only through computers. I argued that more information would travel over the air, telephone calls would be wireless, and television would move inexorably from a broadcasting model to almost entirely being connected via cable. Having been open to the concept of mash-ups ever since Father Joe Durkin and I had combined linguistics, computers, and literature to produce my Hemingway thesis, it increasingly seemed that the mash-up of media and technology would be fast upon us.

I was far from the only person with this vision. However, Redgate was unique in the multiple angles from which we pursued it. We were simultaneously consultants and practitioners, one moment advising BellSouth or AT&T on what content might soon move through their pipes, the next moment working with computer companies like Apple or Sun Microsystems on the content that might be available on computers. In 1987, we actually created a private satellite network where companies could broadcast their messages directly to other businesses.

Well before there was an Internet per se, by 1991, we were the first company to get into the interactive shopping business, with a CD-ROM in which hundreds of catalogs were digitized so that one could, for the first time, use a computer for comparison shopping. Once a consumer had chosen the product he or she wanted to buy, they could connect to the retailer by modem and actually make the purchase. Today, in the era of one-click instant gratification, this may not seem like a big deal; in 1991 this was revolutionary. We called this project 2 Market, and our joint-venture partners included Dow Jones, EDS, and Apple.

It was a moment of great ferment. Interactivity seemed to be moving inexorably from underground into the clear light of day. Once again, it seemed like my own company was in the middle of everything.

There was enough interest by big companies such as Dow Jones in acquiring Redgate that by late 1991, I hired an investment banker. Hambrecht & Quist was based in San Francisco and had perhaps the best investment banking franchise for young technology companies, with their practice run by a man named Dan Case. Dan was handsome, incredibly bright, ethical, and charming. He had grown up in Hawaii, gone to Princeton, and been a Rhodes Scholar. Until the very sad day in 2002 when he died of a brain tumor, he was one of the leading bankers in taking technology companies public, and since we suddenly seemed to be "in play," it was prudent to hire Dan to explore our options.

In early 1992, when Dow Jones became serious about wanting to acquire Redgate, Dan recommended that we stay independent. He felt it was too early in the process for Redgate to be sold, because to do so at that moment would leave money on the table. There was another reason for his reluctance: Dow Jones was a business-to-business entity (notwithstanding its ownership of *The Wall Street Journal*), and Dan knew that my vision, and the promise of Redgate, was ultimately to become a company touching the mass market of consumers.

During the summer of 1992, as the discussions with Dow Jones continued, one night I had dinner with Dan. We were talking about what was happening in this by-now burgeoning technology sector. Dan had told me previously that his younger brother Steve was an executive and co-founder of a company in Virginia called America Online. I was an early member, and found it interesting to be able to email people using an AOL screen name, though at that time it was just one of several online services available. On this evening, Dan said, "I spent the weekend at a family gathering with Steve, and I have to tell you, you and he sound exactly alike. You're both using an identical vocabulary, and I don't hear a lot of other people—even technology executives in Silicon Valley—talking about consumer adoption of some of these services that you guys each seem to be thinking about identically. I need to introduce you to Steve; I think you'll like each other."

It wasn't until the next winter, February 1993, that my path and Steve's finally crossed. I was supposed to give a speech in Boston at a conference, and Steve Case was going to give a talk there one day later, and just as I was making my travel arrangements, Dan called me up. "You're both going to be in Boston within a day of each other. Steve could fly up the night before his speech, and meet with you the next morning, if you'll stay over. You should sit down with him."

At that point, I would do anything Dan asked, so I said yes and made arrangements to stay the night after my speech.

I was staying at Le Meridien Hotel, so Steve and I planned to meet for breakfast there. I got to the dining room first, and in a few minutes,

I saw a guy walk in who was clearly Dan Case's brother. Steve is cool where I am hot, and he's calm and calculating where I am ebullient and outgoing, and so in the first few minutes of our discussion, I did all the talking. I remember talking a little trash about Dan, and kidding Steve about his nickname, Lower Case. (Dan's was Upper Case.)

We went to a table and sat down, and a waitress brought us each a menu and a cup of coffee, and I think I had taken my first sip when Steve announced, "I know a lot about your company through what Dan's told me, and I think we should merge our companies."

It was the first complete sentence Steve had said. I'm pretty sure I swallowed my sip of coffee, though if ever there was a movie version of this scene, the guy playing me would probably spit that sip of coffee across the tablecloth.

I said, "Can we kiss first? Can I meet your parents? You want to get married on the first date?" I was amazed and amused. And it has to be said: intrigued.

And Steve said, "Life's too short to drink bad wine. I have really good instincts and a good vibe about this, and I'm sure that we should merge our companies."

And so we talked. And while Steve went on to deliver his speech, I went home. Over the next month or so, Steve and I would email back and forth, via America Online. We sat down again a little later in the year, and by the autumn, we were in a serious discussion. I was in the middle of a big round of raising capital for Redgate, and Steve felt it was important that I close that deal, as the investors were serious, sophisticated companies like AT&T.

By October 1993, Steve Case and America Online made an acquisition offer for Redgate, and it was the proverbial offer we couldn't refuse. In the end, Redgate would receive approximately 6 percent of

America Online's outstanding shares and an option for an additional 4 percent. Redgate would remain as a standalone company in Vero Beach, where I would live. It took the Board of Redgate a short time to approve the acquisition. The 6 percent of AOL shares (up to 10 percent with options) that we received at the time the deal closed in 1994 was worth about $40 million—less than what I'd sold LIST for ten years earlier. For AOL, acquiring Redgate was accretive: between when the deal was announced and when it closed, AOL's share price had risen sufficiently that the acquisition was essentially free. I had a pretty good feeling that the value of my stake in America Online would be worth more over time.

Chapter Six

Building a Global Medium

T he story I could tell about my time at AOL would make a book in its own right. In fact, there have been at least four books written about the rise and fall of AOL. (Kara Swisher has written the two best, the first about the rise, the second about the post-merger fall.)

But it isn't my intention to chronicle the full history of AOL in this space. My interest is in sharing what I learned during my thirteen years as an executive there, because it was over the span of my AOL career that I achieved genuine happiness and learned many of the lessons I hope to impart through this book.

The most important lesson learned can be summarized as follows: when the company, and its employees, partners, and users were happy, AOL flourished. When these constituencies were unhappy, it spiraled down. It was a simple formula. Make multiple communities happy and all will be well. Fail to do so, and it all falls apart.

From my vantage point, AOL didn't just rise and fall. AOL rose and fell, and then it rose and fell again, and...I can't, at the moment this is being written, actually predict what will happen, as in the autumn of 2009, AOL, like Redgate in 1986, is poised once again to become an independent entity, cleaved from the shanks of Time Warner, after such an unhappy time within a larger corporate entity. After a nine-year detour down what is widely derided as "the most disastrous merger in American corporate history," AOL will again become an independent entity, under an inspired CEO recruited from Google, Tim Armstrong, and will have a fighting chance of reclaiming at least some of its past glory.

For me to write about AOL at this moment is fraught with peril. It's like reentering a battle scene where a million arrows have already been shot off. The smoke from campfires surrounding the carnage is still rising. For someone who helped lead one of the participating armies a long time ago, the impulse to keep moving is strong. This, after all, is a book about happiness.

It's not my intent either to refight the war, or answer the critics, though some historical perspective is needed. I recently read a prominent journalist's account of his sojourn covering AOL over the course of, he said, half of its life as a company. He said that during the time he had covered AOL, there was only an eighteen-month period when we weren't on defense.

Well, now. I suppose that's possible, or certainly that's his perspective, given the moment when he first began to cover the company. All I know is that in the six years between 1994, when I arrived, and 2000, when AOL's acquisition of Time Warner was announced, the company went from a market cap of $400 million to $163 billion. Over a ten-year period, it grew from $60 million in revenue to $10 billion in revenue. When I arrived, AOL had 300,000 members. Eight years later, it peaked at 36 million members. If you tuned into the AOL story in 1994, the company's climb and moment of dominance was not short-lived. It was one of the great business success stories of all time.

Let me state for the record: I was passionately opposed to the merger with Time Warner, and I protested it by not moving to the combined company's New York headquarters as so many of my peers did. I immediately shifted more of my energy to my teams and charitable work.

Once the merger was consummated—it took a year—the company we'd built began to decline, and AOL was on defense.

But I was there, too, for AOL's second period of rapid growth, between 2005 and 2007. This is the time frame when, even as the subscription business we ultimately abandoned continued to unravel, the advertising business I oversaw became the second-fastest growing audience and advertising-funded business among the major online companies (after Google). This second period of rapid growth culminated with AOL persuading Time Warner's professional managers to let us jettison the dial-up subscription business whose decline distorted the underlying strength of our advertising business. Unfortunately, this second growth period ended when Time Warner fired Jon Miller as CEO, and once again, the pros from Dover were sent in. Many of my colleagues and I left—in my case, following a period of less than two months in which, as Vice Chairman Emeritus, despite having a fancy title and a desire to help, I was shut out by the installed professional managers. From afar, my colleagues and I got to watch all of our hard-earned progress dissipate, and AOL once again fall back on defense.

There are business lessons to be learned from AOL's rise and fall, and rise and subsequent fall. Perhaps too many words have already been written about the roller coaster ride we were on. For a long time, I was in the lead car on the roller coaster—sometimes sitting right up front, sometimes shoved back in my seat.

But there were lessons to be learned about happiness, too, and in telling the AOL story from my perspective, that's where I want to begin.

———————————

It took until the middle of 1994 for AOL's acquisition of Redgate to close, and by that time, Steve and I were in constant contact. One morning, I was sitting at home in Vero Beach, and Steve and I were sending emails back and forth in rapid succession. I would send an email with two lines, and he would email right back to me, and it was like an instant messaging session, a precursor to AOL Instant Messenger (which we would introduce to the world two years later as AIM).

I remember that the exchange that morning revolved around my conviction that America Online could fulfill the promise contained in its very name, and that we could get tens of millions of people online. We knew that our job was to take the complexity out of things. Neither Steve nor I were technologists—we were a marketing guy and an English major, respectively. One of Steve's major strengths is the fact that he is fundamentally a very normal person. His view of life is in sync with Middle America. When you're cool, you might be a little snarky, or play to the other cool kids, but when you're mainstream, as Steve is—and honestly, as I am—you play to the middle. And this was an essential ingredient in AOL's success: making the online medium work for the masses.

Our business vision was that by getting people online, we could change the world. In those early days of the Internet, we had grandiose dreams. We believed we could level the playing field for education, for example, as a family living in rural Mississippi might have the same shot at a good education as a family in Manhattan. We could introduce more democracy into the world, and compress the distance between people and their friends and loved ones by introducing a widely used new communications medium. As Steve and I riffed, I remember sending him an email that said something like, "It's our job to make this online communications stuff social and high touch so that everybody can use it and, like the telephone, like the television, not even have to think about it."

I could really envision AOL's higher calling as, first, getting people online by simplifying the process, and then having the medium itself introduce new possibilities in bringing people together. I was taken with the romance of the name America Online; it just seemed to be the logical outgrowth of everything I'd been striving toward for the past decade. And of course, what I was repeating back to Steve was exactly what he and his wife Jean and other early members of the AOL team believed in and had started both to articulate and put into practice.

Steve quickly replied, "Call me. I want to talk to you right now."

So I reached him at home, and in his typically direct fashion he said, "Look, I know we've just closed the deal and that you're supposed to stay in Florida and run Redgate, but I think you should come to D.C. I think I should concentrate on expanding internationally, on our investor base, and on our strategy for acquisitions, but I think you should run AOL, the core service. You should move here and be the president of AOL."

I was stunned, to say the least, but before long, Lynn and I flew up to Washington, and it immediately felt like home. We stayed in Tysons Corner, Virginia, and I took Lynn into Georgetown that night to have dinner and show her D.C. The next day, I had a series of meetings at AOL's headquarters. Steve and I talked at length about the role I should play at AOL. It seemed natural to me to be back in the Washington area, and I understood the logic of moving into AOL's headquarters, but I wasn't an independent agent. I couldn't just make a decision about moving from our home in Florida all by myself.

As Lynn and I flew back that night, she told me, "I think we should do this. I could be really happy in Washington. I have really good vibes about Steve and the company. We need to do this."

In a matter of some weeks, I was in place as the new president of AOL.

When I joined as president, AOL was far from the juggernaut it became. We had 300,000 members. We were on a march to get to one million members, because that was a big number, and we thought that at one million, we'd be taken much more seriously, and see some of our goals begin to come to fruition. We weren't really aware yet of the so-called network effect—once everyone you know has become part of a network, everyone else joins the bandwagon in order to participate with all their friends and colleagues. All we knew was that after one million would come two million, and so forth. Remember: good day, good week, good month; three good months make a good quarter, and it continues.

AOL was a happy company, and in retrospect I wonder if one of the reasons for this was because it had so many great female executives. Jan Brandt, Kathy Ryan, Audrey Weil, Jean Villanueva, and Lynn Cameron were absolutely essential executives in AOL's greatest periods of growth—and happiness. It may not be a coincidence that when AOL later became an unhappy company, most of the top positions were held by men.

I worked day and night, and met every one of AOL's 500 employees and all our partners. I wanted to get as much feedback as I could and found there were a lot of really smart people in the company whose ideas were very good. Naturally, I created a list of what we needed to accomplish in order to fulfill what became our corporate mission of creating "a global medium as central to people's lives as the telephone or television . . . and even more valuable." My goal was that AOL should be transformed from a one-dimensional data communications company into a genuine New Media company, and we redesigned the service around what became known as the channel metaphor—just like with television, you went to different channels to get different programming. We threaded together our "Six Cs"—convenience, connectivity, community, communications, content, and ultimately commerce—which to this day are the basis of Internet business success.

AOL was an Internet service provider—an ISP—and as such would get people online. At first, this meant getting them inside AOL, not the Internet per se. Once there, each channel we created would be the organizing principle for what they wanted to do, from reading the news to getting the weather forecast; or from following their favorite sports team to checking in on the latest entertainment offering. It was always clear to me that the future lay not in connectivity—that was just providing a dumb pipe to get someone online—but in content and the other dimensions of our service. In addition to just connecting people to content, as providers of email, message boards, chat rooms, and eventually, instant messaging, AOL revolved around the concept of community. It was that "third place" where people could reside in between work and home, to paraphrase Ray Oldenburg's *The Great Good Place*.

Each of the "Six Cs" proved to be important, but nothing was so important as community. From these early days, community was central to AOL's success, as more people went online and found others like them organizing around certain topic areas. At first there were hundreds, and then thousands, and then tens of thousands of chat rooms organized by members who wanted—needed—to discuss topics of interest to them. From breast cancer survivors...pet lovers... fans of particular teams...supporters of particular political parties... gays and lesbians...to divorced straight people...everyone, it seemed, was beginning to use AOL to connect with others, to talk, find fellowship, and compare their experiences. From the comfort of your living room, you could be linked with people across the country and the world. This seems so basic now in a world organized around Facebook communities or fan forums for sports teams. In 1994, however, it was *terra incognita.*

Even as I was helping to build AOL as a medium in fulfillment of the insight I'd had a decade earlier—that the computer monitor and television offered essentially the same possibilities—I paid really close attention to what was going on within the AOL community. And because people used their AOL screen names no matter which public chat room they entered, and because the community was still small enough that you could remember some people's screen names, I began to notice the same people popping up all over the service. The same person might, on a given Saturday, be found discussing college football in one chat room, then on Sunday show up in a completely different chat room discussing religion, and then next Friday be discussing the movies she wanted to see that weekend. From the tone they used and the tenor of their conversations, it did not seem like they were lonely individuals. It became pretty clear that many of the people who were moving from one community to another weren't lacking normal lives or normal relationships in the "real world." They were well-established, well-adjusted social animals who understood that the online medium AOL was building was becoming that good third place between work and home, as well-established in the American psyche as the bar in *Cheers*—just gone off the air at its peak in popularity—or the neighborhood Starbucks, which were beginning to proliferate across America.

The people in AOL's chat rooms were *happy*. And the more chat rooms that were opening, and the more time they were spending meeting other people, the happier they were. Consequently, the more time they spent with AOL, the more money we made (the amount of time you spent online was still metered; we had not yet gone to unlimited pricing). I hadn't been at AOL very long before I began to connect the dots.

Happy members were happy customers, creating and expanding a happy AOL community. This in turn made us a very happy company.

———

AOL was a happy company, first and foremost, because it was fulfilling its mission. We really were changing the world in pursuit of the statement we made into a plaque and hung in the lobby at headquarters: "To build a global medium as central to people's lives as the telephone or television—and even more valuable."

While people working inside corporations with office email had, since the early 1980s, been able to communicate back and forth electronically, even in the mid-1990s writing letters while at home still involved taking pen to paper, or typing and printing something, proofreading it, folding it and putting it in an envelope, getting your tongue cut as you sealed the envelope, searching through your drawer to find a stamp, and finally giving that letter to someone, who gave it to someone else, who sorted it, and then gave it to the person who would put it on a gas-guzzling truck, drive it to the airport, and hand it off to the person who put it on a plane. When it came off the plane, someone would sort it again before putting it on the truck where a nice letter carrier would deliver it the person you wrote, at best two days later. Holy cow!

With email, grandfathers could connect to grandchildren with the press of a button. It was faster, better, cheaper, and more convenient. As the convenience of doing things online expanded—as more and more people began going online—we were making people happy. And as we made people happy, those of us working at AOL were happy, too. We were working for a company with a mission, and as we fulfilled that mission, the excitement and innate goodness to what we were doing felt almost tangible.

Working for an online service is somewhat unique in that you receive immediate feedback from your users. AOL's members would show us in real time which of our products worked and which ones didn't. The more time they spent online mastering the new tools available to them, the more they told us what else we should be making for them. The more they liked our products and services, the happier and better our employees felt, and the more money we were making. The more money we made, and the more new subscribers signed up, the higher our share price rose. Our users loved us so much, they bought our shares. It was the definition of a virtuous circle.

The whole company was on a mission, and even though the companies deemed cool by the "digerati" were those like Netscape, which operated as an Internet browser, or Yahoo!, which was a portal, AOL was thriving. It's true that business users could explore the nascent Internet with the faster T1 connections available at work, while their

AOL connection at home, coming in over copper wire, was much slower. Even before the crisis when AOL went to all-you-can-eat pricing, and the resulting explosion of new subscribers trying to get online simultaneously through local access numbers led to busy signals and angry state Attorneys General, AOL was already being dismissed as a pokey online service. But if we were on defense, it was because we were too popular to service demand.

Within a year of my arrival at AOL, a moment arrived when I realized I was succeeding in my own personal quest to become happy.

I was working really hard, but you can work hard and be miserable, or you can work really hard and be happy, which in turn makes you work even harder. In my case, it was the latter.

Lynn loved living in Northern Virginia, and we both enjoyed being parents of young children. Admittedly, I was at the office early and late, and even when I was home, I spent a lot of time working—something AOL, the service, allowed you to do by connecting you to co-workers via email. With me working as much as I was, Lynn picked up a great deal of the responsibility and was a wonderful mother to our children. But Lynn knew she had been correct in believing that moving to the Washington area and my going to work with Steve at AOL was the right move for us and for our family.

My family made me happy. And it must be said, so did fulfilling the higher calling I had pursued in business since starting LIST all those years before. It was fulfilling to witness the long-ago vision I had become a reality: the computer and the television were functionally merging.

AOL was performing well financially and was in many ways the hottest company around. For tens of millions of Americans, "AOL" and "the Internet" were synonymous; we were the category, not just a brand within it. People really loved the products we made and sent suggestions for improvements. Some even sent us love letters. I would spend an hour a day reading through emails our customers sent to Steve Case, so as to learn what we could do to enhance our service. There was constant positive reinforcement for what we were doing.

I went through a somewhat frantic period where I got a number of items crossed off my Life List of goals. My position at AOL made accomplishing some of them just that much easier. For example, I had on my list going to a championship fight, and we had a partnership with HBO, and I called the president of HBO sports in order to go see a Mike Tyson match they were airing. Boom, another item checked off the list. And this did make me happy.

But as I paid attention to what was driving my happiness, I realized that fulfilling the goals I'd written down were just a part of the picture. Writing down the list a few years before had gotten me to focus on happiness as a quest. It concentrated my thinking in the right way. Just as a businessperson can track a set of metrics to understand whether their company is on track, my list had given me a way of keeping score. As I would come to find out, it wasn't the perfect system for achieving happiness in and of itself. And yet I knew that having defined happiness as an explicit goal, and having organized myself in pursuit of 101 separate sub-goals, at least I was facing in the right direction. Was I really making progress? Yes, it sure felt like it. But I knew there was more to it than that.

By the beginning of 1995, I had given my first speech talking about happiness as an explicit goal for us at AOL. It was entitled "Niceness As A Competitive Weapon." I believed—and still do—that if a company focuses on things like happiness and community, it will prevail in the marketplace. I remember talking about AOL's mission as a company, and about the need for us to be nice to one another—and that our purpose was to seek, and become, happy and self-actualized individuals. Even then, I remember having an understanding that there was a connection between our creating happiness for ourselves and building a bigger, better, and yes, happier business.

It was hard to slow down sufficiently to examine and analyze what really was making me happy, but I would look to vacations as times of reflection, when I could tote up the metrics of happiness and assess where things stood. They say you should check the batteries in your smoke detectors every year when shifting from Standard Time to Daylight Savings Time. Similarly, as frantic as we might be trying to get the most out of our limited vacation time, I tried to use these respites from the office to check in on how I was tracking against my goals.

I was making progress on my list—on the big items as well as the smaller ones. What I had instinctively understood to be the most important goals, such as getting married and having children, were providing me with tremendous satisfaction. I was increasingly living my life without regret.

But as I began thinking about it, new elements for happiness were coming to the fore. The first one was community.

Fostering multiple communities was a driver of AOL's success, so I had to pay attention to it. From my own observation, and from reading letters people sent us, it seemed the happiest users were those who participated in multiple online communities. This made me think about my life at that time.

As hard as I was working, the center of my life was Lynn, Zach, and Elle. Having children put us in close contact with both Lynn's family and mine. We spent as much time as we could with each other's parents and extended family. Our immediate and extended family comprised a community, and our participation within that community expanded as our parents wanted to spend more time with their grandchildren.

I spent a large amount of time at work, and I really enjoyed the people with whom I was working. We were comrades in arms, fighting Microsoft and taking on all comers. As a team, we did encounter conflict. Tensions could be high when a new product was gearing up for launch, but we liked one another, spoke the same language, and together developed what was long ago tagged by some consultant in a similar context as our "corporate culture." We spent hours and hours together trying to build a better product and serve our customers. We were a community serving a community.

In my various roles over time at AOL, I had to stay in close contact with our customers, our partners, and participants within the larger technology community, many of whose members I had worked with going all the way back to LIST. I was part of the larger community that was building the Internet, and even though many of the people I saw at conferences or met with in their offices or ours might be viewed as competitors, we were part of something larger and we knew it. We could compete by day and still be friends when day was done. Washington had been a home away from home for me, and I stayed in close contact with the greater Georgetown community—faculty and alumni alike. The Hoyas were one of the elite college basketball teams, and because I lived in the area, I was able to go to their home games, increasing my contact with the Georgetown community.

I also became a season ticket holder to the Washington Capitals' games, and I became a real fan, switching from a lifetime's allegiance to the Rangers, and to a lesser extent, the Bruins. Whenever I could, I would go with Lynn and friends out to the old Capital Center, which later became known as the US Air Arena, all the way on the other side of Washington in Landover, Maryland. We built a community of hockey fans among our friends, and a community of friends from the hockey fans we met.

When Zach, and later Elle, went off to school, as good parents we began spending time with the parents of our children's schoolmates. We soon learned the lesson you never expect before you have children: that through school, your children will create their own community, and as parents participating in your children's lives, your own community expands in a circle around them.

Lynn and I still had a home in Vero Beach, and we maintained our friendships there. Therefore, in addition to the friends we were making in the Washington area, there was an established community with whom we were close and did not lose contact, despite the physical distance.

And of course, the very products we were offering—email and, by 1996, instant messaging—fostered communication among and within communities. I knew at the time that AOL Instant Messenger was launched that the Buddy List was a way to organize the different communities around which your life revolved, from family to work. It was clearly an important precursor to Facebook and Twitter. By the mid-1990s, in addition to creating virtual communities, the emerging communications tools were breaking down the distance between people, and enabling friendship and happiness to spread.

More subscribers signed up every day. Over time, by offering users access not just to the AOL service but serving as the on-ramp to the Internet as a whole, we marketed our service as "the Internet and a whole lot more." Throughout the 1990s, before the cable and telephone companies began to offer broadband connections, for tens of millions of Americans, "AOL" and "the Internet" were synonymous; we were the category, not just a brand within it. And of course, with the exponential subscriber growth we were generating, our share price continued to climb month by month, driving the entire stock market.

Despite our success, we lived in a state of constant fear that we were going to be gobbled up by Microsoft, whose vast resources as an operating system and office-product monopolist left it poised either to acquire AOL, or to launch a service off of the operating system that might disintermediate us from our customer base. This outside threat only helped unify the company. In fact, not long after I arrived at AOL, we held a rally in which I stoked the company's competitive fires by picturing Microsoft as a great dinosaur out to destroy us. It served as a great motivator, reinforcing an even stronger *esprit de corps* among our workforce.

It also served as a preemptive strike against a future reckoning. I knew Microsoft and how Bill Gates thought. If MSN had the jump on us, Microsoft's dominance in computing could be fatal. We had to prevent that from happening.

Our employees bought into our mission. Forced to develop an "us-versus-the-world" response to MSN, our workforce became more cohesive and inspired—and yes, it must be said, much wealthier. At some point, we had 3500 millionaires employed by AOL. The happiness we were generating was making us rich.

━━━━━━━━

As AOL grew at an astonishing rate, it made the transition from being "loved" to being "needed." This wasn't a good thing, in my opinion. I remember the exact moment when I realized it had happened.

In 1996, before Bob Pittman joined AOL, eventually to become our CEO, he and his future wife Veronique vacationed with Lynn and me, as well as two other families, on a chartered yacht in the Mediterranean. It was really important to get away and unplug. I'd been working very hard ever since joining the company, and I really needed to check out from email, phone calls, and meetings. This was, of course, before the era of ubiquitous connectivity, with mobile devices connecting to the Internet (and the home office) in the most remote locations in the world.

One day, Bob and I were sitting on the deck having a conversation about whether it was better for a company to be loved or needed. A veteran of MTV, Viacom, and Warner Brothers, Bob knew as much about branding and media companies as anyone around. I argued that the best brands were loved, and cited Disney, Nike, and Coke as examples of loved brands with staying power. Bob argued that in fact it was good to be needed, and that companies that provided a needed service to consumers—cable companies, for example, which provided connectivity—also had a superior amount of information on their customers. Bob argued that AOL was increasingly a utility for people, and that was okay; to be needed was a good thing. I disagreed; I believed AOL was at that time loved, and that it really was better off than if it were simply needed. No one loves the power company, even if they need electricity.

That evening, all of us went to dinner at a restaurant in Positano. We were high above the port, and it was a really beautiful evening. As we were waiting for our party to be seated, the Maitre' D asked where we were from, and I told him Lynn and I were from Washington. He asked what I did, and I told him I worked for America Online. A look came across his face, and in a moment he had fished a newspaper out of a garbage can behind the counter.

"*AOL E Morte*" was the headline. AOL is dead. All the way over in Positano, Italy, an outage that would knock America offline for nineteen hours was making headlines.

I had to quickly call Steve Case from the restaurant, to find out what was going on, and the worst thing was: neither he nor anyone at AOL at that moment knew. The service was still down, and no one understood exactly what the cause was. He told me not to cut short my vacation; they'd handle it. But I returned to the table shaken.

"That's your answer," Bob said when I sat down. "If the AOL service going down makes news all the way in Italy, it shows that you've become needed."

He was right, and it really bothered me. We'd gone from being loved to being needed. From the standpoint of our share price and importance as a company, that was for the moment a good thing. From the standpoint of whether or not we were a happy company, I suspected that wasn't such a good thing.

Brands that are needed can always be replaced by other brands that fulfill the same need.

Brands that are loved can maintain their dominance over a much longer time horizon.

When Bob Pittman joined AOL as the President of the AOL Network in the autumn of 1996, I moved into a new role as President of AOL Studios. AOL had grown big enough that producing the content and services we would offer our members needed to be treated as a business in its own right. And after presiding over nearly three years of AOL's greatest growth ever, I stepped out of the role of running the service and essentially became our content chief, reporting to Steve Case.

I would serve in this role from 1996 until 1999, at which point I became President of AOL Web Properties, overseeing brands and services such as Netscape, Moviefone, Mapquest, Digital Cities, and Winamp. Between 1996 and 2001, while I was integrally involved in helping to develop the services that would animate the online medium, I was no longer running the AOL service as I once had. You might say that I was running the parts of the AOL experience that we hoped people would love, while Bob Pittman ran the parts that people would need. Bob Pittman is a master marketer, and a brilliant businessman, and he was very adept at taking AOL to another level as a business.

At AOL, I often said, "Today is the worst day the Internet will ever again have." By that, I meant that tomorrow there would be more users who would be online. The speed at which they would connect would be faster, and the bandwidth would be cheaper. There would be more content for them to access. There would be a bigger online community. More investment and innovation would produce great functionality. It's still true. *Today* is the worst day the Internet will ever again have.

Just as Moore's Law posited that computer chips would double in speed every eighteen months even as they cost half as much, I belived that every day there would be more things you could do online, ultimately new media would win out over traditional media, and businesses would charge less and less for their offerings, until many of the best things in life would, in fact, be free.

Even in my days at Redgate, I'd understood that there were "new rules and New Media." The first new rule was that the more people you could get online, the faster you could grow the medium. From the moment Steve Case recruited me to help him, I positioned AOL as a media company. Steve encouraged this, because he understood it was exactly right. This had tremendous implications for our business model.

Traditionally, media companies with a subscriber base—let's say, Time Inc.—have dual revenue streams. They sell subscriptions, and because they have subscribers, and hence an audience, they can also sell advertising. It wasn't long before AOL was able to do the same thing.

AOL built the first online advertising platform which created a second revenue stream after subscription income. Though it ultimately was all-you-can-eat pricing that goosed the subscription business into the stratosphere, AOL's becoming an advertising medium forced marketers and advertising agencies to recognize the power of the online medium as a nascent alternative to print, radio, and television. And when that happened, the last AOL skeptics in the financial community threw in the towel, and soon, everyone was buying shares in AOL.

The stock split, once, twice, okay, it split seven times. If each of the investors and employees who benefited from AOL's acquisition of Redgate had held onto our shares and sold them at the peak, we would have shared in something like a $9 billion jackpot. Of course, that's not how it ever works; no one ever actually holds on to all their shares and sells them right at the top of the market. I sold shares along the way (including a significant percentage of mine in order to buy my sports team holdings—the Washington Capitals, Washington Mystics, and a share of the Washington Wizards), and yet at one point still qualified for the Forbes 400 List of the richest Americans. Albert Einstein once famously said that the most powerful force in the universe is compound interest, but compound interest is actually a pretty weak force when compared to the power of stock splitting.

In fact, the IPOs of AOL and then Netscape Communications were so phenomenally successful, they triggered the "dot.com" era in the stock market. And yet the rise in AOL's share price was so stratospheric, we'd been able to acquire Netscape outright.

By 1997, it seemed like AOL was the most successful business in American life. But it wasn't all good.

AOL continued to exhibit enormous growth—but simultaneously began to lose its vision. From a mission to get America online…to create a medium as central to people's lives as the telephone and television, and even more valuable…we had become a really big business. Unfortunately, sometimes when a business generates the kind of success that AOL was generating, it can lose sight of its higher calling.

We lost out on some big opportunities as we began focusing short-term share price over long-term growth.

During AOL's rise, our workforce was so busy that our single, young employees needed to create an online dating service called "Love At AOL." It solved the problem of which young woman in Network Operations might want to go with a young programmer to see a movie on a Saturday night, but it also held the potential for something bigger. In fact, when Love At AOL launched as a dating service on AOL itself—not just for AOL's employees, but for its members—it was an instant hit. Before long, however, another online dating service called Match.com wanted to become the exclusive dating service on AOL, and they were willing to pay for the privilege. And so not only did we accept a really big check from Match.com so they could take over the Dating channel on AOL, we actually sold them the category, and Love At AOL was merged into their service. Years later, once AOL wasn't doing well and we were trying to develop our strategy to get AOL's mojo back, someone at one of our really long meetings had a great

idea. We could see the success Match had using AOL to build traffic to
their service. Someone asked, "Why did we give up the Love At AOL
franchise? Why don't we build our own service again?" And of course
the answer was that Match.com had written a very big check, and by
taking in that revenue *at that moment*, we had another killer quarter.
Now, and for some time to come, they owned the category on AOL. So
even if we wanted to revive Love At AOL, we'd kicked away our ability
to do so, because at some point, we'd sold the category just to make
the quarter!

In the late 1990s, we began to manage to the quarter, not to the mission. I'd long had as my mantra the progressive formulation of good
days ultimately leading to good quarters, but I also understood the
importance of playing not to the quarter as a god in its own right, but
simply as a metric for measuring success. In addition to financial metrics, I'd always viewed my job as working to please 1 million members,
which became 10 million members, which became 20 million members, and so forth in virtuousness and happiness. But the company
became so successful—such a juggernaut, with such high financial
expectations to justify our share price—that we began to manage not
to 20 million members, but to 15 financial analysts on Wall Street. We
weren't trying to keep our members happy. We shifted to keeping
financial analysts happy, and in that construct, it's easy to sell away
entire categories of future success just to make the quarter.

Individuals are imperfect beings, and anyone of us can lose his way.
Everyone can be lured off the right path. The same is true with companies.

Whenever AOL was in service to its customers, its members, its
employees, it was a happy company. It did good things. It grew and
was dynamic and innovative, and in so doing, it built genuine value.

But when we got off that path and worshipped the false god of a short-term earnings bump, we lost our way.

In a public company, you're constantly in a battle between doing the right thing in the right way and meeting the demands of Wall Street. You are constantly balancing leadership and vision with the expectations of financial managers. And there are times when the pressure on leadership and management to meet what looks like the right management objectives really proves to be the wrong thing to do. Selling out Love At AOL is just a metaphor for the way short-term lucre at times blinded us not just to what was the right path for building AOL and the online medium, but what our long-term best interest might actually have been.

Before Amazon became the most powerful online retailer, AOL had an opportunity to become its most important partner. For an investment of $500,000, Jeff Bezos offered us the opportunity to have Amazon be our exclusive retailer of books. We'd be able to share the revenues from books sold to AOL members, and we'd have an option to acquire 20 percent of the company. That same quarter, Barnes and Noble offered us $14 million annually to be our exclusive partner in the book category—with no revenue share and no ownership prospects. One deal would show up as $14 million of advertising revenue, and the other would show up as a $500,000 investment. Barnes and Noble carried the day, and AOL lost a chance at owning a 20 percent share of a company that in the fall of 2009 had a market cap of $40 billion.

Years before, I'd learned that if you just exercise one arm—if you over-index entirely in one area of your life—you get out of balance. And so it went with AOL.

Our financial results directly translated into a higher share price. The higher share price directly enriched many people at AOL—me among them. At one point we had six executives on the *Forbes* 400 list of the wealthiest people in America.

The momentum we acquired had an impact on our entire industry. Wall Street had started to take lots of Internet companies public and every one of those companies needed the oxygen that a deal with AOL could provide. And so in effect, we had a group within AOL that was almost like an investment bank, and their mission was to extract value from companies while helping them to go public. Because of the size of our audience, because of our dominance in getting people online, a young company would pay AOL a very significant amount of money to do a deal with us that would generate traffic to their service, and they would leverage that deal into a public offering. For a time, it made financial sense to everyone. For a time.

We would get advertising revenue from these deals, and by getting warrants in the newly public company, we could share in their success. But the deals were based on a false economy, which was that companies could raise venture capital, and in rapid order, do a deal with AOL and go public. When the dot.com bubble was inflating, this worked fine. When it was punctured, things were not so fine. And yet with all these companies competing to do a deal with AOL, they created what was, in essence, our third revenue stream.

We had this beautiful, understandable, predictable consumer-based, ongoing revenue stream, which was the subscription business. We built and maintained this business by operating and enhancing a good service that pleased people. We got America online, helped them to communicate, helped them to socialize, and to live their lives on the Net faster, better, cheaper, and more efficiently. Occasionally we would screw up—the service would crash for a day, or some ill-considered marketing gambit would make people think we were trying to trick them—but we would quickly get back on track.

Our second revenue stream flowed from our having become an important media company. The core of our advertising business was innovative and helped to create the online advertising economy. (Later, when we weren't so dominant and we had to persuade advertisers that they wanted to be on our service, this became an impediment bordering on a disaster, but during the rise, AOL's proprietary publishing platform and display ad dimensions forced agencies and marketers to create one set of ads for AOL, and one for the rest of the Internet.)

This third revenue stream, based on corporate development deals, helped turbo-charge AOL's financial reporting. Yet as it turned out, at a certain point, the deals weren't based on business fundamentals. And according to the Securities and Exchange Commission, at a certain point—as the "dot.com era" became the "dot.bomb era"—approximately one handful of those deals also weren't done in compliance with accounting rules.

In addition to the puncturing of the dot.com bubble, there was one other problem looming. The telephone and cable companies understood that AOL had won the first round of the new medium by renting the phone companies' infrastructure and reselling it to consumers with branded software and the AOL client technology. In the dial-up era, we had used their networks to get America online, and even though we were the telecom industry's single biggest customers, and even though they made plenty of money off us, the real value had accrued to us, not them. As the broadband era loomed on the other side of the coming Millennium, they weren't going to let that happen again.

And still AOL's business expanded—now 25 million subscribers, now 28 million subscribers. You could hear the marketing apparatus begin to pant with exhaustion. We became a little tricky trying to sell people new services. The woes people had trying to unsubscribe from AOL became legendary—at every party, someone would tell a story about how difficult it was to quit AOL. In meetings with sophisticated business executives, you'd hear how their 13-year-old had clicked on the wrong link and ended up subscribing to a service neither the child nor her parents knew she'd just signed up for. Even as broadband began to ramp up and churn increased, AOL kept growing. It was getting harder to grow by the same increment as before, but by launching services in Europe and Brazil, the subscriber base continued to rise. And so did the share price, and as the new century loomed, the stock split again, and then one more time.

Before it all came tumbling back down, it had to reach a peak. And the peak, of course, was the acquisition of Time Warner, announced in January 2000, and finally approved and consummated almost one year later to the day. For me, the announcement that AOL was acquiring Time Warner in a "merger of equals" did not produce happiness. It was very fortunate that, for some time now, I'd found other sources of happiness beyond work.

Chapter Seven

Empathy, Charity, and New Avenues for Happiness

Between 1994, when I arrived at AOL, and the dawn of the new millennium when the AOL-Time Warner merger was announced, I really grew up. As a husband and a father, I had learned that happiness could not be achieved by over-indexing on work—even with the responsibilities I had, even at the center of a company that had become a global phenomenon.

I'd say that the biggest discovery I made about happiness over the course of the 1990s and the beginning years of the new century was the role that empathy plays in providing an individual with opportunities to find happiness. Empathy for others led me to participate in charitable activities, which increased the number of communities in which I was involved. Empathy for others made me grateful for what I had, and I discovered that gratitude sustained me when I felt down, and grounded me when things were good. Empathy for others led to a number of relationships and activities that made me really happy. I learned that empathy for others was the connective tissue between the various components of happiness. During a time when I might otherwise have been down, by tuning up my empathy and becoming more involved in the lives of others, I was actually quite happy on a consistent basis. Moreover, I made discoveries that have led me to new business opportunities that sustain and fulfill me to this day.

Even as a relatively callow business success, I knew it was important to participate in charity. You don't grow up in a tight ethnic community without understanding that when you're successful and make a lot of money, you have obligations to provide for those less fortunate.

What I learned was that, even after having started a charitable foundation to provide a vehicle for philanthropy, writing checks to support charities is kind of a lazy way of giving, and whether you're buying a table at a gala, or just writing a check because a friend has asked you to support his pet cause, it's pretty unfulfilling. You're not connected to a mission. You don't have hands-on experience without the output or the successes of the charity.

Over time, I've gotten deeply involved in a number of charitable activities that have increased my awareness of how expressing your empathy leads to happiness. When you work with people who are deeply involved in a charitable cause, you find they tend to be pretty happy people. Whether it's the team working for the charity, or like-minded supporters doing their part, no matter how grim the mission might be—feeding the homeless, aid to those afflicted—charitable activities are by definition driven by a higher calling. This tends to offer new paths to happiness, but as we will see later, adding a community devoted to one cause or another to your network of communities helps drive both happiness and your opportunities for successfully connecting with people whom you might not otherwise ever have met in your ordinary work and life.

My journey to happiness included important stops in support of two charitable organizations in particular, Hoop Dreams and Best Buddies. Involvement in these organizations added dimensions to my life and my happiness. And it was through them that I discovered just how vital giving back to society is as a means of building sustainable and fulfilling happiness.

———————

The documentary film *Hoop Dreams* came out in 1994 and had an immediate impact. Set in Chicago, it told the story of two young African-American teens who dreamed of making it out of the inner city to the glamorous world of the NBA. Two years after the film came out, Susie Kaye, a teacher at H.D. Wilson High School in Washington, D.C., created the Hoop Dreams Scholarship Fund, which started with a one-day, 3-on-3 basketball tournament to raise college scholarship money for African-American youth in the District of Columbia. Susie's dream went beyond just raising money; she knew that one of the greatest impediments to success for young black men is the absence of role models and mentors who can provide the kind of non-financial support needed to make the leap from the streets of D.C. to college. It was easy enough to give money, but after talking with Susie about her goals, I told her I wanted to see how the program actually worked before just reaching for my checkbook.

And so I was paired with a young man named Michael Hendrickson, who was then in his junior year of high school. Michael didn't have the best grades, but he had a perfect attendance record. I read that as, "I'm desperate to be in control of the output of my life. I'm struggling, but I'm willing to do the work to get there." Michael never really knew his father, and he had two brothers who'd been incarcerated, and two sisters who were single mothers. He was the archetypical young adult who could go down the good road, or the bad road. I thought back to my days as a young man in Brooklyn, where the difference between going to college or perhaps being shot while trying to rob a pharmacy was whether you took that extra 100-foot stroll past the park bench where the older kids were drinking and smoking pot, and moved on down to the community center. When I met Michael, I realized he was a really good kid, and I wanted to help him.

So I bought Michael a laptop and got him an AOL account, and I told him that we were going to work together. I said that we would start small, with an emphasis on what he wanted to accomplish every day. I asked him to write me an email every morning with his list of what he wanted to get done that day, and at the end of the day, he needed to write me an email on whether he'd met his own goals. And if he didn't meet his goals, he needed to explain why. This was an effort to get Michael to envision what he wanted to achieve, to write his goals down, and be able to see how he was tracking against his own metrics for success.

We did this every day, and no matter how busy he was, or how busy I was, we stayed constantly in touch. I would meet with Michael at least once each week, and ended up hiring a tutor to help him with his SATs. Michael determined that he really wanted to go to Hampton University, a historically black college in Virginia. While he did better in his grades, he still got pretty low SAT scores, and when he applied to Hampton, he was wait-listed.

I felt really terrible for him. By that point I'd gotten to know Michael, and I admired him for his willingness to work to achieve his dreams. So I called the president of Hampton, five times in fact, but he never called me back. One day, I called around eight in the morning, and by luck, he picked up his own phone. I talked to him literally for an hour about Michael, and at the end he said that they would let him come to Hampton for summer school, and if he could maintain a C average, he could enroll there in the fall as a freshman.

I paid for Michael to go to the summer program, and he did even better than was required: he got all Bs. He struggled a little bit in his freshman year, but got stronger academically as the years went on, and when he graduated, he was on the Dean's List. It was one of the proudest moments of my life, and it made me really happy.

Michael now volunteers for the Hoop Dreams Scholarship Fund. He became a director-level executive at Verizon, but was recently laid off in a big corporate downsizing. Michael and I email back and forth every week, and we are working together on his next phase of career development. We go to Washington Caps and Mystics games together. I've become something like a surrogate father to him. I was there for him when his mother died, and I helped to get him his first apartment. Yet while Michael has benefitted from my being involved in his life, it has enriched my own life as well. Over time, my foundation got really involved in the Hoop Dreams Scholarship Fund. Sadly, in the current economic environment, Hoop Dreams has found it difficult to broaden its base of donors, and after thirteen years, it is beginning to wind down its operations. I can say unequivocally that my investment of time and financial resources in Hoop Dreams has been one of the greatest of my life, and it has paid me great dividends. It has made me happy.

Another organization I got involved in was Best Buddies, which was founded by Anthony Shriver, whose sister Maria, the First Lady of California, was a classmate of mine at Georgetown and a close friend for more than thirty years. The Shrivers are a really remarkable family, and they've helped more people in need than any family I know. Sargent Shriver started the Peace Corps. The late Eunice Kennedy Shriver started the Special Olympics. Best Buddies is a program in which you team up with someone with an intellectual disability and become a mentor and a friend.

When I learned about the way Best Buddies worked, I wanted to find a way of automating the program, and so we created e-Buddies, where you could become friends with someone online, and it's through this that I became a friend and mentor to Big Ken Holden.

Big Ken is now in his early 40s, but when I first met him, he was twenty-eight years old. Neither of his parents felt that Ken was capable of using a computer and having a relationship like this, but we got Ken a Mac, and through some coaching got him engaged in writing every day. Not a day has gone by in twelve years in which I haven't written to Ken. If I'm going away, and know that I won't be able to get to a computer, I pre-write letters and have them sent in my absence.

One time, I was at sea on vacation and I couldn't get an Internet connection, and I knew that Ken would be expecting an email from me. And so I used the ship-to-shore radio to call my assistant, and I dictated a letter to Ken, which she sent. Over time, I've become Ken's best friend—his Best Buddy—and he's become a really good friend of mine. I've also become friends with his sister Kendra. I've never had a relationship with someone with an intellectual disability, and I learned that I had underestimated how capable they really are. I've since helped raise more than $10 million for Best Buddies, because through exposure to them, I became connected to the higher calling of reducing the isolation of those with intellectual disabilities. They need to be able to participate in the broader community. They need ways to self-express.

But whatever I've done to support Best Buddies has paid off in spades for me. You see, taking time during even the busiest days to write an email to Big Ken Holden hasn't simply connected Ken with a friend. It's helped me connect with a friend. It has also made me happy.

———

Telling the stories of some of the charitable activities in which I became involved while working at AOL is not meant to shine the spotlight on my generosity. Most happy people I know are motivated to connect to others less fortunate than they are, to contribute what they can, and be generous no matter what their own financial circumstances are. The reason I've offered these anecdotes is to shine the spotlight on the connection between empathy, giving back to society, and the creation of happiness. And it's meant to explain how it was that even as I was over-indexing in work, and in building AOL, my engagement in charitable activities created happiness—happiness that sustained me when perhaps things at work weren't so great. Showing empathy and gratitude for what one has, and getting involved in the lives of those in need—not through writing a check, but through active involvement—has led to my being a happier and more fulfilled human being.

When I sat on that plane and promised God that if I lived, I would become a better person, and would use my talents to do good, it was a sincere way of bargaining to get off that plane alive. Giving away some of the wealth created by the rise of AOL was a means of fulfilling a promise made under duress. I had no idea at the time that through getting involved in the Hoop Dreams Scholarship Fund, in Best Buddies, and in a number of other such activities, my life would be so enriched. I had no idea at the time that such activities would open me up to greater happiness—happiness that would sustain me no matter what else was going on in my life.

Chapter Eight

He Shoots, He Scores!

My 101 list directly led to my becoming the owner of the Washington Capitals. In 1999, a local reporter wrote a profile about me and included as a sidebar an excerpt from my list, including the goal to own a sports team. Dick Patrick, who was then and is now president of the Caps, had been chartered by Mr. Abe Pollin to find a buyer for the team. So he called me.

Abe was a remarkable man who built and sustained both the Washington Wizards (nèe Bullets) and the Caps, and in the mid-1990s, he'd taken on a very significant financial commitment building a new arena in downtown D.C. (The week this book was wrapping up, we received the sad news that Mr. Pollin, a truly great man, had passed away.)

Mr. Pollin had moved his teams from Landover, Maryland, into the heart of the District because he thought it would be better for the city he loved. He financed this himself, in an act of civic generosity that is increasingly uncommon among sports team owners, who often rely on municipalities—taxpayers—to build them their new arenas or stadiums. In fact, when Abe built what is now called the Verizon Center, he helped restore the commercial center along 7th Street, NW that had been destroyed by the 1968 riots following the assassination of Dr. Martin Luther King. Abe's commitment to downtown D.C. sparked a boom in restaurants and nightlife, but financing the arena didn't come cheap. So Abe decided that he needed to find a buyer for his hockey team, the NHL's Washington Capitals, and when Dick Patrick read that I had "own a professional sports team" on my list, he quickly got in touch.

Dick sat down in my office at AOL, and he had a very intelligent pitch. Essentially, he said that it is very difficult for anyone to purchase a sports team in his home market. Taking Washington as an example, he pointed out that Mr. Pollin had owned the NBA basketball franchise (Washington Wizards) for thirty-five years and the Caps for twenty-four. At that time, our NFL team, the Washington Redskins, were owned by Jack Kent Cooke, and before him had been owned seemingly forever by the legendary Edward Bennett Williams. At that time, D.C. didn't even have a Major League baseball team.

Dick's message was pretty simple. I had stated that one of my life's goals was to own a professional sports team. The Washington Capitals were for sale. I could buy the Caps, or someone else could buy the Caps, but if someone else bought the team, they'd probably own the team for a long time. He said that if I really were serious about becoming a team owner, this was probably my shot.

I thought about what he said. I looked out my window at the AOL campus, and it was rocking and rolling. People were bustling from the large office building known as CC3 over to CC1, an Ultimate Frisbee game was being played on the lawn in between them as engineers who would probably work a 14-hour day took a little break, and every space in the parking lot was full. I was a high bandwidth executive who could manage multiple things simultaneously, but this was a time when AOL was just nailing it, growing in leaps and bounds, and I had a big job. Yes, the fact that the share price was rising exponentially meant I had the financial wherewithal to buy a team, but one reason the share price was rising was that all of us were so focused on improving the AOL service.

So I said, "I'm not interested. I love sports. I really love hockey, and I especially love the Caps—I'm a fan and a season ticket holder. But I'm fully engaged here at AOL. I'm married, and I have young children. Being a team owner involves a lot of scrutiny, and it is a lot of money. So thank you, but I think I'm going to pass."

Dick is a gentleman, and he thanked me for my time, and as he left he said, "If you change your mind, give me a call."

And so that was that. I went about the rest of my day, went home, and talked to Lynn. When I told her what happened, she didn't say much. Later, when it was almost time to go to sleep and we were both lying in bed, she said to me, "When you get old, and you're at number 99 on your list, and you've got just two more things to accomplish, but you didn't buy that sports team when you had a chance, and you didn't win the championship, and so you're never going to have completed the one-hundredth and hundred-and-first items on your list, will you regret not buying the Caps? Think about it."

And it really struck me. I had made my list. I'd followed through on it pretty consistently, acting when I had the opportunity to fulfill something I'd put on it. I'd written my list as a younger man, and I knew that not everything on it would provide me with the same degree of satisfaction. Owning a Ferrari wasn't as fulfilling as getting married and having children. (In fact, I found that owning a Ferrari wasn't really fulfilling at all, and I quickly sold it. The best part is that I actually sold it for a profit, bought a much cheaper Mercedes-Benz, and donated the rest to build two Habitat homes in New Orleans after Katrina—which made me really happy!) But there was a reason why I'd written my list. It captured goals and aspirations I'd authentically believed were things that would make me happy and offer fulfillment. Among these aspirations, Goal #40 was to own a sports team, and Goal #41 was to win a world championship. And here I had an opportunity to buy a team in Washington, D.C.—the town in which my family and I lived—and I'd just turned it down.

I thought about how someone else would buy the team, probably someone my age and a lot like me. And they'd own it forever, and I'd have missed my chance. I supposed I could buy a team in another city and commute to games. And I thought to myself, "What would that be like, commuting to Philadelphia or Charlotte to watch a game played by my team?"

I had vowed that if God let me get off that plane, I'd live my life without regret. And then I'd made a list of things I wanted to accomplish so that by steadily working my way through them, when my time came I'd be happy and able know that I'd done it. And so after thinking about it for one more day—analyzing how much AOL stock I'd have to sell, trying to think through the arithmetic of team ownership, and figuring out just how much I really would regret passing on this chance—I called Dick, and we began a negotiation.

Now, this is a moment when I won't deny that having money gives opportunities for happiness that are special. From my research and observation, I believe that having money and being happy generally correlate, as the social scientists say, about the same as not having a lot of money and still being happy. People who aren't "rich" can be just as happy as those who are, and as the difficult lives of Howard Hughes or Michael Jackson might indicate, maybe have even a better shot at happiness.

But being able to own a team is undeniably cool. I was in a position to sell several hundred million dollars of AOL stock in order to buy the Washington Caps. In fact, I used to joke that I owned the team for free, because later, when AOL's share price fell to $8.00, I knew I'd sold pre-merger shares priced high in order to buy a tangible asset. Today, my sports holdings constitute the biggest part of my family's financial assets.

Over and above the fact that I was wealthy enough by then to buy the Caps, and beyond the fact that, yes, being a sports team owner can be really fun, there's a serious lesson here that universally applies, regardless of how much money is in your bank account. Setting goals is an important way of capturing what would make you fulfilled and happy. Once you've set those goals, you need to take them seriously. You shouldn't put on your list of life's goals becoming President of France if you don't live there. At the same time, if you do put on your list climbing a 14,000 foot peak, you really should go buy some hiking boots and get in shape.

In order to live a life without regret, it is vital to both set goals and take available opportunities to achieve them. I had the opportunity to fulfill item #40 on my list of 101 goals, to own a professional sports team. I didn't blow my chance. There's no question that owning the Washington Capitals of the NHL continues to make me happy.

But there's another link in the chain. I bought the Caps in 1999 when, objectively, most people would have said that I was a highly successful Internet executive. Ten years later, it's likely that I am best known as a sports team owner, not as someone who helped build AOL, or who pioneered the rules of New Media. Today, many people would say that even though the Caps have yet to win the Stanley Cup, they're a more successful institution than AOL is, and that my own greatest business success—as unfulfilled as I am having not yet touched the Stanley Cup—is as a team owner.

Prodded by Lynn, driven by my desire to fulfill my 101 list, I bought the Washington Capitals. Just as I parlayed ownership of Redgate into a big stake in AOL, I transformed AOL shares into an ownership stake in an appreciating asset. It has made me happy. Beyond making me happy, I believe owning the Washington Capitals—an important institution in the Washington community with the double bottom line of both creating happiness and being financially viable—has made me a more successful person on many levels. QED.

———————————

Growing up, I loved the New York Rangers. My father took me to the Garden to see Rangers games, and sometimes at night I'd listen to them over a transistor radio I placed on my bed beside my pillow.

When we moved to Lowell, the Bruins were at the tail end of their great run with Bobby Orr, and it was impossible to live in Massachusetts and not be a fan.

But I arrived at Georgetown just as the Caps came into existence, and for $5.00, you could get a ticket, a bus ride to The Capital Center, and a hot dog and soda. Even within my limited college budget, this was a good deal, and I went to a bunch of Caps games. Consequently, when Lynn and I moved to Washington, one of the first things I did was buy four season tickets.

About five years ago, we refurbished the team's locker room, and in addition to installing new carpets and furniture, we took a number of photos from the archives, blew them up, framed them, and hung them on the walls. One day, I was walking through the locker room and glanced at one of the photos. It was a shot of Abe Pollin and Dick Patrick and the then-captain of the Caps, Dale Hunter, on the ice holding the 1998 Eastern Conference Championship banner. Something caught my eye, and sure enough, there in the fifth row of the crowd were my son Zach and I watching them lift the banner. And I know exactly what I was thinking at that moment: *I wish I could do that.*

In 1998, during the Caps' only Stanley Cup finals, I found myself in Los Angeles on AOL business the night Game One was to be played in Detroit. When my meeting was over, I could have taken the 2:00 p.m. flight to Dulles, but that would have meant missing the Caps game. I booked a ticket on that night's "red eye," extended my hotel room reservation, ordered room service . . . and watched in frustration as the Caps lost a game they should have won against the defending champs. I was pretty tired the next day when I got to work, but I would have been tired and even more frustrated if I'd missed the game.

So for me, buying the Caps wasn't like buying the Phoenix Coyotes or some other team that didn't really mean anything to me. It wasn't one of the "empty calorie" goals I'd put on my list as a young man and then achieved (see: buying a Ferrari). It was buying a team I knew and already loved. I'd turned down the opportunity when it was first presented to me but, thankfully, reconsidered. When I bought the Caps and assumed ownership, it was deeply fulfilling, and has been so ever since.

───────────

When I met Abe Pollin, he told me that owning a sports franchise like the Caps was a public trust, and that nothing brings a city closer together than an exciting, winning team. He also told me that the personal scrutiny that comes with sports team ownership is as intense as it is for a major politician.

How right he was, on all counts. Even during the hottest days of summer, with the hockey season over and a new one months away, fans of the Caps will be on message boards and will email me literally 100 times per day. They are as passionate about their team in the summer as they are at the height of the season. We're all part of an extended community, and when I think about my role in that community, I know I have a large responsibility.

I want the Caps to win the Stanley Cup championship, but that's not even our real mission. Making the playoffs is great, and winning the Stanley Cup is going to be fantastic, when we finally achieve it. But bringing the city closer together—helping all of our fans achieve some element of immortality for having been part ·of a glorious season together—is the larger mission, the higher calling. That's the achievement that is priceless.

When I was a teenager in Brooklyn, the Mets made their improbable run to the 1969 World Series, and the Jets won their only Superbowl. This was the same era in which the New York Knicks won the NBA championship, and the Rangers made it twice to the Stanley Cup Finals. Throughout that magical period from 1968 to 1971, I was with my father constantly—in the stands at games, watching them on television, listening on the radio. When we weren't watching the games, we were talking about them—and so was everyone else in the neighborhood. I remember that time with joy. The nation was in tumult, New York City was on its way to a fiscal train wreck, society was turned inside out over politics and Vietnam and sex and drugs and rock 'n' roll, yet I remember that period with joy. Why? Well, on a summer day, you'd walk by a store and there would be a crowd of people around a makeshift television watching Tom Seaver or Jerry Koozman pitching for the Mets. On a Sunday late in the fall, it seemed the whole neighborhood was alive as Joe Namath took the Jets into the post-season. That whole period glows in my mind. I feel connected to it—to my memories of being with friends and family and strangers alike—and forty years later it brings me happiness.

Sports teams can bring a city together. If you think about it, that's as important as anything a politician can do.

There's no business that can produce happiness like a successful sports team. Last May, when the Caps were in an exciting, ultimately disappointing playoff run, a local reporter named Tim Lenke wrote a column in the *Washington Times* about Alex Ovechkin and the joy he brought the Washington community. I could completely relate to the way he compared the happiness created by Alex and the Caps to the joy just then being created by Zack Greinke, a young pitcher for the Kansas City Royals of Major League Baseball's American League:

> Kansas City as a baseball town is a lot like Washington used to be as a hockey town. Poor attendance, years of struggle. But here in Washington, Ovechkin arrived and things started to change. People started to believe. The team started to win, and all of the sudden the Verizon Center was packed, and now we're the center of the hockey universe.
>
> What Zack Greinke is doing has the same feel of those early days when Ovechkin arrived. 22,000 people watched him pitch last night in Kansas City, which doesn't seem like much except that the Royals usually draw half that on a Monday night. It was the Royals' third win in a row and the team is winning the AL Central and there's a feeling that they won't

fall back to last place like they have in the past. If he continues winning, the excitement could be similar to what we saw with the arrival of Fernando Valenzuela in Los Angeles, or Mark Fidrych in Detroit. It's next-day buzz where people ask "oh man, did you see that last night?"

After Monday's game, Royals head coach Trey Hillman said: "I'm thrilled to death for our fans. Our job is to inject as much joy into people's lives as we can."

That's the perfect way to describe the responsibility of being a sports team owner: to inject as much joy into people's lives as we can. Come to think of it, I can't think of a better description of a happy company, either.

In terms of anxiety and responsibility, buying a sports team is a little like having your first child. From the first day, I wanted to be a great owner, bond with the fans, and do everything right, but there was no *Sports Team Ownership For Dummies* to tell me how. Now, after a decade in the business, I can say unequivocally that winning a championship in any professional sport is the hardest thing to accomplish in business.

First, there are twenty-nine or so competitors—the owners of the other teams in your league—and they're just like you. They're your age, and they're just as smart and accomplished, or else they wouldn't have been able to buy a team. They're as well-educated, as successful, and as rich as you, or even richer. They're really competitive people— just like you are.

Think about that compared to a typical business, where when you bring a product to market, there are maybe a handful of major competitors out there. In a sports league, there are twenty-nine other people trying to build just as good a product as yours. They're competing for the same resources you need to be successful—players and coaches.

In addition to the talent of the best players and coaches, in order to win a championship, you also need some magic, which is not a word typically invoked when talking about a business.

Allow me to explain. A lot of times, you look at a team on paper, and it would seem they should be champions, but they ultimately don't perform well. The magic needed is not so much raw talent—though no doubt that's the first 90 percent of the equation. It's the way the team meshes as individuals who can become a single unit. A sports team is the ultimate people-oriented business. How an owner communicates and creates a culture, a system, organizational pride, and a platform for the players to succeed are all critical factors in a team's success. Understanding the ingredients involved is easy. Procuring the ingredients—right coach, right players—in theory, is easy. Making it all work involves some magic sauce, and that's really hard to figure out.

Then you have all of the quirky things that you just don't have in a "normal" business. Never once while at work at AOL did the HR executive walk into my office and say, "You really need to sit down. Your head HTML programmer's out for the season. I know it's two weeks before the product launches, but he's got really bad carpal tunnel syndrome in his typing hand. We're going to have to call up the head programmer from Netscape."

I can't quantify the number of times our general manager, George McPhee, has come into my office and said something to the effect of,

"The goaltender just blew his knee out. He's going to miss eight weeks." And there's nothing you can do about it, no matter how smart or skillful an owner you are. (Though it helps to have a backup plan, and a good player on the bench.)

When we had Jaromir Jagr play for us, he was the highest-paid player in the league, and many people would have said the best. The day before the playoffs began, someone chopped his wrist with a stick, and broke it. We couldn't tell anyone. Jaromir just had his wrist taped up, and he went into the playoffs against a team every bit as good and tough as we were, and he had to play with a broken wrist. And of course, the public reaction is, "Jaromir stinks. He choked in the playoffs." While the truth is that he could barely hold a stick, and just getting out on the ice was an act of courage.

On top of this, you have a third party involved: the referee. Refs are human, and they do a really good job, but they're not infallible. The Caps have lost two playoff series in the last few seasons playing, in overtime, shorthanded. Why were we shorthanded? Because a ref blew a whistle. Were they right to blow a whistle? It really doesn't matter, and over time, the call is as often going to go your way as the other team's. But the ref is a third-party factor that you can't in any way control.

And then you have pure luck, working for you or against you—usually, it seems, against you, unless it's one of those years in which your whole team is slathered in that magic sauce. A puck hits the cross bar and instead of being ahead two to one, you're still tied. And the other team scores and they win.

The point is that owning a sports team is a tremendous responsibility, and while you have the opportunity to create joy, it's a really hard business, for a number of factors. Businesses normally have a more limited number of competitors. There isn't a human, a third party—a ref—calling the plays in each engagement.

In the first phase of my being a team owner, I was anxious to get a Stanley Cup, and it led me to acquire Jaromir Jagr, the league's biggest star. I increased our payroll beyond what was financially wise. And the not-so-funny thing was, the more money I spent, the worse we got.

I like and admire Jaromir, and wish him well, but as talented as he was, he really didn't want to be part of the Washington Caps community; he just wanted to get out of Pittsburgh. He was extremely talented, but that was actually a problem. The players around him would just give him the puck and watch; they stopped playing. From the standpoint of creating a cohesive team, acquiring Jagr was an absolute disaster. The team didn't perform well, the locker room was divided, and the fans were really unhappy. One year we lost $35 million—a lot of money! By this time it seemed clear that the business model for the NHL was broken, and we were heading for a lockout, in which none of the teams would play games for perhaps an entire season.

As the lockout loomed, I recognized our situation for what it was: a reckoning. It was an opportunity in which we could make the necessary changes to get on track, or not. If we made the right moves, we could start building a happy team. And I was convinced that if we could build a happier team—one that was more cohesive and didn't have such a mismatch between marquee players and all of the rest—we would be more successful.

One of the things people in publicly traded companies complain about is that you can seldom do the right thing and take the long-term view. If the financial analysts expect $11 billion of EBITDA (the standard way media companies measure profitability), by God, you have to produce. It makes it hard to invest in long-term R&D projects.

But when it became clear that there was going to be a lockout for the 2004–2005 season, I viewed the Caps as having an opportunity to transform the kind of team we were. It was clear that a salary cap was coming—a limit on the total amount of money a team could pay for player personnel—and so we did a lot of research on how teams in sports leagues that had moved from a system without a salary cap to one that had one, managed under the new rules. We were determined to develop a plan to be successful in the new reality.

After analyzing a lot of data on teams in other leagues that had been successful, it was pretty clear that we'd taken the wrong approach. We had a very expensive team. And when I closed my eyes and asked myself, "Can I envision this team ever winning a Stanley Cup and bringing the city together while creating joy and happiness?" the answer was no. That was a difficult conclusion to come to because we were already a perennial playoff team—we just could never get through the first round.

So we developed a plan for completely rebuilding the team. We traded every player we had with significant market value—players in their prime—in order to get draft picks and up-and-coming prospects. We didn't trade expensive players to get expensive players; every trade was intended to get a pick-and-a-prospect. It became our mantra.

Because we'd been a playoff contender for so many years, we'd consistently had our first-round draft choice be number fifteen or higher. (In the NHL, as in most sports leagues with a draft, the worse you do, the higher you draft—and we weren't bad enough to get good draft picks.) After a number of years where you're always drafting in the mid-teens, and never drafting one of the top five choices, you become mediocre. You lose the opportunity to spark your team's development with a single young player added to the roster. Smart teams can be transformed in one or two years by building around their high draft picks.

We envisioned a future built around a core of players that we would amass via the draft and trades for prospects. We determined to teach them in a way that we liked. We thought we'd be able to do this because the players we would get would be young. We'd be able to define their behaviors and our expectations for them. Importantly, while it looked to the world like we were deferring our dream of winning the Stanley Cup, even though this sounds like a paradox, we believed that by following our strategy we would increase the prospect that we'd actually get there in a shorter time frame. We knew the press would be brutal, the fans would be mad, the business—ticket sales—would drop, but by facing our reckoning with a real plan, we would actually hasten our prospects of achieving happiness as a team—and with it, success.

So we traded Jagr, and Peter Bondra, and Robert Lang, and on and on. This made our fans really unhappy. I communicated our strategy and thought process in as transparent a fashion as I knew how. I said explicitly that we had to get bad in order to be good. It wasn't what someone who'd shelled out hard-earned money to buy a season ticket wanted to hear. But it was the right thing to do, and I told the truth about what we were doing.

We finished the 2003–2004 season with the third-worst record in the league, after having made the playoffs and winning the division the previous two years. And just to prove the role luck can play in the fortunes of a sports team, at the end of that year, the puck bounced our way. Our third-to-last finish paid off by our getting the Number One draft choice in the lottery. And that was the year that Alex Ovechkin was available to be drafted.

It was a good year to be bad. We drafted not only the most talented hockey player in the world, we drafted a happy guy. Alex doesn't just play hard. He plays with a smile on his face. He exudes gratitude for the sheer pleasure of being able to play the sport he loves. He is a brilliant player, but he's also a wonderful human being. Because he's such a good guy, no one begrudges the money he makes, or who he is, or how he's treated. He is one of the guys, and when he's on the rink, he lifts the playing skills of the players around him. They don't just feed him the puck and watch; they don't stop playing when Alex is on the ice, leaving everything up to him. They play their hearts out because that's what Alex demands.

Drafting Alex Ovechkin set the tone for our team. Four years later, we haven't won the Stanley Cup, but this year we went to the seventh game of the second round against the team that eventually did win it. We sold out every game. We now have a waiting list for season ticket holders. People leave the arena with big smiles on their faces. We've built a happy team, a happy franchise, a happy business, and it translates into happiness for the fans, happiness at the box office, and happiness for the city. I can say with humility that we're not yet where we want to be. I can also say with confidence that the best is yet to come.

Owning the Washington Capitals is not simply being the proprietor of a business. It is, as Abe Pollin said, a public trust. It has also offered me an outlet for personal expression, as I've strived for transparency and continuous communications with our fans. When we traded players like Jaromir Jagr and Peter Bondra, I answered every email, including the ones that began, "I can't believe what a moron you are." There were many emails that were worse.

One of the things about having helped build companies that were innovators in email—from Wang Labs to AOL—is you understand that the hierarchies of organizations have flattened, and that any fan, or employee, who writes the CEO, or the owner of the team, expects to get a reply. No matter what I'm doing, or how busy I am, I attempt to reply to every email I get from the Caps community, and when the volume is simply too great, I try to address fans' concerns through my blog, *Ted's Take*.

Even while attempting to be open and approachable, there can be rough moments, and in the immediate aftermath of the Jagr trade, tensions ran high. In late January 2004, we were playing a Sunday afternoon game against the Philadelphia Flyers. We'd traded Jagr the previous week. It was snowing so hard that I decided not to go to the game, because it would have meant driving in from Virginia through unplowed streets. But then my son Zach said, "C'mon, let's go to the game," and since you have finite opportunities in life to spend a Sunday afternoon with your teenage son, we got in the car. We weren't halfway there before we slid a little way off the road, and my car got banged up. A fender bender, nothing serious, but it was jarring—one of those automobile mishaps that can ruin your whole day.

I remember thinking, "Let's just turn around and go home." But we were halfway there, and the car was drivable, so we continued on our not-so-merry way.

Practically as soon as I got to our box at the arena, I saw a young man holding up a sign that tried drawing a comparison between how the Caps were performing and how AOL was doing. This was at a moment when SEC and Department of Justice investigations of AOL's advertising deals from past years had not yet concluded, and the share price of the corporate entity that was, by then, known simply as Time Warner—the AOL stock symbol had long since gone away—was at maybe 15 percent of its pre-merger high. And the Caps, having just traded our biggest name player had, at that moment, limited prospects. I tried ignoring the sign, and the young man holding it and shouting my way, but the Caps were losing pretty badly. There was no way, at that moment, I would characterize either our team, our fans, or myself as being happy. We had just started to dismantle the team with a long-term strategy in mind, but if you're a season-ticket holder, and all of a sudden, management starts trading away your team's best players, even if you buy into the theory that this is for the long-term good, you do not feel joy. And when your team is losing to one of its archrivals, and you've slogged your way through a blizzard to see it, you're probably not in the best of spirits. Certainly, after a hard week and a minor car crash, neither was I.

While the Caps were losing, I got a phone call from Stephen, my driver, who was off that day. He's terrifically dedicated, and he offered to come pick me up from the game for the drive through the snow back out to Virginia. But even after having slid off the road on the way in, I thought I could make it home. Talking on my mobile phone, I said to Stephen, "Well, how bad can it be?" I wasn't driving an SUV; I was driving a sedan, so I thought I should go see for myself how hard the snow was falling. I left the owner's box and walked across the entrance lobby to catch a glimpse of what was going on outside. A woman stopped me and asked if I would pose for a picture with her daughter, and just as we were finishing, the young man who'd been holding up the sign saying something like, "Caps Losing, AOL Losing, Any Connection?" happened to be coming out of the arena, maybe to go home, and as luck would have it, he walked right by where I was standing.

This was one of those classic situations where "words were exchanged." He got a little too close to me while cursing me out, and I thought he spat at me. And I responded in a way that was incredibly stupid. I grabbed him, and lifted him a little, and more words were exchanged. I didn't hurt him, but what I did was wrong. He was a young man who was a diehard Caps fan, and on this day he had a head full of anger and frustration. I was the adult who should have known better. Moreover, I was an official with the team, and the NHL has rules about proper engagement between team officials and fans.

I put him down, we disengaged, and I went back to the box. Man, was that a crappy day. By the time I got home that night, the story was all over the *Washington Post*. I think the ticker crawling at the bottom of CNN said something like, "Fan-Friendly NHL Owner in Dust Up with Fan."

I got a lot of advice about what to do, much of it concerned with my legal exposure, or the consequences from the NHL. But I knew what I'd done was wrong, and once we got his name and phone number, I picked up the phone and called the fan with whom I'd had the altercation. I reached him at home and said, "I want to apologize. It doesn't matter what led up to what happened. I grabbed you, and that is really unacceptable, and so please accept my apology."

The young man's reaction was, "I'm so happy you called. I really love the team. I'm really sorry that happened."

We started talking, and I said, "Why don't you come to a game with your family, and be my guests in the owner's box." And he agreed, and not too long afterwards, he and his family watched a game in the box, and the episode was over.

I was fined $100,000 by the league and suspended from games for one week. The incident seemed to crystallize the frustrations between the Caps and our fans over the strategy of transforming our team from an expensive collection of high-priced veterans to younger prospects and future stars acquired through having banked draft picks.

From this low moment, even as we began to rebuild the team, I knew that transparency and honesty were going to be the key to being loved—not needed—as a brand. We communicated broadly, openly, and continuously about what we were attempting to accomplish. At first, the fan base only knew that after trading away our star players, we were losing. As we began to win again, they began to see that I'd been telling the truth all along: that by stripping down to brass tacks and rebuilding, we'd be positioned for greater success over a longer term. As this is being written, I'm pleased to report that the Caps are in first place in the NHL East, and that surveys have shown we have the highest level of fan satisfaction in the league.

As the owner of the Caps, I put my tenets of happiness to the test in a business setting. We faced up to our reckoning and made a plan. We treated the fans as our partners by updating them on what we were doing, every step of the way. Some people advised me that I had to limit my contact with fans, and I went in exactly the opposite direction: I increased my contact with them. I said, *I'm not going to let something like that incident get in the way of participation in the Caps community.* I'm happiest when I'm hanging out with fans, and talking to people, and getting their input.

And then we drafted Alex Ovechkin. And Niklas Backstrom. And Mike Green. And over time, we assembled a team that I believe can and will take us to the Stanley Cup championship. I believe we have built a happy team and a happy Washington Caps community. We are grateful for our fans, and I think we show it. We give back to the Washington community that has embraced the team and given us so much. We have a higher calling: the immortality of a championship season.

We still have some distance to travel to get to the magic moment when the city comes together behind a championship team and immortality is reached for all who live through it. But we're a lot closer to that moment than we were that cold and snowy night in January 2004 when unhappiness reigned over everything.

Many people use the phrase "happiest moment in my life" pretty loosely. For me, I view happy moments as a slideshow, with dozens of memories and images. I really don't want to try to rank whether the moment Lynn and I were married was happier than the moments when Zach or Elle were born, and so forth. I will say this: on the last day of the 2008–2009 regular season, as the Caps were winning an essentially meaningless game—we'd captured the division, and our Number Two seed in the Eastern Conference Stanley Cup Playoffs was secure—the arena video display showed me in the owner's box, and I stood up to wave to the fans and thank them for all they'd done to make the Washington Capitals season a really great and memorable time. It was a happy season, for all of us. And as I stood there, I didn't hear boos. I heard an arena full of Caps fans embrace our team—embrace me—with cheers and applause. The incident of five years earlier when the team and its ownership were out of alignment with its fans seemed to be long forgotten. On this evening, the 18,000 people in the Verizon Center were happy, and so was I.

There's no question that as we have built the Caps into a genuine Stanley Cup contender, the net result for all of us has been to increase our prospects for genuine happiness. I stood there beaming, and I'll never forget it.

Chapter Nine

Rebuilding a Happy Company

Enough has been written about the AOL-Time Warner merger that we don't have to belabor it here. But this is how screwed up it really was. We bought Time Warner to sell broadband AOL to their cable company's subscribers. And yet even as a merged company called AOL-Time Warner, we couldn't sell our service to their customers for any discount off the full price of Time Warner Cable's Roadrunner service, plus the full price of AOL. Yes, I know, there were regulatory impediments, driven by fears about how dominant we'd be, that made it complicated for AOL simply to convert Time Warner Cable customers to broadband AOL users. But still, we bought the company, and we were prevented from jointly marketing our service to their customers—not by the government, but by Time Warner. How dumb was that? It was what it was because that was the way Time Warner was managed.

Not being able to sell our service to Time Warner Cable customers was a very big deal, but we were stiff-armed in smaller, albeit equally annoying, ways as well. Soon after the merger, Time Inc. balked at having to use AOL email. At this point there were probably 75 million active AOL email accounts worldwide, but our email just wasn't good enough for the employees of Time Inc. They cheered at being liberated to go back to Microsoft's Outlook.

Time Warner Cable had literally 1100 separate home pages for the websites of its local cable franchises. Each local jurisdiction had its own design, and while some were highly professional, others looked like they'd been created by the local cable guy's brother-in-law. Time Warner Cable was spending about $15 million annually to design and maintain these sites. AOL, which at that point was the most successful company in the history of the Internet, offered to redesign and manage the sites at our own expense, but were told that if we really wanted to do this, we would have to negotiate with each of 1100 local cable companies.

When I look back, I understand exactly why Steve Case went to China to meet with Jerry Levin in an effort to merge Time Warner with AOL. I understand exactly why Jerry said yes.

As the CEO of Time Warner, Jerry knew this new digital medium was going to change everything about how Time Warner sold its products, and at that moment, Time Warner—the world's largest traditional media company—was zero for lifetime in making digital media work for its magazines, films, record labels, and television networks. (The only thing that was beginning to work was Roadrunner, the broadband pipes sold by Time Warner Cable.)

Steve's theory and motives were also easy to figure out, and completely rational. Like me, Steve had always believed what we called convergence would happen—that all media would be digitized and available online, or over the air, on multiple devices. When I'd stared at my Apple II and thought it looked a lot like a television, the dream I had then could be characterized as a vision of convergence.

Steve Case's desire to merge AOL with Time Warner was partly based on the practical need to find a broadband outlet, but far more important to him personally was a higher calling. He really believed in convergence, and thought a mash-up of AOL and Time Warner was the natural mechanism to achieve this. We all know how that turned out, but objectively ten years later, it's clear he was conceptually correct. Take all the bile out of the conversation, all the bashing of Steve Case and AOL, all the snarkiness, the disappointment over the collapse of the AOL share price, all the revisionist history about Time Warner's viewpoint on the merger (many, if not most of their senior managers initially welcomed the sprinkling of dot.com magic on the "dead money" tied up in their perennially moribund share price—even if they never wanted to lift a finger to make the merger an actual success.) Conceptually, if you were to merge the leading New Media company with the leading traditional media company, it would not be irrational to expect it to become the leader in this next-generation media platform.

Ah, but execution is the killer. It was the execution—not to mention the culture clash—that went just a little bit awry. Time Warner may have known that the digital medium would change the way it sold its products, but it had no intention of actually changing the way it did its business. Though Time Warner executives in theory understand the higher calling of convergence, in practice, they just weren't about to change the way they operated.

The financial architecture of the merger was delicate and difficult. Time Warner had $30 billion in revenue to AOL's $10 billion, but we had the far higher market capitalization, based on what the financial markets valued at that moment. The day the merger was announced, financial analysts started spinning the beads on their abacuses. By the time the first headlines had screamed across the screen, a company whose higher calling had been to create a medium more valuable than the telephone or television had been reduced to a single number: the combined AOL-Time Warner would generate $11 billion in EBITDA.

In the various books written about the merger, I've read the scenes in which Jerry Levin announced to the Time Warner execs that AOL was acquiring their company. I understand that some Time Warner executives were shocked and unhappy, and some saw Internet dollar signs and were shocked and pleased. (Most claim to have been in the first camp.)

In January of 2000, Bob Pittman held our regular meeting for senior management (OpComm, as we called it) and announced that AOL was buying Time Warner.

By this point, AOL had a very good, very sophisticated senior management team. The deal wasn't put to a vote, and there was very limited discussion. The person who spoke up loudest was me.

I thought acquiring Time Warner was one of the worst ideas I had ever heard in my life, for numerous reasons, and said so.

First, I had worked with Time Warner since my days at Redgate, and I knew that there really wasn't any such thing as "Time Warner." Nobody you ever met said they worked at "Time Warner." They said they worked at *Sports Illustrated*, or HBO, or Warner Brothers. Many of them were spectacularly successful managers with high bandwidth and in their own way, a higher calling: to publish the best magazine that would please sports fans, or to run the best music label for artists and consumers alike. Time Warner's profits were based on individual units that rolled up, eventually, to a $30 billion company. But Time

Warner executives' identity, and their vantage point, was parochial. I don't mean that as a putdown; it's just a statement that no one at Time Warner identified with Time Warner per se. The business units competed with one another, and there was no *esprit de corps* across the empire. Time Warner as a corporate entity was almost like a conglomeration of fiefdoms run by fiercely protective dukes.

AOL wasn't like that at all. We worked in service of a single mission. We had multiple lines of business, but as senior managers, we didn't look at ourselves as running individual P&Ls. We were all in service to the AOL brand and the AOL shareholders. AOL was bigger than any of us.

I had spent the last fifteen years saying that traditional media was, if not bad, at least increasingly irrelevant. Traditional media had high priests. They decided what you could read about. They were not interactive. In fact, interactivity threatened their priestly authority. Their distribution system was petroleum-based, and they chopped down trees. And now we were going to own the biggest conglomerate of traditional media extant. How could we forge ahead in exploring the possibilities of New Media when we had to protect the old media we'd just acquired? Finally, I couldn't understand how Bob could refer to AOL as the "crown jewel" in what would become AOL Time Warner, yet intend to work for the new corporate parent along with Steve and so many others of my AOL peers. They would be helping to improve the operations of Time Warner. If AOL was the "crown jewel," shouldn't *we* have been recruiting Time Warner talent to help *us*?

All the objections I laid out that night came to pass. And much as I loved all my friends and colleagues around the table, to many, I was the skunk at the garden party. Some of my colleagues were looking forward to their new lives as part of the World's Largest Media Company. They were New Yorkers. Virginia was square. They thought they'd be happy. But I knew AOL-Time Warner wasn't going to be a happy company. It gives me no pleasure to say I was right.

———————

AOL and Time Warner were granted the government's approval to merge in the winter of 2001, and it did not take very long it all to go wrong. It was a hard environment, as the dot.com boom became the dot.bomb bust, as the terrorist attacks on September 11 ushered in a harsh new era in American life and the economy soured. The AOL service actually kept growing, both in revenue and the size of our subscriber base, until the 3rd Quarter of 2002 when, having peddled furiously to the top of the hill, having huffed and puffed to get to 36 million members and $10 billion in revenue, the whole thing made a wobbly turn and began going right back down the hill again.

One reason membership peaked was because the number of U.S. households seeking a dial-up Internet connection was saturated. We really had gotten America online—and now people wanted something more: speed, and the kind of media delivered to their home allowing their television and computer to converge. AOL bought Time Warner in order to provide AOL service on a broadband connection, which was up to ten-times faster than the dial-up service we offered. Yet, even after becoming one entity known as AOL Time Warner, AOL was stymied from gaining broadband subscribers at a price that worked for our members. Our members could afford AOL, or they could afford the higher-priced broadband line, but they couldn't justify the expense of both—and besides, along with the broadband line came the cable company's software, and an email address, and other things that duplicated what we were offering.

In January 2000, the AOL Time Warner merger had been heralded as an epochal triumph. Less than two years later, it took on deep symbolic resonance as the failure of an almost instantly diminished era. Old Media, some of it resident within AOL-Time Warner itself, was quick to declare New Media a sham, and as evidence, pointed to the way the AOL service had suddenly gone into decline.

Rather than the "crown jewel," AOL was now just a division in the sprawling behemoth. Despite the fact that in any given quarter, more than one of AOL's divisional siblings might be sucking wind, after the merger closed, all of the attention fell on AOL's performance. This was fair, sort of, because the merger was predicated on AOL being able to sprinkle the Internet's magic dust on the rest of Time Warner's stodgier divisions. But therein lay a problem that, I have to admit, I'd predicted. The AOL division comprised about 25 percent of the combined company's revenues. This meant that the analysts who covered the company were principally drawn from the ranks of those who covered "media companies," not "Internet companies." They viewed AOL as simply one more media business, whose progress could be tracked as if it were Time Inc.—how many subscribers and how much advertising revenue did it have at the end of a given quarter—with very little understanding of, or appreciation for, the transformational imperative of trying to inject Internet/New Media DNA into the larger, older corporate entity.

What was perhaps a little less than fair in the harsh judgment of AOL was the failure of commentators to focus on the active resistance of Time Warner's divisions to work with AOL. When we think of the phrase "passive resistance," we envision demonstrators going slack and forcing the police to pull them to the bus that's going to cart them away to the hoosegow. Time Warner's divisional response to the partnership with AOL was a more aggressive stiff-arm move, the most important being the flat-out refusal of Time Warner Cable to assist in AOL's efforts to convert its dial-up membership to broadband. The first real effort to jointly market AOL to Time Warner Cable's subscriber base took place in 2005—five years after the merger was announced, four years after it closed, three and a half years after it was pronounced the biggest failure in the history of the universe. That's not the whole story of the merger's failure by any means, but it really should be Article One in the indictment.

———————————

Post-merger, I was told to throw away my stump speech, the delivery of which for the previous few years had made me really happy. I was told I could no longer say, "Print is dead!" You see, now we owned the world's biggest magazine company.

One of AOL's employees had invented an online music player called Winamp, and in the summer of 2000, before the companies merged, he developed peer-to-peer software under the brand name Gnutella that would enable anyone to share music with anyone else on their service. Before we really even knew that we'd built the technology, news of it leaked out on the British tech site Slashdot, and it couldn't have been more than an hour before Bob Pittman, who was then AOL's CEO, and Jerry Levin of Time Warner, were both on the line from New York telling me in no uncertain terms that we had to take Gnutella down. Here someone at AOL had innovated a radical new technology, and when the new corporate brass called me up, I thought I was going to get fired! The conversation wasn't about how one of our engineers was so talented he'd created a file-sharing service that we might have profitably turned into a subscriber-based Universal Jukebox of myth and lore. It wasn't, "Wow, we have a new thing to offer music lovers who might want to subscribe to the AOL service over, say, Time Warner Cable pipes. And maybe, if we work on it, and put all this great talent we have on both the Internet and traditional media side together, we can figure out a way of boosting music sales, while making consumers happy." The message wasn't, "Isn't the Internet amazing, and how do we turn this technology into a really profitable business?" Without reflection or debate, it was, "Don't you realize we own a music business? Shut it down!"

We wanted to be a leader in Voice Over Internet Protocal, or VoIP telephony. And from on high came the message that this would compete with the cable company, over which we needed to be very protective, because it generated so much revenue and EBITDA. And remember, $11 billion in EBITDA was AOL-Time Warner's higher calling.

And while we could do nothing that might in any way threaten their business models, there was little concomitant desire at any business unit within Time Warner to assist us in ours. It's not that they were evil, or when measured parochially, dumb. With the exception of an entrepreneur like Ted Turner who'd created Turner Broadcasting, and as a visionary innovatively developed everything from CNN to widespread cable distribution of the Atlanta Braves games, Time Warner's business units were run by professional managers. They were rational people who responded to the incentives by which they were compensated, and none of these included building AOL-Time Warner into a genuine example of convergence. So long as there were a few token examples to hold up during the earnings calls—"And in the last quarter, promotion on the AOL Welcome Screen helped Warner Brothers' *Cats and Dogs* have the highest grossing opening in the first weekend of August of any film in Warner Brothers' history"—that would do. There was just zero recognition that working for a company that had only one set of shareholders, you might do something to benefit the shareholders as a whole, as opposed to your immediate P&L.

AOL went in the blink of an eye from the plucky outsider taking on the world to a massive establishment company. Like any outsider parvenu we certainly weren't loved by the establishment we'd bought into. That might have been okay, but for the fact that "Time Warner" comprised hundreds of reporters, editors, and media figures who had other friends in the media business and loved the snarky leaks that soon flooded the business press. The real problem was that almost instantly we also weren't loved by consumers. Even as AOL's subscriber base continued to grow—it peaked at 36 million members in the 3rd Quarter of 2002, seven quarters after the merger closed, largely on the basis of our international momentum—surveys showed the AOL brand began to decline literally the month the merger with Time Warner was announced.

Very quickly, we became an inward-focused company. We became a company that managed for Wall Street. I used to say that if you were in your staff meetings and you talked about products and told vignettes about your customers, those were happy days. And when you had meetings where the entire conversation was about sales, and financials, and cash flow—and yes, eventually, layoffs—those were unhappy days.

When the merger went forth, and AOL was suddenly going to be defined by whether or not we, in conjunction with Time Warner, pleased the industry of financial analysts that followed us by delivering the $11 billion in EBITDA they'd figured we should produce, things changed abruptly. While so many others went to New York to be part of the combined company, I stayed in Dulles. And the meetings there changed because our dashboard changed. It was no longer, "What great product did we release this week?" Everything—everything—was about whether we were going to send enough money to New York to help our new corporate parent meet its $11 billion EBITDA number and generate the cash flow to pay off Time Warner's debt. I remember coming out of meetings and saying to people, "We could be making nuclear power plants, for all you could tell from that meeting." You'd look around the room and see the stress on people's faces. Everyone just seemed so unhappy. And this was before the business actually declined! At this point, we were still growing subscribers and revenues.

I remember one day, I was frustrated with what we'd been reduced to, and I walked out of a meeting on AOL's fifth floor, where all of the executives had offices. I decided to just go home, because I was really upset about the turn the company had taken. Downstairs, right by the elevator was our mission statement up on a wall plaque. "To build a global medium as central to people's lives as the telephone or television—and even more valuable." I hadn't merely participated in the writing of that statement, or in making it a reality. Years before, I'd helped hang it on the wall. Now I took a piece of paper out of a notebook, and I wrote, "$11 billion in EBITDA." That was our new mission, that's what remained of our higher calling. I stuck it on the plaque, and I left. If you'd been there, you could probably have seen that I wasn't happy. Neither was the company I worked for. And neither were the consumers that we served.

In the history of the merger as you've probably heard it, AOL tried forcing its ways on Time Warner divisions. If that were the case, than someone like me would have been put in charge of, say, Time Warner Cable. We would have put Michael Lynton—who left AOL to run Sony Pictures—in charge of Warner Brothers. In fact, Time Warner rejected any AOL cultural transplants like a post-surgical patient expelling a donor's heart. And after the summer of 2002, they felt completely justified.

For it was then—eighteen months into the merger—that AOL had its reckoning.

In mid-summer 2002, Bob Pittman, who'd been the CEO of AOL when the merger was announced, and who was co-Chief Operating Officer of AOL-Time Warner, resigned from the company.

Just a few months earlier, in late March of 2002, Bob had actually returned to Dulles and once again taken over the reins as AOL's CEO, even as he continued in his corporate position with AOL Time Warner. On some levels, we welcomed Bob's return to AOL because Bob is a highly talented manager, who having helped build the company, understood what AOL was all about. Bob was forced to return and try to fix AOL, because as the sentiment about the merger at the corporate level soured, the biggest point of contention was the way AOL's growth was decelerating. AOL was missing all of its internal numbers, which in turn was undermining the rationale for the merger. The stock market had peaked two years before, but the shares of AOL Time Warner were steadily dropping, largely because of AOL's performance. Therefore, it made logical and political sense for Bob to step back into his old role and try revving up AOL's engines before it fell completely back to Earth.

I thought Bob would have been better off making a last stand at the corporate level, trying to force Time Warner Cable to work with AOL, among other things. Instead, he took on the thankless role of trying to "fix" AOL, even as his corporate position deteriorated, along with support for the merger. And to be sure, as an architect of the merger, and as someone who when running the AOL service had helped move the company from its focus on our members to a single-minded focus on profitability and Wall Street, Bob may not have been the best person to "fix" AOL. In any event, he wasn't back for long.

Bob called me in Hawaii, where Lynn and I had gone on a brief vacation, to tell me he was resigning. It was clear that a reckoning for AOL was imminent, and I would have to engage in getting the company back on track. Thinking of the great Michael Corleone line from *The Godfather III*, I said to Lynn, "Just when I think I'm out, they pull me back in."

Bob's resignation in late July 2002 coincided with the publication of a highly critical series in *The Washington Post*. Those stories looked at a number of deals done just before or after the merger in which AOL had booked as advertising revenue money emanating from smaller companies who needed to show they were partners with AOL in order to gain credibility or go public. It was a really toxic environment for questions to be raised about the company's accounting practices. Several months earlier, Enron's accounting manipulation had become front-page news. Closer to home—I could see the company's head-quarters from my office window—WorldCom had become subject to a Securities and Exchange Commission and Department of Justice investigation over its accounting. Within a week of the newspaper series on AOL's advertising deals, both the SEC and DOJ announced an investigation of AOL.

With Bob gone, Time Warner CEO Dick Parsons announced that Don Logan, who'd built the modern-day Time Inc., would become Co-Chief Operating Officer of AOL Time Warner, along with Jeff Bewkes, who ran HBO. Don was assigned to oversee AOL, and while he is a

decent and brilliant man who was to work extremely hard over the
next three years to help AOL recover momentum, his frame of refer-
ence was as a classic Old Media executive. Bob's departure, and the
ascension of Don Logan and Jeff Bewkes, meant that from among the
AOL team that had initiated the merger, only Steve Case, AOL Time
Warner's chairman, was still in a senior position at the corporate
headquarters. What had started as AOL's acquisition of Time Warner,
described at the time as a "merger of equals," was clearly a takeover by
Time Warner of AOL.

At that moment, AOL's business was in a classic squeeze. The marketing machinery that had built the company could not overcome the
shift from dial-up access to broadband, which was beginning to
achieve genuine market penetration. The telephone and cable companies—such as Time Warner Cable—toyed with us, and even as our
dealmakers camped out in their offices trying to find some formula
that would work for them, for us, and consumers, AOL was shut out of
the broadband world, except for customers who could afford to pay
for us to ride on top of their broadband pipes. Following the dot.bomb
bust, the online advertising business was in free fall, and AOL's proprietary standards and frankly, the arrogance we'd shown with advertisers and their agencies when we were riding high, now came back to
haunt us. We were still hugely profitable—the most profitable business in the Internet by an order of magnitude, more profitable than
Amazon, eBay, and Yahoo! combined—and we'd made some very
smart moves, such as bringing in a plucky little company called
Google to handle our Search business. (Typically, by giving them our
business, we'd also acquired significant pre-IPO warrants in the company.) But AOL by this time was a most unhappy company, and this
was even before the investigations by the SEC and the Department of
Justice got fully cranked up.

Following Bob Pittman's resignation, AOL Time Warner hired a veteran of Barry Diller's Interactive Corp to become AOL's third CEO in five months. Jon Miller came to AOL with solid media credentials—he'd been a cable network executive and a dealmaker at the NBA. He had good instincts about the Internet and a bright and engaging mind. Jon walked into AOL to find the company's revenues about to contract; its subscription base peaked; multiple Federal investigations into its practices; many of the senior executives who had built the company having left to go to the corporate parent, which by this time had gotten rid of them; a toxic press environment, in which AOL had become a morality tale of what happens when Internet executives from Virginia dare to take on Manhattan/L.A. media institutions; and extremely low morale among a workforce that felt bewildered, beleaguered, and compared to a year or so before when the share price was high, suddenly poor. Other than that, it was probably fun to become Chairman and CEO of a big company with a well-known brand.

Within a few weeks after Jon's arrival, he asked if I would serve as his Vice Chairman, once again running the AOL core service, with the additional title of President.

At that moment, I was gearing up for my third season as owner of the Caps. I was deeply involved in charitable activities. My children were in middle school, and I'd gotten used to being home early enough to spend time with them and Lynn instead of just to tuck them in. I'd built a really happy life in addition to my work at AOL. I was involved in multiple communities, and had found new ways of expressing myself through speeches and my regular communications with the Washington Capitals fan base. Despite the conflict and turmoil that had followed the merger, I was grateful for where my life had brought me. With my commitment to Best Buddies, Hoop Dreams, and other organizations, I was genuinely giving back to society in a way that was commensurate to what life had given me. I had begun to understand that my higher calling was to leave the world having given more than I had taken.

In fact, when Michael Jordan, who in 2000 became President of Basketball Operations for the Washington Wizards, heard the story of how I had gone from being on a plane that had an emergency landing to building a happy and fulfilling life, he introduced me to Oprah Winfrey, and in the spring of 2002, I'd gone on *Oprah*. We did a segment on how I'd embarked on my path toward happiness after having faced my reckoning. The segment was entitled, "Living Life Without Regret." It was a pretty accurate way of describing my life at that moment.

For the previous two years, I had been as helpful as I could be during the transition period between the announcement of the merger and AOL and Time Warner actually getting hitched. While I'd done whatever I was asked by Barry Schuler and Bob Pittman—Barry's predecessor and then successor as CEO—I'd kept some critical distance from the business. When AOL was negotiating with Microsoft over how the AOL service might be offered on Windows XP on equal terms to MSN, I'd put in the long hours, because I had a 20-year history with Microsoft. Yet I'd long ago stepped back from really running AOL, as Bob Pittman and others had stepped in to create a marketing juggernaut.

I'd dissented from the biggest strategic move the company had made since it went to unlimited usage. For a good year before the merger, I'd understood that AOL's share value gave us an opportunity to initiate a big acquisition, but I'd been part of an internal team that had considered a roll-up with other online brands—Amazon, eBay, and Yahoo! To me, linking our business with other online companies made more sense than acquiring a big media company that didn't have Internet DNA. From the earliest moment I'd heard mention of a plan to acquire Time Warner, I'd communicated all the reasons I thought that was a bad move. The merger had gone forward anyway.

So I had a big title and a big office and on any given day I was busy, but it wasn't like it had been a few years before when I was essentially running AOL. The merger had gone forward over my objections, and virtually everything negative that I'd predicted had come to pass.

We were now a big media company with a declining brand that had to find ways of helping the biggest magazine company and other Old Media franchises find relevance on the web. We'd given up our New Media positioning even as AOL was stymied from getting access to the broadband pipes at a commercially viable price that we needed to keep growing.

But I loved AOL. That was why I was still there. That was why I put on a jacket and tie and came to work in the morning. I didn't have to, but I did, and the reason why was simple. I believed we still could recapture some of the magic we'd lost.

From my own experience, I knew this dark moment in the summer of 2002 was an opportunity. So when Jon Miller asked me if I would really step up my involvement and help him revitalize the company, I didn't hesitate. I said yes.

—————————

A crisis *is* a terrible thing to waste, and from the day Jon arrived, we changed things. I recognized our situation for what it was. We were still alive, and we'd made it to the tarmac in more or less one piece. But if ever there was a corporate reckoning, this was it.

The first thing we did was draw up lists of what we needed to do, in a long series of strategy meetings.

We needed to rebuild our advertising business, almost from scratch, this time with industry standard ad units and a humble, traditional sales force.

It seemed we needed to transform AOL into a broadband service, quit being landlocked in dial-up country and find a path to the sea.

I was adamant that we needed to rebuild the AOL community, and put the interests of our Members front and center in our decision-making. When I'd run the AOL service, I used to say that I answered to its tens of millions of members. In recent years, we'd lost that focus. We had shoved pop-up ads in our users faces and been tricky in the way we'd dealt with them—offering them second accounts when they didn't want them, or making it difficult for them to cancel their account. Our employees knew that we'd lost our focus on our Members, and spontaneously around the campus, signs went up saying, "Members rule." These were the handiwork of a group that called themselves "The Optimist Movement," or "T.O.M." God bless Amy Arnold for secretly starting a rebellion by employees, reminding us of our higher calling. This sentiment nicely captured what we needed to get back to. It also was a protest against what, over the past year or two, we had become.

We needed to rebuild the morale of the AOL workforce, get them to tune out the corporate drama in New York, the bad press, and the unhappiness attendant to a company that had lost its way.

We had to recapture our higher calling.

And so began a very hard and long slog. The great myth of American business is that it is only entrepreneurs working in garages who put in the long hours building companies from scratch. Anyone who's ever worked in a once-successful company that has faced a reckoning and had to try to find a way of recapturing its lost magic knows that rebuilding such a company is much harder than building one from scratch. (What GM will go through in the next five years will make its first five years seem like an extended vacation.) Building a happy company that has a higher calling is just a lot easier than turning around a great company that has lost its way.

I believed we had to recapture the status of being loved, because as our users were leaving us to get broadband connections, we were no longer needed. I would have meetings each week with executives who reported to me, and I asked them to grade our performance on how we were doing each week in pleasing our users. There were only three grades: a green arrow, a yellow light, or a red light. Each week saw more green arrows as we set about fundamentally fixing the user experience.

Between 2002 and 2005, AOL's strategy went through multiple revisions. AOL was consistently profitable, with the ever-declining dial-up subscriber business responsible for shipping boatloads of cash north to New York. But profits can be like heroin; it's really hard to break a habit and do things differently if you've gotten hooked on profits coming from a particular source. AOL's profitability at this time stemmed almost entirely from the subscription business—from AOL's role as an ISP, connecting people to the Internet, even though it was obvious to everyone that without a way of migrating our dial-up subscribers to the better experience of a broadband connection, eventually we would lose them. Our users still liked AOL, and most switchers moved to broadband reluctant to give up their AOL screen name and the familiarity of the AOL client software. But they didn't love us enough to keep a dial-up connection when a broadband connection was available.

They needed a faster connection, and it didn't matter whether they loved the company that provided them with that functional service.

The single biggest strategic mistake we made at this time was to require departing members to leave their screen name at the door. Once you left AOL, you no longer had use of an AOL email address. We tried exploiting Members' reluctance to give up their online identity. But the tide was too strong, and broadband really was a superior way of actualizing your Internet experience. And so began the time period when millions of people sent out emails saying, "Hi, beginning next week, my new email address will be..." We were obstinate; our reply was, "Have to get the heroin shot of subscriber revenues, have to get the heroin shot of subscriber revenues..." Let's just say it led to some pretty great years for Yahoo! Mail and Gmail.

We did what we were asked to do to enable what by now was officially, and accurately, called Time Warner, to fulfill its higher calling: pleasing financial analysts by meeting profitability targets. (The name "AOL Time Warner" had been dropped, at Jon Miller's behest, in the fall of 2003, as Jon realized it had become a radioactive corporate moniker, and we needed to find a way of protecting the AOL brand.)

So our focus shifted in a meaningful way. We tried to keep AOL subscribers using the service by actively targeting elements of the online experience that made Internet users unhappy. We were vigilant about killing spam, because logging into email in the morning and finding forty ads for mortgage refinancing, pornography, and drugs didn't really brighten people's lives. On a weekly basis, I would grill our Network Operations team on what progress they could show in keeping spam from getting to our members, and virtually every week, they had good news to report: all green arrows. In fact, over time, offering Members tools by which they could train the computer servers to understand what they considered to be spam—some people wanted commercial email; others didn't—even as spam proliferated on corporate email and email offered by other services, it dramatically dropped for AOL users.

We targeted all the elements of safety and security that bothered users. There were a lot of them. Spyware. Phishing attacks, in which bad guys tried tricking members into giving them personal information that could lead to identity theft. The Internet was full of nastiness that could mess up people's computers and ultimately their lives. Because AOL members were protected, when many ex-members went to the always-on environment of broadband, they didn't even know they needed such protections as antivirus software and a firewall. So we began to offer such protections for free, so that subscribing to AOL in addition to the cost of a broadband connection would be seen as a greater value. In fact, we were so serious about fighting spyware that we passed on an opportunity to buy MySpace before Rupert Murdoch did. MySpace's parent company was embroiled in a nasty legal battle with then-New York Attorney General Elliot Spitzer over their notorious spyware practices, and so for us, MySpace was untouchable.

We were very public about efforts to clean up the online environment. Because the state of Virginia had the most aggressive laws when it came to spam, we worked with law enforcement and then-Governor Mark Warner to go after spammers. In fact, after suing one spammer and seizing a Porsche he'd bought with his profits, we held a lottery and awarded it to an AOL member. I remember watching the man's wife drop him off in our parking lot, and seeing him drive away with a smile on his face—possibly the first person ever made happy by Internet spam.

I testified before Congress on the steps we were taking to protect members from the hazards of going online. When we'd envisioned the online experience years before, I think we pictured Woodstock, with everybody happy and entertained and no police necessary. And it was like the Hell's Angels had shown up with pool cues and knives. Now we were forced to clean the place up.

Cleaning up the Internet by blocking spam, prosecuting spammers, and attacking identity thieves and purveyors of malware really did help AOL recapture some measure of our higher calling. If earlier we had achieved, beyond our wildest dreams, our mission of getting America online, now we could offer something that went beyond what was available via a fast broadband connection: a better online experience.

Our workforce was on a mission again—to improve the experience of our members, to offer a "better Internet." In October 2004 I wrote with my collaborator John Buckley something we called "AOL's Commitments To The Online Community," in which we pledged to protect members and safeguard their children from the threats they faced by offering them the best tools available, for the price of their AOL subscription. The Internet had become the Wild West, and after our reckoning, we were able to reclaim aspects of our higher calling by helping to clean it up.

In the Bible, the disciple Matthew declares, "For what shall it profit a man if he should gain the world, but lose his soul?"

In AOL's case, we were still losing subscribers, month-by-month and quarter-by-quarter. Despite this and our many other challenges, during this period in which I reengaged with AOL and ran the core service, we went a long way toward recovering our soul.

———

Looking back on the post-reckoning period at AOL, a number of things are clear to me. Despite long hours, grueling days, and a certain amount of turmoil and frustration, I was happy. Objectively, you might ask why.

AOL's revenues were continuing to decline, though the company met every profitability target demanded of it by Time Warner. Unhappily, this was in part accomplished through lowering expenses via a steady series of employee layoffs. During the period between 2003 and 2005, the Washington Capitals struggled. My altercation with a fan had led to splashy headlines and a $100,000 fine by the NHL. My life was not without conflict, anxiety, and even controversy. And yet I was happy. Why?

I was happy because on any given day, I was living my life according to certain tenets of happiness that through my own experience and observation clearly contributed to fulfillment and success. On my quest for happiness, I read everything you can on the topic and actively observed happy people and emulated them. This makes it harder to get thrown off stride by the bumpiness of everyday life. When you determine, as I had, to manage your life with a continual focus on how what you do each day contributes toward the goal of happiness, you increase the odds of getting what you wish for.

There were a lot of negative environmental factors in my life, but I believe these were overcome by important positive forces. If you think about what was happening at my two principal places of "employment," AOL and the Washington Capitals, in both cases we were striving to find our higher calling. At AOL, we were struggling against gravity and the downward pull of our subscriber numbers. But we were being reborn as a service that answered to its membership, and tried to genuinely help them achieve a higher quality of life in an Internet ecosystem that was increasingly nasty and brutish. With the Caps, we were seeking immortality bringing the city together through building a championship team that could bring joy to people's lives. These goals were conscious.

After having fallen so low, AOL rose again between 2004 and 2007, because we were focused on making our customers happy. This was not Time Warner's highest priority; they wanted EBIDTA, profits. I knew that if we concentrated on creating happiness for our Members, we'd become a happier company. We'd be more successful.

By now I was president of what we called AOL's Audience business, which is to say, the business of building a large Web audience supported by advertising. It was where the action was, and Jon asked me to take responsibility for it. It was clear to me we had to develop compelling content, available for free on the Web at large. AOL had been built as a proprietary service even before ordinary people accessed the Internet per se. We were a "walled garden," where only AOL subscribers had access to our content. We'd tried building compelling, proprietary content offerings to get people to keep their AOL subscriptions in a broadband world—exclusive concerts with the Foo Fighters and Lou Reed that you had to be a Member to access. But as cable and telephone companies fought through a price war offering broadband for a lower price than you could get dial-up AOL, the dial-up subscription business was, in a word, doomed. AOL E Morte. We had to find an escape route.

AOL had some of the most talented programming executives in the business. Jim Bankoff and Kevin Conroy were steeped in what worked online even as online was changing rapidly. In Mike Kelly, who is now CEO of The Weather Channel, we had a fantastic leader of our advertising sales efforts, which was especially vital for monetizing our investment in content if we were to offer it to non-subscribers. By 2005, we pushed virtually all AOL content out onto the

Web at large. AOL.com went from being a basic website through which AOL subscribers could check their email into a free portal with virtually all of the content available that previously had been locked behind the wall. When Bob Geldof, Bono, and others announced the Live8 concerts around the world—created to raise money and awareness for the cause of African debt relief—AOL stepped in as the global carrier of each of the concerts. On July 2, 2005, AOL streamed simultaneously every musical moment from shows in South Africa, Berlin, London, Paris, Moscow, Japan, and the U.S. Interestingly, MTV had the television rights in the U.S., and botched the coverage when their VJs spent a lot of time talking while AOL was flawlessly streaming the concerts in their entirety. It was a moment in which the computer was a superior delivery vehicle of content, and television was a medium hobbled by its conventions. It was a moment when my epiphany from 1978 was embodied by events; the Internet could be a superior content delivery vehicle to the television. It was also a moment when AOL's strategy shift of being reborn as a worldwide audience business, unencumbered by the need to have subscribers, reached fruition.

AOL had a giant audience. On any given day, we had the second-largest audience online in the world. (Yahoo! had the largest.) We had more than 100 million Unique Visitors to the AOL network each month. The AOL network was defined as the AOL service itself, AIM, Netscape, and many of the properties we'd acquired along the way, such as Mapquest, Moviefone, Spinner, etc.

In the summer of 2004, AOL purchased the largest advertising net-work on the web, a business called Advertising.com that a brilliant young entrepreneur named Scott Ferber had built in Baltimore. Advertising.com had built a really big business by identifying unsold advertising inventory on websites and placing advertising on it from marketers in search of an audience, with technology that allowed them to charge advertisers a higher price for access to the websites with the highest consumer response to their offering. To their credit, Time Warner let us do the transaction, which meant that AOL could monetize Internet advertising in more than one way.

We had a thriving business selling ads across the AOL network of sites, and we produced content that brought people into the network. We made some smart acquisitions in order to build low-cost content that would attract an audience. For example, before the phenomenon of blog networks reached critical mass, we acquired Jason Calacanis's Weblogs Inc., and had some of the most popular blogs on the Web—Engadget, Autoblog—in addition to AOL's homegrown content verticals. We also grew new sites, like TMZ.com, one of the only truly satisfying collaborations we ever had with a Time Warner entity—in this case, a subsidiary of Warner Bros.

With the acquisition of Advertising.com, we had a way of profiting from advertising sales on websites that weren't part of the AOL network.

Finally, we had a fantastically profitable partnership with Google, which brought in hundreds of millions of dollars of revenue each year while aligning us with the smartest company offering the best service on the Internet.

Because I was in charge of AOL's Audience business, which was funded by these multiple advertising streams, it was clear to me what AOL ultimately needed to do. By now, our advertising revenues were growing by better than 25 percent—every quarter. We hadn't seen growth numbers like that since the 1990s. By 2005, we had one billion dollars of advertising revenue. I declared then that by the end of 2006, we would double this to $2 billion per year, and while some people were skeptical, I knew we could do it, given the velocity of our momentum. We were rocking and rolling; AOL was once again on fire, growing rapidly in the portion of our business that counted for the future. We knew we were really hitting it when we had our first $500 million quarter in advertising revenues.

For the first time in years, I'd go into meetings and see smiling faces around the table. People would make their reports on how their business was doing, and it would be all green arrows. This was certainly not true across the entire company, as the subscription business decline dragged down revenues and forced AOL into laying off employees on an annual basis. There were portions of the company that were genuinely happy, and other areas where fear and anxiety ruled. But for a broad swath of the company, we were winning again. We were offering consumers content and services that made them happy, which in turn made our advertising partners happy. We were hitting our numbers while not doing anything tricky or sleazy—our fight against spyware meant we did not engage in partnerships with some advertisers that could have been highly lucrative. Fighting bad online advertising practices and holding ourselves accountable to a standard higher than mere profitability was an outgrowth of the way AOL had changed since our reckoning in 2002. By growing our advertising revenues dramatically while simultaneously avoiding bad practices, we were fulfilling our higher calling, and had become a happy company once again.

I knew we needed to make one very big change, and I argued my point privately with Jon Miller and other senior executives. I believed we needed to declare our subscription business a vestige of the past. We could keep counting the revenues and profits, which, even as the business declined, were considerable. But we needed to find some way of segregating the declining subscription business revenue away from the growing advertising business revenue. We needed to be able to say, "The subscription business is Old AOL, and the audience business is New AOL; judge us by the latter, and don't let the former distort the picture of what AOL really is all about now."

I knew that GE had found a way of booking revenues from its moribund nuclear power plant construction business, which they had declared a "discontinued operation." They got credit for the revenue, but weren't dinged for its declining growth. Why couldn't AOL make some similar declaration about our subscription business? It would never grow again, and there was no use pretending it would, but while we could still squeeze it for the profits it produced, why not declare it discontinued and move quickly to being known for the business we had moved to? I asked this question of senior executives at Time Warner. They thought it was a fascinating question and then did nothing.

By 2006, AOL was one of the fastest growing, most successful businesses on the Web. You would never know it from the way Time Warner reported our numbers. You would never know it from the way the analysts or the media, who took their cues from the analysts, who took their cues from the way Time Warner, reported the numbers. Each quarter, we'd report to Time Warner that we were nailing it—that our Audience business was now one of the fastest-growing, large scale advertising businesses on the Web. And every quarter Time Warner would report that AOL had lost so many subscribers, and that revenue had dropped again. Every quarter the message downplayed how AOL's smaller advertising business was growing like gangbusters, because the bigger subscription business, surprise surprise, was still failing:

another million subscribers had slipped away. It was a distortion of what really was going on at the company. By being addicted to the heroin of the faltering subscriber revenues, Time Warner could not cast AOL in terms that accurately reflected its future state. They wouldn't even cast AOL in terms that reflected its current state.

In the early summer of 2006, there were two important developments for me and for AOL. In my case, I could see the way the company had turned around, and it made me really proud. I'd been called back into action at AOL four years earlier, and I'd helped stabilize and improve the AOL service, before concentrating on growing that portion of the business—monetizing our giant audience through advertising—that would survive the inevitable winding down of our predominantly dial-up subscriber business. In the portion of the business that, in terms of AOL's future state, actually mattered, we'd brought AOL back to its rightful position of one of the Web's great properties.

At the same time, I was increasingly happy and fulfilled by multiple elements of my life. While on a family vacation the previous Christmas, I'd read the heartbreaking obituary of a writer named Iris Chang, a Chinese-American woman who had chronicled events in the late 1930s when Japan invaded China. Her book, *The Rape of Nanking*, told the story of an unknown holocaust in the Asia theater of World War II, and was published to great acclaim—but Iris was in a state of post-partum depression and tragically she took her own life. I'll have more to say about my film *Nanking* in the next section, but for now suffice to say that by the summer of 2006, I was firmly launched on the project. Winning an Academy Award was an unfulfilled item on my Life List of 101 goals, and in order to win an Academy Award you have to actually make a movie. Doing so was making me really happy.

I went to New York and saw Jeff Bewkes, Time Warner's CEO, and told him I wanted to retire from active management of AOL at the end of the year. Jeff was surprised, but supportive. I told a handful of people about my plans, and we quietly drew up a press release announcing my impending retirement.

But this quickly was overtaken by a development at AOL itself. In mid-June, Jon Miller held an off-campus strategy session for the company's 100 top managers, and a remarkable thing happened. As the dilemma we faced was discussed—AOL's advertising business growing by leaps and bounds, but our subscription business dwindling every quarter, pulling down revenues, even as the bottom line continued to show profits—there was a groundswell from the company's senior managers.

"Why are we insisting on propping up a dying subscription model? Let's give away AOL for free." I don't remember who first voiced what we needed to do to cut the Gordian Knot, but I remember the way the expressed thought hung in the room.

Jon asked the group as a whole how many people supported the concept.

We all did. Everyone in the room.

And the remarkable thing was that many of the managers there were in positions overseeing the subscription business. They knew what this meant. If AOL was going to willingly give up hundreds of millions of dollars of subscription revenue, undoubtedly faster than we could make it up by transforming subscribers to AOL "users" whose presence within our network could be monetized, the company would shrink, and jobs would go away. It would be wrenching. Many of the people in the room wouldn't be with us anymore when we came out the other end of the tunnel. But AOL would be transformed into a free service for anyone with a broadband connection.

And everyone said go for it.

But first we had to persuade Time Warner. It took a few weeks, but by August of 2006, AOL announced that if you had a broadband connection, we would no longer require you to pay a monthly subscription fee to use the AOL service. By this move, we placed the subscription business in wind-down mode, whether or not it was accounted for as a "discontinued operation." If Time Warner could just figure out how to talk about it without making the subscription business the lead sentence in the AOL section of every earnings release, we would now be judged on the basis of how we grew the size of the AOL audience, and how we sold advertising based on that audience. It was a leap of faith, but the early results were fantastic. Yes, AOL's subscribers called to cancel, and we let them. For the first time, people leaving AOL left with their AOL email address and a pleasant experience. Yes, the company announced it would lay off an additional 5000 employees, which was sad for all of us, and disruptive, as the company divided between those who would be staying and those who would have to leave. But the company was transforming itself for a viable future.

I felt like I'd done my duty. I'd seen this transition through. Production on *Nanking* was finishing up, and the film had been accepted in the 2007 Sundance Film Festival, Robert Redford's quintessential showcase for a limited number of high quality independent films. The Caps were gearing up for the 2006-2007 season, and while we knew we weren't quite at the level we'd need to be to get to the Stanley Cup finals, we had high hopes. I was happy; thoroughly and completely happy. On September 14th, we announced that I would relinquish my day-to-day responsibilities as President of the AOL Audience division, but would remain as Vice Chairman Emeritus—out of the day-to-day fray, but still involved with the company I'd built, and helped rebuild, following its reckoning.

In October, Time Warner announced its 3rd Quarter earnings, and reported that the AOL Audience business had grown by 49 percent over the year-ago period. We were now the second-fastest growing major online advertising network behind Google, our growth rate having that quarter overtaken Yahoo! It was a moment of triumph that was a long time coming.

One month later, the same group of senior managers that in June had called upon the company to jettison the subscription business met in the same conference center a few miles from the AOL campus. Jeff Bewkes of Time Warner came to speak to the group, and he metaphorically put his arms around Jon Miller, praising him and all of us for what we'd accomplished. We left that day filled with purpose and commitment. We'd turned the corner. AOL was back. Back, we believed, even in the good graces of the Time Warner hierarchy that had shown such bitterness toward us since the merger had been completed.

I remember driving home with a smile on my face.

And then the next day, reporters from the *New York Times* and the *Los Angeles Times* called to ask whether AOL would confirm the rumor that Time Warner was firing Jon Miller and replacing him with an NBC network executive.

With impeccable timing, Time Warner threw a monkey wrench into AOL's machinery and broke it.

Jon Miller is a smart and decent man who deserved better. He had worked 365 days a year for four years trying to make AOL grow. He'd been sent by Time Warner's corporate management to "clean up AOL," and while there had been bumps along the way, objectively he'd done so. Unfortunately for him, Time Warner's management thought he'd gone native; he'd become an AOL executive, not a Time Warner executive ensconced in the "troubled AOL division." So in the worst possible way, even as he'd delivered on what was expected of him, Time Warner ritualistically took him behind the building and put a bullet in his head.

Once again, the pros from Dover were sent in to "fix" something that this time didn't need fixing. Time Warner's spin on the situation would have been funny if it hadn't been tragic. They told the press that Jon had done a really good job transforming the company, but now they needed operational executives to make it all run smoothly. Of course, their idea of an operational executive for a business competing with Yahoo!, and now Facebook and other online entities with large audiences, was a television network executive who was rumored to not even read email.

The fifth floor of AOL's Dulles headquarters, which had been comprised of a very cohesive group of senior managers who together had fought against all challenges since the company's reckoning four years earlier, rapidly depopulated. At Christmas, it seemed like all my good friends were leaving. Joe Redling, Randy Boe, John Buckley, and Jim Bankoff left immediately. Others would soon follow. Having months before planned to depart AOL at that time, I found myself in the really weird position of offering to help the newly installed Time Warner team. There was no one else at the senior level who could show the new guys where all the switches were.

The company's new leaders were polite and said they appreciated the help. Then they went ahead with their new senior staff meeting without bothering to inform me. I'd send emails with suggestions on things that the new team might do, but didn't get replies. Maybe it was true that they didn't read email.

I took the hint. By the end of January, *Nanking* had debuted at Sundance and was nominated for the Grand Jury Prize in the Documentary category. (It won a prize for its film editing, and later would win a Peabody and an Emmy.) The Caps season was underway, and I had many responsibilities as a team owner. I had begun investing in a number of start-up technology ventures. I was working with Steve Case on some business and not-for-profit projects we both thought had high potential.

The AOL chapter of my life—thirteen years in which the company rose, fell, and rose again—drew to a close. I could walk away into a new life with ideas to explore for creating and building businesses that would have a double bottom line—they would both make profits and have a higher calling. *Nanking* was set for theatrical distribution, but even before it was shown to a non-festival audience, it had a significant impact in focusing attention on the events chronicled by Iris Chang in *The Rape of Nanking*. I would probably never make back my investment in the film, so in a way, my filmmaking was an act of philanthropy. I began thinking about how "filmanthropists" like me could have a positive impact on society by using our resources to fund more such films that would right a wrong or shine a spotlight on injustice.

It gave me no pleasure to watch how the team Time Warner installed at AOL botched the success we handed them, and as this is written in the fall of 2009, as AOL prepares to be spun off from Time Warner, I'm hopeful that a company that played such an important role in my life, and vice versa, succeeds from this point forward. Certainly all the momentum we had in late 2006 was squandered by Time Warner in the interim. I've rooted for AOL for too long not to be rooting for it again as it regains its independence.

When I left AOL in the winter of 2007, I was sad on some levels, but on so many other levels, my journey to happiness was complete. My happiness will increase further if you stay with me now, learn lessons I'll share about the tenets of happiness, and start your own journey to happiness. I'll tell you about the businesses in which I'm involved today, and how they are based on a model of creating happiness that can apply to all companies. I believe I can show you that if you consciously work to increase your own happiness, you'll achieve that goal and a different one as well: you'll increase your prospects for becoming more successful.

Having told you about my journey to happiness in this first section of *The Business of Happiness*, in the second section of this book I'll show you how to increase the prospects for happiness and success in your own life.

It's the least I can do. You see, I was given a second chance some twenty-six years ago when the plane I was on didn't crash, and I told God that if given the opportunity, I would try helping others. I've done some good things in the years since then. And yet nothing I've yet done is as important as what I hope to accomplish in the pages of this book.

PART TWO:
Your Journey to Happiness

Chapter Ten

How Did I Come to Know What I Think I Know?

I began my journey to happiness with a list, but without a map. I knew some things instinctively. Others I had to learn the hard way. As Yogi Berra once said, "You can observe a lot just by watching." And Yogi was right, as he always is. Ever since I embarked on my quest, I've evaluated the people I've grown to know and spent time sorting my friends and colleagues into categories. There are those I believe to be happy, and those I believe who aren't, and it is always my preference to spend more time with the former than the latter. Among my happy friends, I've tried determining what exactly makes them so.

The happiest people I know share many common elements. They have productive and positive relationships with their families and friends. They are authentic and honest. They seem to know what their higher calling is—their purpose in life. The happy people I know might have great accomplishments, but they are humble. They measure their success not by how much money they have, but often by how much they are able to give back. They are active within their communities of interest. They are empathetic and think of others, not just themselves.

As common patterns emerged among the people who I knew were happy, it became easier to recognize what I needed to do to complete my own quest.

As I went about my analysis, I didn't actually need scientific research to know that money can't buy happiness. After all, as a young man with millions of dollars, when that plane started circling the runway, I knew I wasn't happy. That was my social science experiment, under real world conditions. I'm a quick learner, and it was clear in an instant: money had bought me nothing but material goods and a ticket on the wrong plane.

Of course, there is plenty of scientifically validated research proving the cliché is true—money doesn't buy happiness—and from the earliest days of my quest, I sought it out and absorbed it. Dr. Ruut Veenhoven at Erasmus University in Rotterdam has catalogued more than 1,000 studies in more than 200 countries in the World Database of Happiness. He has found that in order to achieve some threshold level of happiness, minimum standards have to be met: one must have food, shelter, and sufficient clothing to stay warm when the weather is cold. Genuine poverty and the existential fight for survival prevent even the possibility of one being "happy."

And yet, after certain basic needs are met, the data shows there is no correlation between having money and being happy. Or, as it is sometimes put, "making $100,000 does not make you twice as happy as making $50,000." In fact, in the most recent ranking of countries published by Dr. Veenhoven, the United States—one of the richest nations on Earth—is the 17th happiest nation in the world. Colombia,

Guatemala, and Mexico are all "happier," even though they're significantly less affluent.

At some level, I knew this even as a freshman at Georgetown, when I first encountered classmates with families who were really, really rich. My wealthy classmates weren't necessarily happier than I was, and in fact, some of them seemed certifiably miserable. Even now, divorce, chemical dependency, and alcoholism seem more prevalent among my rich friends than my working-class buddies.

Happiness has been "studied" for thousands of years. Before the social scientists, it was the province of religious prophets and philosophers, and equally so in both the Western tradition and what has come to us from the East. It's not my goal here either to deliver a dump truck full of academic studies, or go beyond my expertise in discussing what my Greek forebears such as Socrates, Aristotle, and Plato could have told you more than 2,500 years ago. I'm not the Dalai Lama, though I have read his work, admire it deeply, and absolutely recommend *The Art of Happiness* and *The Art of Happiness at Work,* which are basically conversations between the Dalai Lama and an American psychiatrist. Type the query "Happiness" into the Amazon database and you'll find that 420,000 items are so tagged. I've read a lot—I personally make Amazon a happy company by being among the biggest customers of Amazon's "Happiness" section—but it's not my intention here just to repeat what others have written, or as a businessman-adept, to try to condense the work of academics and experts.

My job here is to tell you what I think I know and why I think I know it. I've told you a fair measure of my story in order to illustrate how my quest for happiness informs my beliefs. From this point on, I'm determined to shift from telling you strictly about my journey to happiness to offering some practical information that can help you on your journey to happiness.

I believe that for many of us, the path to happiness begins with some kind of reckoning. Something shakes you up to such an extent that you have to examine yourself and the life you have led, and from there you have to make an affirmative effort to change things in pursuit of happiness.

Once you have committed yourself to becoming happy, you have to define your terms and get organized. The best way I know to get organized is to make a list of your goals. It's the first concrete step in your affirmative campaign to achieve the happiness you desire.

———

For more than twenty-five years, I have actively, consciously, managed my quest. What I've learned along the way is in roughly equal measures a synthesis of published research, my personal experience, and my observation of friends and associates. I had to discover things for myself, but once I had done so, I found my beliefs to be supported both by the work of social scientists and other academics and by the experiences of others.

Bono is an international rock star, social activist, and deeply committed human being with a calling far higher than simply making lots of money by singing pop songs. I know he is a happy human being. Once again, some might react by thinking, "Of course Bono's happy, he's a rock star with a gazillion dollars; if I were a rock star with a gazillion dollars I'd be happy too." Well, not necessarily. Kurt Cobain, Michael Jackson, and Janis Joplin might have something different to say, if they were still with us. From my interactions with Bono over the years, I believe he is happy because he embodies certain tenets held in common by other happy people.

Bono's longevity and unique standing as perhaps the music world's preeminent "star" is not simply because he's got a great voice, and not just because U2 is an amazing band. It is the result of his being a happy person who actively manages his quest for happiness.

I believe a big part of the magic that has made Bono so successful is that efforts on behalf of his own happiness and fulfillment have allowed U2 to reach a broader audience than they might have otherwise. Inherent in the sentiment of "I Still Haven't Found What I'm Looking For" is that Bono, too, is on a quest. I believe the quest he is on makes him even more appealing than his great voice and songwriting abilities would, absent this connotation of his search for something greater.

A few years ago, I was the chairman of the annual YouthAIDS gala, and Bono was our honoree. He told us that one of the things that had propelled him to become as active as he was in helping Africa was the realization that U2 had become the biggest band in the world, and he wanted—needed—to find out what else he could do with his life beyond, well, being a member of the biggest rock band in the world. When he went to Africa, his empathy really kicked in. It was a life-changing moment—perhaps you could call it a reckoning. Bono told us that he discovered that celebrity could be a curse, but also a very powerful tool. Instead of being distrustful of it, he would use it to effect positive change.

And so he began his effort to, among other things, fight AIDS in Africa, which was why we were honoring him. That trip to Africa spurred his commitment to alleviating the challenges the continent faces, like high levels of international debt, disease, and the absence of jobs. So he became a champion of lowering the massive debt African nations owe Western financial institutions through promoting debt forgiveness. Bono became an advocate for enhanced trade and foreign aid from the world's wealthiest nations. You may not agree with all of the policies for which Bono is an advocate, but spend two minutes with him and you won't doubt his sincerity, or that he has found his calling. I believe that in advocacy on behalf of Africa, Bono has found what he was looking for.

Bono scores high across my list of the tenets embodied by happy people. For more than a decade, through DATA, the ONE Campaign, and RED, Bono has worked tirelessly in pursuit of making life better for those living in poverty in Africa. He is a member of multiple communities—as much at ease meeting with presidents and aid workers and activists as ever he was with members of the rock 'n' roll fraternity. He is able to express himself not merely through the songs he writes with U2, but in dozens of speeches and meetings where he is a passionate spokesman on behalf of his cause. He is grateful for his status as a celebrity, but because of the high degree of empathy he has, able to give of his time, and the benefit of his name and notoriety, on behalf of a higher calling.

I have met with Bono at AOL, the Sundance Film Festival, Live8, and YouthAIDS events. He is always upbeat and positive, with a twinkle in his eye. He contributed the use of "Where the Streets Have No Names" to our film *Kicking It*, and I still thank him for it when I see him.

When I look at Bono, I recognize the model of happiness and success called for in this book fully actualized and at work. Do you have any doubt that Bono is a very happy person? When I am with him, I see a kindred spirit—a fellow happy man. Importantly, I believe that he and U2 are far more successful because of this happiness than they would otherwise be. There is a double bottom line to the "corporate" entity known as U2, and to the "brand" that is Bono. Bono is not simply trying to make records that will hit the charts. He is working to create happiness—his own, as well as for the people who listen to U2 in stadiums or through headphones. Because he also has a higher calling, which includes alleviating the suffering of the planet's most troubled continent, what he does achieves nobility. I believe this makes him happier than he would be if he were simply one more superstar. I believe this nobility, almost as much as their great music, helps U2 sell more records.

I was recently surprised to find that a good friend of mine, someone whom I have known and worked with for many years, is a recovering alcoholic. In discussing my beliefs about the path to happiness, he nodded his head vigorously and said, "You're almost perfectly describing Alcoholics Anonymous and the premise of 12-step programs." I was stunned, not just because I hadn't known my friend was an alcoholic, but because I didn't know all that much about AA. Now I do, and while I'm no expert, my sense of Alcoholics Anonymous and the way it helps recovering alcoholics fits my model of happiness attainment perfectly.

An alcoholic finds himself, either figuratively or literally, sleeping in the gutter. Alcohol has brought him low. Because of his addiction to alcohol, his life has fallen apart: maybe his wife has left him, or he's lost his job, or is in danger of bad things happening. And so one day he hits bottom, and he recognizes it for what it is. He has a reckoning.

The 12-step program developed by Alcoholics Anonymous includes a step in which the alcoholic conducts a "fearless moral inventory" of his failings. Among the steps to recovery, alcoholics have to develop a list of all of the people whom they've hurt through their drinking and to whom they must make amends. So you have a reckoning, and, following this, list-making.

AA is, first and foremost, a community that those who wish to get and stay sober need to join. Joining this community is a vital element to their staying sober, to their getting well. Embracing a community of people with a common interest is a key to their becoming happy. It is essential to their becoming successful, because it helps them move past their disease.

At AA meetings, alcoholics learn to express themselves, to discuss their feelings and fears. They learn that the act of expressing themselves within the community of their alcoholic peers helps them sort through their feelings in a way they simply wouldn't be able to do on their own. They are given a respectful hearing. They can say anything, and by expressing themselves in this manner, sometimes even the most taciturn of people can find an important outlet and a connection to others.

Alcoholics are grateful for every day of sobriety. They are grateful for the opportunity to get sober, and for the community that is helping them do so. They learn how much they have to be grateful for outside of drinking, and how much more important it is to connect with family and friends, or to preserve their employment, than it is to have that next drink.

As they progress, they commit themselves to giving back to their community. Each recovering alcoholic in Alcoholics Anonymous is committed to helping others get and stay sober. Someone committed to the program will literally leave his house at 2:00 a.m. to help prevent a virtual stranger from having the drink they desperately want—and desperately don't want.

The recovering alcoholic in AA has empathy for others who fall off the wagon. Without judging them, they welcome them back into the AA community. Importantly, the act of helping others reinforces their own efforts to stay sober.

Finally, members of AA have a higher calling: not just to stay sober every day, but also to help others achieve sobriety.

As my thinking on the tenets of happiness progressed over a quarter of a century, it never dawned on me that the model I'd arrived at so closely paralleled the recovery process used in Alcoholics Anonymous. I find it validating that what has been called the most successful self-help program in history is based on identical principles. A reckoning leads to reflection and a determination to pursue a path to happiness. Involvement in a community of like-minded people pulls one out of himself and into society. Outlets for self-expression provide fulfillment. Empathy for others and gratitude for the small things available every day keeps one grounded, and prevents lows from being too low and highs from being too high. Fulfillment is found from giving back to others. The quest for happiness leads to a higher calling.

If ever there was a question about whether the systematic pursuit of happiness also leads to the potential for greater success, the AA model answers it. Society is filled with successful people who would not be where they were if they had not embraced Alcoholics Anonymous at some low moment. Their path to success began with a reckoning.

In recent years we have learned that happiness is contagious. A study of more than 4,700 people over a 20-year time span found that being around happy people increases the likelihood that you will be happy. I started this chapter saying that I sort my friends between those who are happy and those who are not, and prefer to spend time with the ones who are. Science validates this, and reinforces the notion that connecting with a community of other people—happy people—is a way of increasing your own happiness.

Neuroscientists have recently overthrown the belief that humans are by nature and biology entirely driven by self-interest. Instead, according to *Forbes*, research by University of Chicago neuroscientist John T. Cacioppo shows that humans "are inherently unselfish, or at least they need to be for their health and the perpetuation of their genes." Of course this makes sense, if you believe that happiness and self-actualization comes, in part, from engaging with other human beings within communities of mutual interest. The headline of the *Forbes* story was perfect: "Loneliness Can Kill You."

Recent research indicates that as you get older, having a higher purpose in life correlates to living longer. Of course it does. Dr. Patricia Boyle of the Rush Alzheimer's Disease Center studied more than 1,200 elderly participants and found that someone with an intentional effort to derive meaning from life was half as likely to have died over the studied period as a person without a similar sense of purpose. Put more starkly: someone without a sense of purpose in life is twice as likely to die as someone with one.

Many people derive a sense of purpose from their communities. In his fascinating book entitled *Blue Zones*, Dan Buettner studied societies around the world where people live the longest and most fulfilling lives. Buettner believes that focusing on community-building contributes to long life.

We know from a welter of survey research that consistently the happiest people in America are evangelical Christians, which to me makes perfect sense. For an evangelical Protestant, to be "born again" means that you have had a reckoning and have decided to accept Jesus Christ as your Lord and Savior. The act of going to church each week is a willful expression of joining in a community in support of a higher calling. Evangelical Christians are generous with their money and their time, volunteering at higher rates than those found among non-church goers. Habitat for Humanity, in which so many ordinary people take up hammers to help those less fortunate achieve housing and homeownership, started out of a single evangelical Christian church in Georgia.

We know that in this consumer-driven culture, purchasing material goods does not provide us with the same degree of happiness as purchasing an experience. That is, the vacation at the beach that you take with your family is a far better investment in happiness than that new watch, or car, or iPod. Unquestionably, you want that new watch, or car, or iPod, and when you get it you are happy. You may even be momentarily happy every time you put the watch on, or drive the car, or listen to U2 on your iPod. But an important 2003 study by Professors Leaf Van Bolden of the University of Colorado at Boulder and Thomas Gilovich at Cornell, entitled "To Do or to Have? That Is the Question," found that people quickly adapt to their new possessions. They then need other, newer possessions to continue to feel the same degree of wellbeing. In contrast, the pleasure derived from social interactions—going to see U2 play in concert, going on vacation with your family, or screaming your lungs out as the Washington Capitals (hopefully) win the Stanley Cup—lasts much longer. "Kodak moments" simply provide more happiness than buying a new camera, even if you've anticipated buying that new camera, and even if it makes you happy every time you use it.

A 2008 study undertaken by University of British Columbia psychologist Elizabeth Dunn found that spending money on ourselves provides far less happiness than spending money on others. Employees at a firm who used their annual bonuses to make a contribution to charity were happier than those who used their bonuses entirely to purchase things for themselves. In another instance, researchers gave a group of people between $5 and $20, and told them to spend it that day however they liked. A different group of people was told they should spend the money on others. Guess who was happier at the end of the day?

I could go on, telling you about other new research or about item number 420,001 just added to the Amazon "happiness" category, all of which back up the premise of this book. But that might quickly become repetitive.

So instead let me put it this way: since the 1980s, I have read just about everything I can get my hands on concerning the topic of happiness. I haven't yet found research that contradicts my beliefs. Nothing I've ever read suggests it is better to stay bottled up than to find some outlet for personal expression.

I've never read any actual scientific research suggesting it is better to eschew empathy than to have it, nor that it is better to horde what you have and resist being charitable than to try giving back to society.

Every day, I look to find examples of behavior or research that undermine my beliefs. And every day, I find my beliefs are reinforced by the research of others and by my own observations.

———

I began *The Business of Happiness* declaring that I'm not a social scientist, which by now should be self-evident. But on the path to writing this book, I decided to try testing out my beliefs with some research of my own. I worked with a survey researcher who cautioned me that because of the self-selecting nature of who responds to online research questionnaires—as opposed to surveys conducted from a statistically valid random sample of adults—the data we would generate wouldn't pass muster with the American Association of Public Opinion Research. With that caveat understood, together we wrote up a set of questions and published them online as The Happiness Questionnaire.

We put the questionnaire into a widget (developed by Clearspring Technologies, a company whose Board I chair) that could be found by anyone who either comes to my blog, *Ted's Take*, or to the Washington Capitals website. More than 200 websites grabbed the widget and it was seen by more than two million people. Among the more than 3,500 people who took the entire Happiness Questionnaire, just over half said that they consider themselves to be happy "all or most of the time." They were the cohort we were most interested in—the half that were happy all or most of the time. As it turned out, the common tenets of happiness I have shared with you were at work among the 1,500 people who identified themselves as happy all or most of the time.

Among the happy respondents, 90 percent could list their top goals in life. Nearly 60 percent had gone through some kind of reckoning. Nearly every happy respondent could cite a community of interest in which they participated, and 75 percent could cite three or more. More than 60 percent could cite three or more outlets that they'd found for personal expression—writing in a journal, playing a musical instrument, going to AA, dancing, gardening, writing poetry, singing, engaging in prayer. Eight respondents in ten said they could regularly reflect upon the things that made them happy. More than seven respondents in ten ranked themselves in the upper half of generous people contributing money or time to charitable causes. Nearly three-fourths of the happy respondents (72.6 percent) said they believed they had a "higher calling, or a higher purpose to their lives."

I'm mindful that this was just an online survey. (And if you want to take the survey, go to www.BusinessOfHappiness.com. I encourage you to match your own answers with that of the happy cohort who've gone before you.)

I accept that there is no "scientific" validity to our survey instrument. And yet it is reinforcement that what I believe I know about happiness is backed up by the real world experiences of real people. I had a great time developing and posting the survey and seeing the responses. In fact, joining the community of people who responded to The Happiness Questionnaire made me happy.

Chapter Eleven

1. Your Life List

It would make me happy to know that my reckoning could stand in for your reckoning. In other words, I'd be pleased if rather than you getting on the wrong airplane and having an emergency landing, the mere act of reading this book could lead you to assess your life, the goals you have, and spur you on to mounting your own journey to happiness.

You don't really need any gear to start your quest to happiness. But you do have to envision what you believe your state of happiness and fulfillment would consist of. When you go through that process of envisioning happiness, it would help to take some notes on things you'll need to do to get there. The notes you take will probably pretty quickly get formulated as a list.

Writing my Life List—the goals I wanted to accomplish in life— didn't make me happy. And fulfilling my list has not, in and of itself, made me happy. And yet I credit the writing of that list, and my dogged, faithful effort to accomplish the goals I put on it, as a necessary aspect of my quest for happiness. I also know that by putting on my list certain goals that would require personal growth to accomplish, I have become a more three-dimensional person, and genuinely more successful.

Writing my life list was a very business-like approach to becoming happy. It was the only way I knew to approach it at the time, and in hindsight, it made for a good start. Managing your achievement of happiness as if it were a business venture, as if you were managing your career, takes clarity of purpose and organizational skills, but it makes it far more feasible. If you think through what it would mean for you to be really happy, and then set down on paper the events and achievements and ingredients to get there, you've already started your journey to happiness. It's not just an incidental bonus that this process of pursuing happiness can also deliver you to success.

I say this even accounting for the fact that for some people, happiness may lie in a state of non-accomplishment. That is, for some, the happiness they envision may consist of lying in a hammock all day long, reading Proust or comic books. You could probably go set up the hammock, and check out Proust from your local library (though maybe not the comic books), and do just that. And maybe you'd be happy. But you do have to eat, and own or rent the two trees to string the hammock between, and then you've arrived at needing to do some actual planning to achieve the happiness you've envisioned.

Just write the list. Start now.

———

Of course, most happy people haven't written out their list of goals. From The Happiness Questionnaire, we found that just over four in ten happy people had actually written one down. And yet twice that number of respondents at least kept a list in their mind. This accords with what I know from studying happy friends. Most, if not all, have been operating off of a rough list of things they want to accomplish in life. They carry the list around in their head. If you ask them what their life's goals are, and how they're progressing in fulfilling them, it only takes a moment before they can tell you. Few have actually ever written a list like I did.

Consistently, however, when I've given speeches to audiences and suggested that every person in the room have a written-down list of their life's goals, at some subsequent point I've gotten an email from an attendee, or run into a member of the audience at another event, and been told that writing down their goals helped them get started on their journey. People tell me that it has helped them sort through what's really important to them. Some tell me that they did it with their spouse and found it generated real discussion about where they wanted to live, and how they envisioned retirement, and about whether accumulating wealth was more important than traveling to India to see the Taj Mahal, or whether their single greatest goal revolved around their kids, which necessitated a total focus on their family.

Writing your Life List is important for clarifying your conscious desires and needs. It can also tap into your unconscious desires and needs and offer the chance to do some exploring of side roads off the highway you thought you were on.

When I put "own a sports franchise (basketball, hockey, or football)" on my list of goals, I'm not really sure how important it was to me at that moment. I loved sports, but having such an aspiration seemed like a lark, something that would be fun, like owning a Ferrari. It turned out to be something much more than that. I've recounted already the story of how, fifteen years later, when Dick Patrick asked me if I wanted to buy the Washington Capitals, I first said no, before being reminded by my wife Lynn that in doing so, I was failing to fulfill a goal I had set. She was right—and owning the Washington Capitals not only has given me joy, but plunging into sports-team ownership developed into my single biggest business venture as an investor and entrepreneur. The serendipitous timing that led to my selling shares of AOL in order to buy the team one year before the shares plunged in value meant that fulfilling my goal of owning a sports team took on even greater resonance.

Admittedly, when I wrote my Life List, the possibilities I had for achieving such a goal were probably greater than they might have been for a more typical 28-year old. I had made a lot of money; it wasn't too far-fetched to dream of owning a sports team. And yet by envisioning that I would find fulfillment as a sports team owner—if ever I were to have that opportunity—when the chance came, I took it.

It's not like I put down on my list *playing* for the Washington Capitals or a professional sports team. That would have been in the realm of Walter Mitty, the character in the famous James Thurber story who fantasized a life of heroism and triumph. Owning a team was an aspiration that may have been grandiose, but it wasn't entirely removed from reality.

<hr />

The idea of winning an Oscar (goal #88: "Win a Grammy/Oscar/Tony/Emmy Award") was far more Mittyesque for a young man who'd never gone to film school. It is still the longest of long shots, and I can say this even though both *Nanking* and my second film, *Kicking It*, were accepted into the Sundance Film Festival and went on to win awards. *Nanking* even made it to the short list of films that get circulated among the Motion Picture Academy as they determine their Oscar nominees. (It did not make it onto the final list of five.) By the time *Nanking* had its premiere, I was a member of a team that won an Emmy—for AOL's 2005 webcasting of the Live8 concerts, the first-ever Emmy awarded for an online broadcast. I've now also won a Peabody Award for *Nanking*, and in September 2009, I won a second Emmy—this time for *Nanking*. Still, given the level of competition, you would have to consider the odds very much against my ever having a shot at ticking the Oscar portion of this goal off my list.

Yet in 2005, when I read the story of Iris Chang's tragic death, and learned about the events that took place in Nanking seventy years earlier, I immediately realized that it was a topic I wanted to turn into a film. Making *Nanking* opened a whole new chapter in my life. It rang all the bells of happiness. It offered me a chance to express myself. I entered new communities of interest, including the Chinese-American community for whom the events in Nanking during World War II are an unappreciated Holocaust. It offered me an opportunity to give something back and ultimately put me on a path toward a higher purpose— as well as steering me toward a new business venture.

You see, it was through my experience as the producer of *Nanking* that I developed the concept of "filmanthropy"—making movies to right a wrong or shine a light on an injustice in order to use the power of documentary filmmaking to move people to action. *Nanking* was a success—by the standards of documentary films. It was accepted in Sundance. It had theatrical distribution. It was bought by HBO. It aired on the largest television network in China. It won awards. Yet at the end of the day (other than in China), few people saw it, and I just bare-ly broke even on my investment.

From this experience, SnagFilms was born. In early 2008, with co-investors Steve and Jean Case, and another friend and former senior AOL executive named Miles Gilburne, I created an online site with a library of documentary films that anyone could watch for free, either at SnagFilms.com, or on a video player encased by a widget "snagged" by a blog, website, or Facebook page.

Our first goal was to fix a broken distribution system. Because inex-pensive digital tools have led to an increasing number of fantastic documentary films being made—just when there are fewer and fewer venues in which to watch them—there's a fundamental mismatch between supply and, if not demand, certainly distribution. SnagFilms fixes that by getting thousands of films before a global online audience that can access them on demand, for free. We share a portion of the advertising revenue with the filmmaker.

Our second goal was to showcase "filmanthropy" in action, as any-one moved by one of the featured films could easily "snag" the widg-et in which the films are played and open his or her own "virtual movie theater" on their own social network page or blog. Anyone touched by a film he or she saw could "donate their pixels"—the online real estate they own via publishing their own website, blog, or social network page. We also made it easy for anyone who saw one of our films to quickly be able to make a financial contribution to a charity associated with it. When we drew up our list of what we con-sidered metrics of success for SnagFilms, I wrote down, "Opening one million virtual movie theaters, generating one billion page views, and having one trillion pixels donated." We're not there yet, but we're making progress.

Working with a very talented founding CEO named Rick Allen, we launched SnagFilms in July 2008. As this is being written, SnagFilms is a thriving business, with over 1,000 films in our library, more than 25,000 "virtual movie theaters" distributed across the Web, and more than 200 million monthly page views across our network—one billion page views in our first year. We stream millions of minutes of free films every month. Every single documentary filmmaker whose work we've hosted has received a check based on the advertising revenues their film has generated. We've liberated the documentary libraries of major companies like National Geographic and PBS, and premiered films simultaneously with major film festivals. We've connected contributors to hundreds of charities. Filmanthropy is working.

I recount this story, as I earlier recounted the story of how I bought the Caps, for this reason. It is no accident that I've created a successful online business, which in turn has created a new distribution system for documentary films, while also enabling the work of really talented filmmakers to inspire people to action. If you want to trace the antecedent to how a "double bottom line" venture like that got going, if you want to work all the way back through the chain of events that led to this really terrific company getting created, you have to go back to that day when I sat around the pool in Vero Beach, Florida, still shaken from my near plane crash. For it was there that, as I wrote down my list of 101 goals for life, I envisioned #88: "Win a Grammy/Oscar/Tony/Emmy Award."

Even if it were for only a moment, I envisioned winning an Oscar. It was a realistic enough aspiration to me that I wrote it down on my list. Years later, after reading an obituary of a young mother who committed suicide following the publication of her important history of events during Japan's invasion of China, I had an inspiration. Bing.

I decided to make a movie, because moviemaking had always been lurking there as something I might do. *It was on my list.*

If you're going to put winning an Academy Award down on your list of life's goals, you have to make a movie, right? I made the movie, and learned about the challenges of distributing documentaries. Bing.

Theatrical distribution of documentaries isn't working, therefore—bing!—movies should be distributed online. And since documentary films like *Nanking* would probably never make money, but could genuinely shine a spotlight on injustice, there was a social benefit to creating them. It should be easy for someone to act on their inspiration, once they've seen such a film. Filmanthropy should be achievable via an online site from which you could take a movie, open your own theater, inspire your friends to watch it, and help channel money to an associated charity. Bing.

And so, SnagFilms was born and became a success. And it all stemmed from my having put an item on my list of life's goals, more than a quarter century earlier.

Go on, write your list.

Your reckoning, whether it follows some dramatic and negative development in your life, or stems from your simply deciding you want to get serious about living a life on offense and without regret, will concentrate your mind. When my reckoning was delivered courtesy of Eastern Airlines, I was probably searching for it in some way. After that plane landed, I was scared straight.

I said to myself, "Okay, I just had this scare and it's a crisis of confidence in myself. What can I do about it? How can I know that the rest of my life will be one filled with reflection and getting to where I want to be?" I wasn't at a place of peace, happiness, and contentment, and I knew it, because when I had that wake-up call, I really didn't like the person I was.

I'd been fighting for success and recognition, and I'd found it. And suddenly I came face-to-face with my own mortality, and had to negotiate my survival. I believed I had a binding deal to work toward happiness by leading a far less selfish life. The list I wrote around that pool was a fun, possibly feeble attempt to create a scoreboard of what would make me happy. It was, however, deliberately created with a sense of balance, because the Jesuit ideal I had learned at Georgetown was that in order to achieve fulfillment, your life needed balance.

I wanted to think big, and I really did have aspirations. In hindsight, removed from that process by a quarter-century's greater maturity, I am as ashamed of my list as I am proud of it, because so much that was on the list revolved around possessions, material things. I didn't have the tools to really reflect on a mature hierarchy of needs and values. Buying a Ferrari did not contribute to my happiness, and I quickly sold it. A Ferrari has a price tag. Getting married, having children, and taking care of my family are priceless.

My goal at the time was to ensure that when I really did die, I would have all 101 things checked off my Life List, and the process of doing so somehow would add up to happiness. I've been faithful to the list, and as you'll see in the appendix where the list is published, along with checkmarks denoting those items I've fulfilled, it is almost complete. (No, I haven't taken a trip into outer space—but who knows, Richard Branson's offering the service, and I'm still a comparatively young man...)

I have treated my life as a systematic plan of aspirations. I believe you should, too. You don't have to have a long list. By the time you write your list, you may already have accomplished more than half of the things that will lead to a happy life. I wrote my list as a single man; maybe you're already married and have children, and the family portion of your list is checked off before you even write it.

My list was written without my fully understanding that the things you strive for are not ends in themselves, they're all in service of your overarching goal, which is to be happy. As you write your list of life's goals, include on it the things you've already accomplished and the things you've yet to achieve. Already run that marathon? Put it down with a checkmark beside it, because when you were training for it, I'm certain you viewed those long hours running as adding up to a major event in your life, one that you would cherish forever.

Think through your list of life's goals in as many dimensions as possible. Write goals for yourself that relate to your dreams for your family. Write goals for yourself that can help steer your career to where your ambitions are meant to take you. Write goals for your life that will broaden your life—the places you want to see, the books you want to read, and the skills you want to acquire. Add some whimsy, because life should always have some whimsical goals. Who knows, you might just be able to fulfill them.

When I look at the verbatim answers in The Happiness Questionnaire, so many of them relate to a poignant desire for self-improvement. To lose weight or quit smoking. To get out of an abusive marriage or find a better job.

Writing your Life List of goals will help you clarify what you want and need from life. Fulfilling those goals probably isn't sufficient to make you happy. Yet a trait I hold in common with happy people I have known is that we've all embarked on a journey to achieve certain things, that this journey has directly and indirectly led us to some measure of happiness, and that it has made us more successful than we otherwise would have been.

Write your list. And let me help you!

Visit www.BusinessOfHappiness.com.

A Listing of Things to Consider When You Make Your Life List:

1. Are the things you want to accomplish in life realistic, given your talents, opportunity, and resources?
2. How will the accomplishment of each item make you happy?
3. Is your list consistent with what your life partner wants for his or her life?
4. Do you feel strongly enough about each item on the list that you would regret not achieving every one of them?
5. Are you really serious about these goals, or are these just things you want to talk about at cocktail parties?

Chapter Twelve

2. Multiple Communities of Interest

The most popular television show in America at the time I joined AOL was *Cheers*, a situation comedy depicting a bar in Boston where "everyone knows your name." I remember a seminal episode that began with four people sitting at the bar, each lost in his thoughts, not connecting in any way with the other customers.

Sam Malone was the name of the character played by Ted Danson, who captured America's imagination as maybe the greatest bartender of all time. In this episode, Sam noticed that the individuals at the bar were isolated from one another, and so he turned on the television to a Boston Red Sox game.

"I really think this could be the year for Sox, Norm," he asked one of his customers, "what do you think?" Norm started to talk, and the guy next to him commented on what Norm said, and then all four of them started talking about this team they loved, the Red Sox. A community was formed, and Sam poured a beer or two, and before you got to the commercial break, they were singing a song together.

It was a comedy, but it made a pretty important point. If you are alone in your thoughts, disconnected from everyone else, you're probably not as happy as you could be. You're probably not as productive as you could be. While being alone with your thoughts is necessary some of the time, it's no way to live. Your potential for happiness is greater if you are connected in some way to the community around you. For Sam, by simply using content (a television broadcast of a Red Sox game) to start a conversation, he activated a community, which created happiness in the room and drove commerce.

Which bar is more successful: the one where four guys drink beer all by themselves, or the one where people sing songs together?

When I arrived at AOL in 1994, I told everyone that we should think of ourselves as bartenders like Sam. I gave speeches in which I told the story of Sam and the Red Sox game, and explained that our job was to bring communities together just like he had in that bar. I put it in these terms: we needed content to activate community to activate commerce. It was the *Cheers* bar, right?

AOL became the success it was because of the community it built. AOL was itself a giant community, in which you could communicate with others simply by addressing their screen name—no other domain name was required. ("Where everyone knows your name...") Within the AOL community there were thousands of smaller communities arranged by affinities, interests, and needs.

Then we created AIM, where you could organize your various communities in clusters: family, work, and social groups. It may seem trivial, but there was magic in the way we enabled users to structure their sub-communities as they wanted, because it gave people an opportunity to think about, and thus manage, the multiple communities in which they participated. Managing your Buddy List was a metaphor for actively managing the communities in which you operated. AIM proliferated as both a social tool and a business utility, and through its success AOL took further advantage of the network effect, where once a large number of people are participating in a network, others naturally join, because...that's where a large of number of people are. It was the ultimate virtuous circle. (Unless you were Microsoft or Yahoo! and found your community was smaller because AIM's was so large.)

The innate human desire for community has, from the Internet's earliest days, been a driver of success for the biggest businesses on the Web. Facebook is the natural successor to AOL in that it created a giant community, and it is built on many of the tools we pioneered—presence detection (allowing you to see if your friends are online), instant messaging, email, personalization, active management of your communities of interest, and of course tools to publish information about yourself. Most genuine online phenomena are driven, at least in part, by the concept of community.

Twitter enables people to express themselves, and is built upon the concept that you follow people in a community, as you define and organize it, and other people in that community follow you. The fact that Twitter is both a means of personal expression and has become a vibrant business tool indicates that some of the smartest companies realize that their success is built upon the need to keep a community informed and engaged.

eBay wasn't just a place where goods could be auctioned; from the start, there was an eBay community of buyers and sellers. How the community ranks you as a seller has a big impact on whether your goods, or someone else's, spark a competitive bidding process.

The Washington Capitals' website isn't simply a promotional or informational tool—it is the hub of a vibrant community. In fact, many of the most successful sports sites—from SBNation.com to the thousands of official and unofficial team sites—are built around the idea that sports fans are members of specific communities with tribal affiliations.

The same increasingly is true for musicians and bands, whose websites or MySpace pages are community centers for their legions—or maybe it's just dozens—of fans. The old-fashioned concept of the fan club has moved online, and members of a band's community share information and rumors, get a first listen to new music, get early notice of where the band's playing next, and maybe even special offers, including advance notice when tickets are going on sale.

Products with devoted followings—like Apple—have online communities that dissect news and information about the goods and services around which they affiliate. Communities can give thumbs up or down recommendations on new products. They can be an incredible source of technical information about problems a consumer might face in properly utilizing a new product. The smartest businesses understand this, and utilize their community in their marketing and consumer communications.

Tools harnessing social networks enable communities—through the wisdom of crowds—to steer commerce, as Amazon or iTunes recommend books or songs that other people *in their community* are buying. In fact, one of the great aspects of the online revolution is the way community recommendations have supplanted those of designated high priests in creating viral enthusiasm for music or films or books. For thousands of people, LivingSocial.com is a more relevant authority on what to read or listen to than *The New York Times Book Review* or *Rolling Stone*. Our innate need to connect with others is one of the main reasons the Internet so quickly became a necessity.

In my final year at AOL, we really were successfully reclaiming our lost Mojo and transforming ourselves from a business built upon access to the Internet to one based on engaging and entertaining an audience. My late friend Brandon Tartikoff, who had been the president of NBC, once told me that there are only three acts in the American drama. Kid makes good, and achieves success. Kid stumbles and falls. Kid redeems himself and rises again. AOL was fulfilling this sequence by rising again.

It was time we updated our mission statement. In the early 1990s, we said our mission was "to build a global medium as central to people's lives as the telephone or television...and even more useful." Well, mission accomplished. By now it was time for that third act: redemption. We needed a mission statement to go along with it.

In 2006, John Buckley and I, along with a small group of like-minded collaborators, updated AOL's mission statement: "To serve the world's largest and most engaged community." There was a little bit of bravado in the statement, but not too much. At that moment, the AOL network had about 110 million "unique visitors" (UVs) domestically each month, and about 200 million worldwide. We had more domestic UVs (unique visitors) than Google, and about exactly as many as Yahoo! (though Yahoo! had a bigger audience outside the United States). The fact that we saw community as central to our success wasn't an accident; community was always central to AOL's success. This was something that, after Jon Miller and so many of us left at the beginning of 2007, Time Warner forgot at its own peril.

The Internet is a global community, and millions of smaller communities. Fostering a sense of community among people with common interests is one of the Internet's great gifts. Offering individuals the ability to connect within communities is one of the Internet's central benefits to humanity. Participating in multiple communities is innately linked to our desire to be happy, and a common tenet of the happy people I know is their participation in multiple communities of interest. Here's how I think it happens.

———————————

A child is born and joins a community. That first community may only have two other people in it: the child's parents. From our earliest moments on the planet, we seek sustenance and happiness from the communities in which we participate.

Innately as humans, we're meant to bond with others. While our first community is our immediate family, from there it often is our extended family. By the time we're conscious of going to church or school, we've already plunged into multiple communities. The family is the fundamental building block, and if you are fortunate, this is as true for you as an adult as it was for you as a child. From that essential building block, we add others, and the more building blocks you stand on, the greater are your prospects of rising high as a happy and successful person.

You go through your childhood and school years building friendships, participating on teams, organizing your activities around varied interests—Little League, Glee Club, your Spanish study group, your passion for U2. By the time you're in college, you've learned how to navigate between social groups, cohorts formed by the classes you're taking, affinity groups shaped by similar interests.

When your career is launched, you start to add business relationships, while still trying to maintain friendships from each of the stages in your life thus far. You meet someone and fall in love, and suddenly you join the communities your girlfriend or boyfriend has participated in, starting with their family—just as they join yours. When you have children, suddenly your community revolves around their community, as time spent at your child's school or sporting events brings you into contact with the parents of their friends.

Later, you gravitate to people with whom you have common interests. You find yourself posting messages on forums affiliated with the teams or brands you care about. Maybe you join Facebook and participate in multiple sub-communities within the larger Facebook community. You play cards or go skiing with a regular group of friends, and you don't just read books, you join a book club. Professionally, you keep in close touch with people outside of your company who might have an insight into your business, and have lunch with them regularly. You celebrate friends' birthdays with certain rituals, guaranteeing you never lose touch with the social network that revolves around them.

The happiest and most successful people I know have in common with one another not just an ability to function within multiple communities, but a real desire to do so. The best of the best are connectors—virtual file servers connecting not data but people. Lest this point be lost, I believe that measuring the level of happiness one person may have compared to another is more complicated than simply multiplying the number of communities each person participates in. To really glean whether one person might be happier than another, you also have to factor the intensity of his or her participation in more than one community, the dexterity with which they move from one to another and back again, and their skill at mash-ups, in which they bring their communities together.

Managing your participation in communities may not just happen; you have to be conscious of the notion that these networks you operate in are separate, sometimes overlapping communities. It is easier for some people to flow within communities than it is for others. I believe being conscious of your engagement with communities offers great possibilities for friendship, fulfillment, and yes, success.

If you ever go to an event or a party where you see friends from various stages of your life and career, and from a number of your separate social groups, there's a strong likelihood that you'll have a good time. Whereas if you go to the same event and see no one you know, you may or may not have a good time meeting new people, but it's less likely you'll feel comfortable and at ease. My sense is that the happiest, most successful person in that room is probably the person whose social networks have overlapped the most. He or she might be the one who has been able to mix the most within various groupings, introducing people from one community to another. I'm guessing that the person able to do this is successful in his or her career, in addition to being a happy person.

In my own case, I view my communities as starting with my immediate family, my extended family, and the friends I grew up with in New York and Massachusetts. There are the people with whom I went to Georgetown, and because I'm still very active—I'm on the Board—it's a significant community for me. Then there are my business lives, from my earliest incarnation to the Boards of the start-up companies that I've either founded or invested in. Then it's my sports teams, and within and around my teams, it's all the circles of influence from investors to bankers, players to staff, to the media, and to the fans themselves.

When you start thinking this way, you can actually map out these concentric circles in which all of your communities are represented. It can seem a little overwhelming, especially if you have so many diverse interests.

I have my creative side and the people I work with in making my films. I have my charitable side and the causes I support. I have this ever-expanding universe of interests and friends and communities. But I work it; I'm actively conscious of the importance of paying attention to communities as such, and trying to manage my relationships with them. I've actually written down the concentric circles in which I operate. And of course I believe that the more friends and circles I have, the happier and more successful I am.

I once was asked to write an article on the most successful executive I knew, and without hesitation, I listed John J. DeGioia, the President of Georgetown University. Under Jack's leadership, every indicator of Georgetown's success has gone up: its rankings and endowment have all increased significantly. Jack DeGioia's greatest skill set as the leader of as complex an institution as Georgetown is the way he manages his relationships with multiple communities. Consider the many worlds Jack lives in: Rome, the local archdiocese, the Society of Jesus, all the other denominations at Georgetown, plus the students, teachers, employees, parents, alumni and athletes, the Big East conference, the Georgetown neighborhood and downtown D.C., researchers, politicians, corporations, sponsors, and donors. Plus, he oversees the law school, the business school, the medical school, the School of Foreign Service, and so on. He simultaneously spends time with students, faculty, alumni, parents, the Jesuit order, the Georgetown neighborhood, Washington, D.C., and it revolves outward from there. Circles within circles within circles. Jack is so good at being the President of Georgetown—and a really happy guy— because his immersion in these concentric circles is something he finds joyful.

As you may have gathered, I'm an extrovert, and understand full well that some people are more outgoing than others. I am certainly not saying that an introvert, or someone who is innately shy, is destined to be less happy than an extrovert. I know introverted people who brilliantly manage their participation within multiple communities, and are happier for it—just as I know flamboyantly extroverted people who haven't mastered the trick of making themselves welcome within communities, and thus don't achieve the happiness they'd like.

On many levels, my friend Steve Case is an introvert. The business press sometimes used to describe Steve as "aloof," and more charitably, "shy." Shy or not, Steve is one of the most successful entrepreneurs of the past half-century. It was Steve's vision and drive that helped AOL become a mass-market phenomenon. There are many reasons AOL succeeded, but a critical ingredient was Steve's insight, gleaned before I ever showed up, that there is a human need to participate in a broader community. What always differentiated AOL from so-called Internet Service Providers were the multiple online communities we hosted.

The press might call Steve aloof, but over the sixteen years I've known him, I'd call him happy. As the Chairman and CEO of AOL, Steve had a deep and real connection with that community—through emails sent to and received from strangers, the welcome letter that he sent new members, and other elements of community connection.

I recently asked Steve to list the various communities in which he's involved, and from what he provided me, you can get a good sense of why he's so happy. Steve's concentric circles start with his parents and his siblings, and the family he's created as an adult. It includes his present-day co-workers and the team at Revolution, the post-AOL business he created in order to have a transformative impact on health, financial services, and leisure-time activities. It includes his co-workers and the broader set of contacts he and his wife Jean have developed at the Case Foundation. He is involved in various alumni groups, including Williams College and Punahou, the high school he attended when growing up in Hawaii. (Steve and his fellow Punahou alumni last year celebrated when one of their own was elected the 44th President of the United States.) And then there are the alumni of AOL, a company whose former employees, perhaps owing to the nature of the business we developed, tend to stay in close contact, at least online. (Is it ironic, or simply a logical extension of what we started, that so many of us stay in touch through Facebook?) There are Steve's Facebook friends, and the people in his Twitter community. And because Steve is active in his native state, he lists the Hawaiian business community as one of his most important communities of interest. Finally, there is the church he and Jean belong to, and the network of parents and friends developed around his own children's school in Washington, D.C.

The list of communities in which Steve participates reveals a great deal about him. Most importantly, it gives insight into why Steve says he is happy "most of the time." He is very close to his family, the innermost circle for many happy people. At each stage of his life, the friends he's developed, he's kept. For someone journalists call "aloof"—for someone I just called an introvert—he seems pretty tightly connected to the people with whom he's gone through life's passages: high school, college, business success, as well as challenges.

An introvert may have a quiet but cherished presence within his company, church, or social group. An extrovert may be domineering and turn people off. The real test is developing the tools to authentically participate within the various communities that comprise your life, and it's my contention that the happiest people are those who find a comfortable role. You don't have to be the leader, or have the loudest voice. You just have to enjoy the benefits of participating with other people in shared pursuits.

There is a reason why at its peak, AOL Instant Messenger had more than 100 million users on what was the first online social network, and why Facebook now has 300 million members. In both cases, people can participate at whatever level makes them comfortable. Instant messaging and Facebook aren't for everyone. But participating in some form of community activity is a necessity. The happiest and most successful people I know are those who are comfortable managing their relationships within formal and informal social networks. Those who seek out networks to participate in are more successful than those who try to reduce their participation.

In my early years at AOL, we had an employee who'd been a bartender, and had natural skills at making people feel comfortable with one another. We really worked to develop this young man, and eventually he was asked to start our sports channel. He was a really terrific guy, and pretty soon he started a softball league on the campus. Within weeks, AOL departments were playing against each other. He didn't live all that far from AOL, and one day he asked permission to have his church softball team play some of the AOL teams. A short time later, the AOL teams were playing all sorts of teams from across greater Loudon County. We ended up recruiting literally dozens of these softball players into the company. We imported their communities, and in so doing we imported their happiness. I remember that it struck all of us how well this young man was able to bring communities together.

He seemed really happy, and he became a highly successful employee, retiring from AOL at a young age as a multimillionaire.

This doesn't mean that just because you are social you're going to be a millionaire, necessarily. It does reinforce what research shows: that positive relations with family, friends, and business acquaintances are fundamental building blocks of happiness. And guess what? The same is true for success.

———

Robert Redford embodies all the tenets of this book. I met him three years ago in what was going to be a half-hour meeting, which turned into a long conversation, and since then we've met on several occasions.

Bob Redford is one of the biggest movie stars of all time. He is a creative artist, an actor, and Oscar-winning director. He made a lot of money as a movie star, but he felt like he was isolated in the 30-mile zone around Hollywood—the "TMZ"—and he wasn't happy.

He felt that he was happiest when working with other artists and young filmmakers, and yet there was no way within the Hollywood system to nurture the kind of community he had in mind. Grateful for what life had given him, he created Sundance with a charter to bring the expertise of directors, actors, and producers together in an independent, thriving filmmaker-artist community for mentoring and the growth of creativity. Sundance is Robert Redford's good third place between work and home.

When Redford's in Sundance, he's in the mountains, he's horseback riding and skiing, and he's working within an artistic community he created. He's giving back, and he's found his higher calling. In my first conversation with him, he told me, "I can make movies, either as a director or an actor, but my legacy will be that I've touched thousands of young artists and filmmakers. I will have brought thousands of films to a wider community and done it in a way that has turned into a pretty good business."

When I think of what makes Robert Redford such a happy and successful person, what first comes to mind is the way he both builds and participates in various communities. At seventy-six, he is still one of Hollywood's great luminaries. But he's correct about what his legacy will be: the most notable thing about a career in which he has worked with virtually every major star and director is that he literally built from scratch a *community* in Utah called Sundance. Let's think for a minute about what Sundance is.

"Sundance" is an institute dedicated to nurturing independent filmmaking—filmmaking taking place outside of the large studios.

"Sundance" is an annual film festival, in which the best independent films are showcased. I have been honored to have two films debut at the Sundance Film Festival, and it is because of *Nanking* that I first got to meet Bob and find out what a remarkably happy and interesting man he is.

"Sundance" is a cable television network notable for quality programming that often cannot be found anywhere else. It is an archetypal "double bottom line" business, in that it gets quality films that might otherwise never see the light of day aired on television, and was recently acquired by Cablevision for a nine-figure sum. (That meets anyone's definition of "a pretty good business.")

"Sundance" is a lifestyle brand as a successful catalogue retailer, offering Western clothes and furnishings to customers all around the world.

"Sundance" is big business and it is a brand—Robert Redford's brand.

But Sundance is an actual town, with a ski area and resort accommodations. It is the hub of a community—physical and virtual—that Redford created in the late 1960s with the earnings from his star turns in everything from *Barefoot in the Park* to *Butch Cassidy and the Sundance Kid*.

In January, the Sundance Film Festival brings to nearby Park City a gathering of independent film's extended family. Bob Redford figuratively is the paterfamilias of a large family, and he thrives on bringing this community together physically every year—and conceptually, on an ongoing basis.

He is a forthright liberal and environmental activist, and circulates within Democratic circles. No matter what your politics are, however, it's hard not to admire a happy man motivated by a higher calling, giving back to the film industry that nurtured his success—and subsequently able to sell a cable channel which wasn't created for commercial reasons for a very large amount of money. It is also inescapable that having built the "Sundance" brand as a community, Bob Redford is even more successful as a businessman than he would have been had he merely been a superstar in Hollywood.

If you really want to understand why, in his seventh decade, Bob Redford is one of the genuinely most successful entrepreneurs in the history of film entertainment, you have to understand that Bob envisioned Sundance as a community, outlined goals he had for it, and then fulfilled those goals. He skillfully manages his participation, and that of the multifaceted conglomerate he founded, within the larger Hollywood community. He participates within the environmental and political community. He's a genuinely happy man.

To me, Bob is a hero and a role model. Just getting to know him has made me happy.

———————

A few years ago, someone at AOL had the great idea of trying to determine who had the most members in his AIM Buddy List. A fun tool called AIM Fight was born, based on an algorithm that measures not just how many people you have you on your Buddy List, but also how many people have the people on your Buddy List on *their* Buddy List. The algorithm factors in three degrees of separation; that is, they take your AIM Buddy List community out three degrees. You put in your screen name, and an opponent puts in hers, and with the click of a mouse, you can find out whose extended community is larger.

I like AIM Fight because it captures an important element of what AIM has always been about: it's not merely a tool for communicating with someone in real time; it was the original online social network in which people can connect to one another. Okay, I'll admit that I also like AIM Fight because I usually win!

You see, I was one of the first people to ever send an instant message over AIM. *Newsweek* recently published a list of the first messages sent over various media from the telegraph ("What hath God wrought?") to Twitter ("Just setting up my twttr"). The first AIM message listed was from me to Lynn: "Don't be scared . . . it is me. Love you and miss you."

The record shows that Lynn's response was, "Wow . . . this is so cool!"

Ever since that moment, I've been an active user of AIM, and have built a giant list of Buddies. A great many people have me on their Buddy List. The people who put me on their Buddy List tend to have many other people put them on their Buddy List. It's a pretty good indicator of how broad my community is.

On Facebook, I long ago reached the limits of how many "friends" you could have. I tell you this not to boast, but to indicate something you've no doubt figured out by now: I really like participating in communities. I like being a participant in social networks. I believe it makes me a happy person. I know that it makes me more successful than I would otherwise be. I could tell a dozen stories about someone with whom I've kept in touch over the years being in the precisely perfect place to greenlight a deal, or add the missing piece to a business puzzle. There isn't a doubt in my mind that by having actively built broad and overlapping communities in my business and personal life, my prospects as a businessman are brighter.

I've never met a happy hermit. To me, the movie *Castaway*, in which Tom Hanks is a plane crash survivor alone on a South Pacific island, was a complete horror film. My idea of torture is solitary confinement. In terms of happiness and success, I don't know any recluses who've built big businesses or managed successful careers. Howard Hughes was the world's richest man at the same time he was the world's most famous recluse, but in fairness, he inherited the basis of his wealth; I doubt that an entrepreneur today could become as rich as Howard Hughes was while remaining as isolated as he was.

From the earliest days of my earliest professional career, I was an active participant in the community that created the personal computer. It was enjoyable to me, and being part of a community helped me build LIST, then Redgate, and ultimately AOL.

At AOL, I would check out various message boards, forums, and communities. I paid attention to what was going on within the service, not just because it was my job, but because I was a member of the AOL community, too.

As the owner of the Caps, I am not isolated from our fans. I am a fan! I want to participate in discussing the team's prospects with my fellow fans—who happen to also be our customers. I answer as many emails as I can personally. When too many emails come in on the same topic—a trade, a loss, something we screwed up—I tend to answer everyone simultaneously via a blog post. I'll drive readers to the blog by tweeting about it on Twitter. I read the comments that people post on my blog, and I read what's posted on message boards and in forums. When I walk into the Verizon Center, yes, I'm the owner of the team. But I never forget that before I owned the team, I was a member of the Capitals community. In that regard, nothing has changed. The 18,000 people all dressed in red shouting their lungs out in favor of the Caps . . . they're not just customers, they're my community.

I believe this is the way you, too, should think, as you pursue your journey to happiness.

Your co-workers aren't just the people you work with; you and they are fellow members of the community hosted and harnessed by your employer. You participate with them in a broader network comprising shared business interests. To this end, think about the role you play not simply according to the hierarchy of your position relative to others. Think about your participation in your company as a member of a community, and your interactions will qualitatively improve. Just as important, the management of your company is also part of the community, and just as you have community obligations to them—to work hard and behave honorably—they have obligations to you: to treat you equitably and communicate honestly. A business is a community. You really are all in this together.

When you go to your church, synagogue, mosque, or temple, you're not simply entering a house of worship; you are entering a community of co-religionists. For literally billions of people, the religious community in which they participate is among the most important sources of sustenance in their lives. It is fashionable to be negative about aspects of the world's great religions, and certainly there are negative elements to people overly identifying with their religion in a way that creates conflict or tension with people who don't share their faith. To be a Catholic, a Muslim, Greek Orthodox, or Shinto, is to be part of a community, and the community aspect is in some ways as vital as the actual tenets of the faith. Some religions—I'm thinking in particular of the Church of Latter-Day Saints—are built around community prosperity and shared interests.

When you play golf, or go the gym, you're often not just exercising. You are joining a community. People exercise at "health clubs." People play golf at "country clubs." Implicit in the notion of a club is community. Obviously, many sports are built around being on a "team"—an organizational unit that comprises a community. But whether you play softball with co-workers or bike with your family, there are often social benefits, not just physical benefits, to your participating in sports.

Your children's school is the community center for their lives—and yours, so long as they're students there. Many parents find this still to be true, long after their children have gone to college.

It has to be said that not all communities are positive. Sometimes going out with old drinking buddies connects you not to happiness but to dysfunction. Street gangs are a community, and a must to avoid.

But you get the point. The people who recognize the various social networks that we all participate in as separate but often overlapping communities are, I believe, well on the path to happiness. The more such communities you participate in, the happier you likely will be. I have no doubt that this happiness will make you more successful in your work and business.

A Listing of Communities of Interest:

1. **Family:** the inner-most circle of people with whom you share common history.
2. **Alumni:** people you went to school with, as well as those with whom you "graduated" from various stages of life: teams, jobs, military service, political campaigns, and charitable causes.
3. **Children:** life revolves around children, their schools and their network of teachers, coaches, friends, and friends' parents.
4. **Places of Worship and Other Community Hubs:** church, synagogue, mosque, or temple; a local coffee shop; each of the central gathering places within our physical community.
5. **Work and Workplace:** so much time is spent at work, and our common interests with our co-workers are so important, work is a vital community in its own right.
6. **Teams:** whether a fanatical follower of your city's baseball team, or the local high school soccer team, each us is likely linked with a broader sports affiliation.
7. **Politics:** Democrat, Republican, or Independent, those who support similar causes comprise a vital community of interest.

A Listing of Communities of Interest (cont.):

8. **Cultural Affiliations and Hobbies:** from James Bond to Harry Potter, our local symphony to the Rolling Stones, whether knitters, photographers, fishermen, or poker players, we are linked to others by common tastes and entertainment enthusiasms.

9. **Charity:** whether mentoring kids, helping out at an animal sanctuary, preparing tax forms for those who need help, or feeding the homeless with a local ministry, we find community in giving back to society.

10. **Online:** from AIM to Facebook, MySpace to Twitter, eBay to our favorite forum or chat room, our present-day gathering spaces are often online.

Chapter Thirteen

3. Finding Outlets for Self-Expression

Writing a book about how to become happy and successful in business is making me happy, and if enough people join you in reading this, it will make me more successful. *The Business of Happiness* is an outlet for my personal expression—and managing such outlets plays a role in my prospects for happiness.

Having outlets for personal expression is one of the things that happy people have in common. Not everyone can write a book, just as not everyone can paint portraits or play guitar. But everyone can find a medium for expressing himself, especially today when there are so many outlets: blogging tools, software for publishing online photo albums for friends or strangers to see. More than fifteen hours of video are uploaded to YouTube *every minute*. There are more than 200 million blogs. The desire for personal expression is real—and the means of fulfilling those desires are many, close at hand, and frequently cost nothing.

I have many avenues for personal expression. I give speeches, mostly to business audiences. I am a blogger, updating *Ted's Take* on a daily basis. I actively manage my life on Facebook and view it as a daily requirement to report in to my friends. Rarely do I send fewer than 200 emails in a day. I produce movies and put my heart and soul into them. The impetus behind writing *The Business of Happiness* was a combination of wanting to give something back, to share with people some of my observations about happiness, and also very much to express myself.

Perhaps you're not inclined to blog. Participating in Facebook or other social networks may not be right for you. It's possible you don't have the kind of hobby or outside interest that lends itself to public expression. I don't think that matters; literally everyone in a free society has the ability to express himself—if not through what we think of as "speech," or through the creative arts, then through interactions with customers, co-workers, and clients.

Personal expression can be at the center of what you do at work, whether you're the bus conductor who calls out the stops in a lively manner, the greeter at WalMart who welcomes people into the store, or the receptionist in the office who is literally the company's first line of contact with customers. You might not be able to sing, but you might really be able to sell. You might not be able to paint, but you might make the best and most creative Powerpoint presentations.

All people have some manner of communicating in a way that gives expression to who they really are, and being able to do so helps drive the potential for happiness. Though only one person wins *American Idol*, thousands of people show up for the tryouts to these shows, because they want to be able to express themselves in front of an audience. Just to have done so makes them happy.

Let's look at some of the tools available for self-expression.

YouTube is now the 4th largest website in the world, measured by its audience. More than 300 million unique visitors go to YouTube every month. YouTube didn't even exist in 2003, but since its launch, it has been on fire. Hundreds of thousands of people, all across the world, are making and uploading their own videos, responding to YouTube's invitation to "broadcast yourself."

Close to 200 million people around the world have started a blog. That's the equivalent of the entire population of Brazil. According to a 2007 report by eMarketer, more than 22 million Americans had a blog that year, and while I don't have current data, we know the number is higher today, because in 2008 blogging by individuals and companies grew by 68 percent. Technorati, the search engine for blogs, tracks close to one million new blog posts every twenty-four hours.

In 2009, more than 600,000 people—the equivalent of the city of Boston or San Francisco—joined Facebook *everyday.* The implications of this number speak to our need to participate within social networks, but moreover, show how important it is to people to have an easily updatable avenue to express themselves.

In 2007, there were 2 billion photos posted on Flickr, the free photo gallery. By November 2008, the figure was 3 billion. By November 2009, it is estimated that figure will be 4 billion.

The widespread use of YouTube, Facebook, and Flickr illustrates our innate desire for personal expression. In some cases, it's a need for people to express themselves within a community they define, like password protected photo galleries. In more cases, people just want to showcase their creativity and point of view for all the world to see, like on blogs.

It has been said that the average number of visitors that a typical blog will get in a given day is one—the author, checking on what she just wrote. I don't really believe that the size of the audience matters to that blogger; she had something she wanted to say, and she said it. It made her happy to do so.

I post on *Ted's Take* daily. Some days I'll have five posts, some days only one, but I try to post something every day. It makes me happy to comment on movies I've seen, link to items I've seen in the news, discuss a game that the Caps won or lost the night before. I like to give call-outs to people who've done good things, and offer my point of view on people who've done things I don't really think have benefited society. What I post on my blog isn't profound, but it expresses my perspective, and makes me happy.

It's easy to blog. Put the query "blogging services" into Google and you'll be amazed at how quickly you've found a free service that offers you the tools you need to get started.

It's easy to upload photos to a public gallery, and Lord knows, it's easy to upload videos to YouTube, given the number that have been uploaded by 9-year-old children.

We've established that people are taking advantage of the available tools to express themselves online. The broader question is why do people need to express themselves, and how does expressing one's personality lead to happiness?

———

I believe happy people are multifaceted and have an innate desire to have the different dimensions of their life receive recognition. The

Jesuits at Georgetown taught me that everyone's life needs balance, and I learned as a young man that over-indexing in one facet of my life—business success—prevented me from being happy.

Perhaps the most important insight I had when sitting down and writing my list of 101 things I wanted to do in life was to ensure that the list was varied. It wasn't all about business or accumulating things or achieving success within the narrow boundaries of commerce. My goals for life included being able to express myself. After all, you can't win an Oscar if you don't make a movie.

If you over-index on any one thing, you limit your potential for happiness. As I explained earlier, exercising only one arm might make that one arm strong, but it throws you off balance. Sometimes we hear that specialization is the route to success, and it may be in certain fields, but it's probably not the ticket to happiness and fulfillment as a three-dimensional human being.

Even though I was the Vice Chairman of AOL and ran our Audience business—the growth engine for the company's transformation—when I read Iris Chang's book, it didn't take me long to want to turn it into a movie. Producing a film while being a senior executive of a major online service, as well as the owner of sports teams, was an enormous amount of work. I enjoyed every minute of making the film, from the casting of the actors to the negotiation with Chinese television. Only later did I realize that fulfilling my need to express myself had been a strain. It made me happy. And it led directly to my creating SnagFilms in 2008. I had a need to express myself, and a few steps down the road, I'd created a really fast-growing business.

I got the idea for *Nanking* while on vacation, reading an obituary in a newspaper. Maybe it was the fact that I was on vacation and not simply exercising my work muscle that opened me to the prospect of making a movie.

I remember meeting a gentleman named Nolan Bushnell, whose name may ring a bell because he was the founder of the early computer game company called Atari. Nolan was an engineer and scientist, and history will show that he was a critical player in creating the videogame industry. That's not the business he ever intended to get into. He created an industry that today is literally bigger than the motion picture industry, because he went on vacation and started expressing himself while playing on the beach.

It was the early 1970s, and Nolan had been working really hard as an engineer. So he forced himself to take a vacation. As he was sitting there, trying to decompress, he stared at the water and idly began playing with the sand. He started pushing the sand around and drew a box, and then put a line through it at the middle, dividing it in two. He started moving his finger from one side of the line to the other, sort of like he was playing two-dimensional tennis, or ping-pong. He realized it was kind of fun and relaxing to move the ping-pong ball from one side of the box to the other. When he got back to the office, he talked to a colleague named Allan Alcorn about creating a computer version of it, and pretty soon Atari had a huge commercial hit. The game was called Pong, and it was the first video arcade game to really catch on.

Today the video gaming industry is bigger than Hollywood. A key element to its creation was Nolan Bushnell's decision to get out of the office and go to the beach. When he let his imagination go, he doodled in the sand. When he expressed himself in an entirely unfamiliar way, he turned his knowledge of science into a leisure activity that is now a giant business.

Nolan Bushnell expressed himself, outside of work, playing in the sand. There are millions of gamers all around the world who are glad that he did. There are thousands of people who have jobs in the United States and Japan because of it. Going to the beach helped make Nolan happy. It also created an entire industry.

―――――――

Self-expressing activities such as blogging are a common trait of happy people, because happy people have multiple dimensions to their lives, and need to express themselves on topics that perhaps don't relate to their everyday business. Wikipedia—the world's most vital "group blog"—is constructed upon the expertise of unpaid amateurs—not professional encyclopedia writers—who have learned enough about a particular topic to be able to write about it and who really have a need to participate. The mechanic at the Exxon station who is also an expert on trench warfare in World War I may not be able to talk about it with customers who come in with a busted radiator, and probably by now his wife and kids are bored with the topic. It would certainly make him happy to be able to share his expertise with someone, and now he has an opportunity to do so. He reads something on the Wikipedia about the Battle of Ypres and he knows, for a fact, that it's mistaken. So he becomes a Wiki participant and corrects the mistake. But if he makes a typo in the number of casualties he types in, another World War I hobbyist can correct him. Or the original author of the disputed point on the Battle of Ypres can start a discussion challenging the mechanic on his correction. It makes them all happy, because now they can apply what they knows from all the hours spent developing their expertise and participate in a community of enthusiasts while doing it. Tools like Wikipedia offer users an opportunity to learn about something quickly, but importantly, they offer contributors the opportunity to share their expertise with others. It is an avenue of expression.

Morley Safer is known by millions of Americans for his droll pieces on *60 Minutes.* He is known to just a few thousand people for the watercolors that he paints while on the road, week after week, which he occasionally exhibits in galleries. I don't really know Morley Safer, though we met when we both received Honorary Degrees from Emerson University in Boston, but I'm betting that he gets as much, if not more, happiness from having his paintings seen by dozens than his reportage seen by millions.

Creating and producing documentary films has made me happier than virtually any other endeavor I've pursued as an adult. *Nanking* was a topic that fascinated me, and I felt compelled to transform Iris Chang's research and story into a movie that would reach a broader audience than her book. *Kicking It,* the second film I produced, was directed by Susan Koch and Jeff Werner, who had already filmed the participants in the Homeless World Cup by the time they brought the project to me. Nonetheless, getting this incredible story to the screen was a creative outlet for me that brought me great happiness.

Neither of the two award-winning movies I've produced had anything to do with a topic at the core of the businesses I've been in. Producing films was flexing a different muscle. Flexing different muscles from the ones you use at work forty or more hours a week is as important to do in your creative life as it is to do in the gym.

———

Individuals in the workplace express themselves through social interactions with co-workers and customers. The clothes you wear to the office, and how you decorate it—whether you're in the executive suite or a cubicle—can be an element of self-expression. That guy you know at work with the really loud tie? Wearing it makes him happy. You may get satisfaction from writing a well-crafted email or making a PowerPoint presentation to an audience, or just delivering your sales pitch to one customer at a time. There are ample opportunities for virtually everyone to express himself in the context of work, either through contact with others, or through what you actually produce.

Expressing yourself outside of the context of work can lead to satisfaction equal to that which work provides—and in some cases, can provide new and more satisfying business outlets.

The literary world has long benefited from talented people whose writing was not their vocation, but something they wished to do while holding down their "real job." The typical example for creative artists—writers, actors, painters, dancers—is to support their dreams via some service job: waiting tables, working in retail. But there are also many examples of writers and artists with real business careers. Wallace Stevens was an executive at the Hartford Accident and Indemnity Company. He was also a genius whose modernist poetry led to him being awarded the Pulitzer Prize in 1955. Louis Auchincloss was for years a partner in a white-shoe New York law firm—while producing approximately one highly regarded novel, book of short stories, or collection of essays each year since 1947. Anthony Trollope was one of the most successful novelists of the Victorian era, and he worked as a barrister; it's said that he would finish a novel while riding public transportation to work in the morning, and start a new one while going home at night. John Grisham, Scott Turow, and David Baldacci all worked as lawyers before being able to turn full time to writing best-selling novels.

There may be something unique to the drive lawyers have in expressing themselves outside of their profession. Lawyers have to be able to write and express themselves clearly. They are analytical and thorough. I am an investor in SBNation, a really successful network of sports blogs covering every professional sports team in America. My friend and colleague from AOL, Jim Bankoff, who runs it, has told me that lawyers comprise the majority of the bloggers who write for him.

This makes perfect sense. Bloggers, like lawyers, need to know how to frame an argument. They passionately marshal their facts. It's possible that always advocating on behalf of others while being a buttoned-down lawyer is like having a straightjacket on, and so lawyers yearn for an outlet to express their true selves.

The Scott Turows, John Grishams, and David Baldaccis learned to express themselves through writing novels while working as lawyers, and it led to their becoming professional writers. The economics of blogging may someday lead to more lawyers leaving their profession to write about the sports team they love, or whatever topic they wish to express an opinion on.

However, one of my favorite examples of someone whose desire to express himself led to creating a successful business wasn't a lawyer. Arnold Kim, medical doctor by day, was fiercely devoted to Apple computer products and published a blog on them in his spare time. His blog, MacRumors.com, built such a large following, Arnold was able to quit his medical practice and turned his avocation into his job. His pursuit of self-expression has enabled him to be happy and successful.

Not everyone can turn their avocation into their vocation. Not everyone who plays in the sand will use the experience to create an entire industry. More lawyers will write briefs than novels. Some people are more private than others, and don't want to post anything about themselves online.

But everyone can express himself in some way. For millions of people, the ability to have a private conversation with a single listener provides them with the expressive outlet they need. They don't sit at a computer to do this. Instead they get down on their knees and put their hands together. Their outlet for creative expression is called prayer.

A Listing of Ways to Express Yourself:

1. Start a blog. Search for the word "blog" and many free services pop up.
2. Keep a journal for your more private thoughts. It doesn't have to be literature—any meaningful thoughts you have or events that happen are worth writing down. (This would be a great place to keep your life list!)
3. Pick up an art set or camera. Your local crafts store or art supply business can get you started in any type of art. Start dabbling in drawing, watercolor, oil, clay, ink, photography...the possibilities are limitless. There are dozens of websites such as Flickr or Etsy on which you can post your photos or sell your art.
4. Write a letter to the editor of your newspaper if you have an opinion about an article you read or an event happening in your community.

A Listing of Ways to Express Yourself (cont.):

5. Decorate. Painting a room in your house, buying new throw pillows, or putting an interesting object or vase of flowers on display is a form of self-expression.

6. Take music lessons. Nearly everyone wishes they had learned or kept up with a musical instrument or voice talent. Find someone online—try craigslist.com—to work on your musical abilities.

7. Meet with your elected representatives when they come to town and share your point of view.

8. Develop the culinary arts. Trying new recipes from cookbooks or online sites like epicurious.com will add to your skills while providing food to share among your multiple communities.

Chapter Fourteen

4. Gratitude

I once made the mistake of trying to drive from my office at AOL to a Washington Capitals game via the George Washington Parkway just as the evening rush hour was getting under way. Even on its worst day, the George Washington Parkway is among the most beautiful urban commuter highways in America, running through a national park parallel to the Potomac River directly across from Georgetown. And maybe this *was* its worst day, because traffic simply would not move. In both directions, cars were parked bumper-to-bumper.

As we eased slowly down the ramp onto the Parkway, in front of me, remarkably, was the most beautiful cascading sunset I'd seen in years and years. Orange and pink and red, the sky was completely lit up. I called Lynn at home and said, "I'm on the way to the game. By chance, are you near a window?"

Lynn said she was.

"You should go look at the sunset. It's spectacular. It reminds me of the time we were in Hawaii together."

Lynn knew exactly what I was talking about: a walk on the beach one evening as the sun melted into the Pacific in a really dramatic fashion. We'd been really happy together on what I recalled was a pretty glorious day, and the capper was a sunset that lingered in memory, an experience that created happiness far deeper than any new possession or simple accomplishment might have done.

Just now the traffic moved a little bit, and I looked at the guy in the car next to me, and he was screaming at someone on the phone while simultaneously blaring his horn. What he thought he was accomplishing by blaring his horn, I couldn't really tell; traffic was backed up for the next quarter mile at least.

But it was weird. We were in the same physical space, but we may as well have been in different solar systems. I could see the sun as it set, and apparently he couldn't.

I was so grateful to see this beautiful sky, and to be on the phone with my wife with both of us transported back to this wonderful moment in our lives. And one car away from me is a guy who's screaming on the phone and beeping his horn.

I felt really bad for him. My empathy kicked in, and I felt kind of sad that he couldn't have a moment of gratitude for one of those rare sunsets that really ought to stop everyone in his tracks and force us all to contemplate how incredible it is simply to be alive.

The ability to stop, take account of the moment, and feel grateful for what life offers is a common tenet among the happy people I know.

—————

One of my favorite scenes in *The Life of Brian*, the great Monty Python film, happens when a prisoner is waiting to be taken out of the dungeon and be crucified. "Oh my God, we're going to be crucified! What could be worse than that?" he cries.

And so another prisoner says, "Well, look on the bright side. You'll be out in the fresh air. You're with your friends. They could kill us in here. So, crucifixion isn't so bad."

When I had my reckoning—when I sat on an airplane that likely wouldn't land—I vowed that if I got to the ground safely, I would live my life to the fullest. I have been grateful for every day I've spent on earth since then.

I have a lot to be grateful for, more than most. The ability to be grateful for what I have is a driver of the empathy I can feel for others. When that fellow leaned on his horn as I was trying to enjoy the moment with my wife, when anyone conscious and alive in that area of Virginia should have been able to see a beautiful sunset, I wasn't mad at him for sort of ruining the moment. I felt terrible for him. He had no sense of gratitude about the wondrous moment. He wasn't in a place where he could see the sunset, even though it was right in front of him.

Empathy is the ability to feel another person's pain as if it were your own. Research shows it's a fundamental element of primate development—that the minds of chimpanzees and humans alike are hardwired to respond when another is facing pain. But as I have analyzed it over many years, I've come to the conclusion that a basic element of the empathy we feel for others is being able to place your current position in its context. It could almost always be worse; you could be executed in the dungeon, not out in the fresh air with your friends. And you could be the one who is homeless and asking for a dollar on the sidewalk.

As this is being written, I have been working with a young man name Kyle Maynard. Kyle is a congenital amputee, born without arms past the elbow or legs past the knee. Kyle is a wonderful, inspirational human being who wrote a memoir called *No Excuses,* the basis for a documentary film we're working on that should be released in 2010. Kyle recently went to Walter Reed Hospital in D.C. where wounded servicemen and women from the wars in Iraq and Afghanistan are recuperating after having lost a limb or an eye.

All of these wounded warriors are unimaginably brave and admirable people, but it's only human that once or twice a day they might feel sorry for themselves and ask, "Why me?"

And then Kyle shows up. He has lived his whole life without arms and legs, and has made himself into a world-class wrestler, owns his own gym, and can bench press 400 pounds. He is the most charismatic, upbeat person. He talks about everything he can do with the tools he has, wasting no time on pity for himself.

The reaction is almost universally one where the wounded soldiers begin to think, "Compared to him, I'm fortunate." They see that Kyle can do virtually anything, and really, maybe they can too. That moment of empathy changes their lives. It gives them permission to be grateful for what they have, not be bitter over what they don't have. That sense of gratitude is a step along the path to their recovering the happiness that was snatched from them by a bullet or a bomb.

———

To me, empathy, gratitude, giving back to society, and having a higher calling are all part of a continuum. Because empathy underlies each of three tenets of happy people that I focus on—gratitude, giving back, and having a higher calling—I don't call it out as a single specific tenet. It is, however, the super ingredient in driving happiness.

Before the economic crisis hit in 2008, America had several years in which, by historical standards, it was easier for low-income families to buy a home. We know now the real price that people who took out subprime loans are having to pay, and the price our economy is paying for lenders forgetting about basic underwriting standards. However, in the middle part of this decade, when the economy seemed really strong and unemployment was low, it seemed like homeownership was in the grasp of just about anyone who wanted it. Even at that moment, voluntary participation in a program like Habitat for Humanity—in which ordinary people devote a day to building a home for someone less fortunate—was at an all-time high.

Why would someone spend a day building a home for someone else? I believe the chain of motivation starts with empathy for others. They're grateful for what they have—presumably, a home of their own, or at least shelter. This makes them want to give something back to those with less. Doing this, of course, makes the volunteers happy.

A hit television show for the past several years is ABC's *Extreme Makeover: Home Edition*, in which good people who have faced some kind of a calamity have their homes renovated by friends and neighbors. You can see the joy on the faces, and I'm not talking just about the people who receive a new home. I'm talking about the neighbors who saw and hammer all night to build it. Sometimes it's hard to tell who's happiest—the person on the giving end, or the receiving end. Empathy was the driver of their effort, but a critical integer in the equation was the sense of gratitude the neighbors had that their own home was intact.

One of the most moving stories I've seen recently concerns the New York City firefighters and policemen who every September 11th, goes somewhere in America that has faced a disaster—a hurricane, fire, or flood—from which a local community needs help to recover. They do this because they remember how, after the terrorists destroyed the World Trade Center, people came from all around America to help excavate the remains of the fallen heroes buried under the collapsed buildings. You can see the happiness in the faces of these tough New Yorkers as they rebuild a Boy Scout camp in Iowa destroyed by a tornado, or [second example].

Why do they take their vacation days and fly to Iowa on their own dime to do this? Because they are filled with gratitude for how people helped them out when *they* were in need. They are grateful for what they have now that others don't. They're able to show this. And it makes them really happy.

———

A few years ago, a New York City construction worker named Wesley Autrey became a hero to the world when he jumped down in the subway tracks, pressed his body on top of a young man with epilepsy who had fallen while having a seizure, and protected him from sure death as the train rolled into the station.

I was completely moved by his story, and especially the seemingly nonchalant way in which the New York City Subway Hero, as he was instantly known, asked other people on the platform to look after his young daughters, standing there beside him, while he jumped down to the tracks to save someone's life.

I noticed in a photograph that he was wearing a Washington Capitals hat, and after asking around, I found out his brother was an usher in the Verizon Center. Through his brother, I was able to meet Wesley, and I found him to be remarkable—and remarkably happy.

When I asked him how and why he could have so calmly have put his life on the line to save the life of a stranger, he told me that as soon as he saw the lights of that train coming into the station, he knew someone would have to try saving the life of the young man who was having the epileptic seizure down on the tracks. As soon as he knew someone would do it, he realized he should. He thought that if it were him down on those tracks, someone certainly would try to save him.

He was grateful in his realization that someone would have helped him in that situation.

So without hesitation, he decided he should be that "someone" for the Columbia University student lying in the tracks.

When I heard this, I could only say, "Wow." Here was someone who was so empathetic, he would risk his life out of gratitude that if a similar calamity happened to him, someone else would act.

Like I said, Wesley Autrey is a remarkable man.

Gratitude is a motivator and ingredient in the happiness of some other remarkable people I know.

Ashley Judd is a movie star who can make millions of dollars for a single picture, and yet, as we shall see in the next chapter, she devotes an incredible amount of time, and a significant amount of emotional energy, to her job as Global Ambassador for YouthAIDS. Ashley is actually happiest when she's going deep into cities in India, sleeping in tents with prostitutes, and helping them get tested for AIDS. What is her underlying motivation? Empathy, of course. And she is one of the people I know whose life is most oriented around a higher calling. Yet I also know from conversations with her that she helps others because she feels gratitude for all that she has. Empathy, gratitude, giving back, a higher calling: elements that combine to do good for others, and to make the benefactor at least as happy as the beneficiary.

What is the underlying reason for Bono, a rock star, to devote so much time and energy to the plight of Africa? In my opinion, the question answers itself: it's the fact that he is a rock star. He is grateful for all that he's been given.

A great many public figures—actors, movie stars, athletes—are ridiculed sometimes for the causes they champion. A movie star showing up in New Orleans after Katrina, or traveling to Namibia to adopt an orphan is immediately suspected to be seeking PR points, and maybe sometimes that's true. But the Christian Bible tells us that to those whom much is given, much is required. I believe that the gratitude felt by people at every level of society, from the time we have enough food to eat and shelter over our heads, all the way up to the moment when some us might have a mansion and a fancy car, the gratitude we acknowledge enables us to process what we have compared to others, and through motivating us to action, whether it's making a donation or volunteering to build a house, it helps make us happy.

When I found myself grateful for that beautiful sunset and sharing the moment with Lynn it didn't matter whether or not I was wealthy. What mattered was that I was able to stop and reflect upon what life serves up every day. Stopping for a moment and reflecting upon the simple virtues of being alive on an afternoon when the cosmos kick up a spectacular sunset is a hallmark of being happy.

On those days that you feel low, having gratitude for what you have can bring happiness. It could always be worse. You may have lost your right arm in Iraq, but Kyle Maynard has no arms or legs. At least you have the use of one arm. You could be executed in the dungeon, not crucified in the fresh air with your friends.

And besides this, you should think about what you do have: the love of your family, your health, a comparatively good life. Happy people have connections to communities of people who, on some level, care about them. They have a means to express themselves. They have a higher calling. They have much to be thankful for.

And on days when you feel high, because something great has happened—a business deal came through, you win an Emmy, you capture the Stanley Cup—feeling a sense of gratitude for what life has given you adds an element of humility that grounds you. You are lucky, and your exultations should be limited because others are less fortunate than you. It is an excellent time to remember your obligations to others. If you're a rock star who has just come off the stage after 70,000 people in an arena have cheered your encore, knowing that next week you're going to help people in Africa adds texture, balance, and context to the legitimate pleasure that you feel. Reminding yourself that we're all children of God is a good way to keep your feet on the ground and your head from getting swelled.

Gratitude for what you have is a leavening agent, keeping us from getting too high, or too low. It is a motivator, to help others who are less fortunate. It is a reality check, to keep us from self-pity. It's also, I believe, an indicator of character.

John Thompson, who is now retired but is still legendary as the longtime basketball coach at Georgetown University, told me that when he recruited players, one of the first things he considered about a young prospect was whether he said "please" and "thank you." This wasn't a test of the young man's manners. It was a test of whether he would be a good teammate—and whether he would be coachable. His reasoning was that if the young man could show gratitude for the opportunity to play for Georgetown, it meant that he would work hard, listen to advice, and help his teammates when they were in need. It meant on some fundamental level that he was happy, and since we know that happiness is contagious, you want to build a team with happy, empathic players grateful that they have the God-given talent they were born with.

Alex Ovechkin, who plays for the Washington Capitals, constantly communicates gratitude in his everyday life. Alex is the ultimate team player. He makes the players around him better. He infuses whatever room he walks into with happiness, because he is such a happy person. He was the NHL's Most Valuable Player two years in a row. He has a long-term contract with the Caps that will earn him more than $100 million dollars. He has a lot to be grateful for.

What he communicates in his every interaction is not the arrogance of someone who is young, rich, and incredibly talented; he continually broadcasts how much joy he has in simply being alive. And what he communicates unmistakably every time he steps on the ice is how much gratitude he has just to be able to put on skates and play. Sure, he's driven and tough and a competitor nonpareil. Alex is the player who arrives earlier and practices harder than anyone else. That he also has more talent is not quite irrelevant to him—he knows he's really good—but when he's on the ice, he's going to do everything to the max because he really loves playing hockey. He's the greatest hockey player in the world, but it's still a game to him, and I know from my interactions with Alex that he's grateful he gets to play the game he loves and is really good at.

Some opponents think Alex is too flashy and that maybe he shows off too much when he scores. He gets under the skin of at least one of the game's other superstars. But Alex has connected with the entire hockey community not simply because he's so good, or an engaging young man. He's connected with his teammates, the Caps' fan base, even with many of his competitors on other teams, because of the infectious joy he shows on the ice. In 2008, when Alex accepted his first Hart Trophy as the Most Valuable Player in the NHL, he began his remarks by saying, "What a life!" He is grateful for the chance he has to live it.

Not all hockey players get that same joy out of stepping on the ice. And not all athletes say "please" and "thank you." The gratitude Alex has for being a hockey player makes him better, not the other way around. He is successful because he's happy, not happy because he's successful. Like many happy people, he is able to step outside the moment and be grateful for things as they are.

Have you ever known someone who loves his job so much he says, "All this, and I get paid too"?

That's Alex Ovechkin. Happy guy.

———

There is a flip side to the discussion of gratitude that helps prove my point. I have been placed in turnaround situations at various times, either working in a business, as a Board member of a company or nonprofit, or simply as an interested party trying to help improve a bad situation. Some business executives come in and say, "Everything here is so screwed up. This place is awful. I'm going to lead us to success despite the mess I was left."

There are other people who come in and say, "This organization has some incredible assets. There are really very bright people here.

Look at what we have to build on. This is an unbelievable opportunity for me to build on the success that may be eluding the organization right now. We've been left a pretty tough hand to play, but there's no place else on earth I'd rather be."

Just that difference in body language, in vocabulary, in the point of view expressed is the difference between successful and unsuccessful turnarounds. The turnaround artist who expresses gratitude for the challenge and opportunity is the one who often succeeds.

Jon Miller arrived at AOL in 2002 in the midst of total and complete chaos—he was the third CEO in five months, there were investigations underway by the SEC and the Department of Justice, the relationship between Time Warner and AOL was rocky to say the least, the press environment was toxic, revenues were peaking and about to plummet, and so were subscriber numbers. Jon's attitude as he expressed it to me was, "Thank you for everything you've done at AOL since you got here. Please stay and help me make this work. I am grateful to have you and so many smart people who we can now channel in the right way to restore the company to its rightful place. We've got great assets, and if we can just get harness them, we'll be okay. Let's get to work."

I was happy to take him up on it. Rather than viewing this as a great moment to extricate myself from the mess that AOL had become and to go apply myself to other activities, I stayed and worked long hours. It took a few false starts, and I don't mean to minimize the bumps along the way, the detours we took, the arguments we had, or the mistakes we made. But almost four years to the day after Jon arrived at AOL, our Audience business, which was by then the core business of the company, was growing 49 percent per year. We'd figured out the going-forward strategy, jettisoning the dead weight of the dial-up subscriber business and floating high on the Internet's online advertising boom.

When you look at Tim Armstrong's approach to fixing AOL now, he speaks in a similar way. He believes in the AOL brand. He is grateful for the opportunity to be CEO of a company with the power and the legacy that AOL has. He has a massive audience, and he can build on that. In spite of AOL losing an entire layer of senior leaders who walked away when Time Warner fired Jon Miller, Tim Armstrong still has some really good AOL people in place, and he'll continue to augment them with new recruits.

In between Jon's tenure as AOL's CEO and Tim's came a management team that communicated clearly, "You wouldn't believe how screwed up things are here. No one knows what he's doing. Oh my God, when we got here it was a mess! We're taking on this chore, not because it gives us pleasure, but because it's important for our careers." Figuratively, and literally, this is what people were told.

During Jon Miller's tenure—which was based on gratitude for the assets he had to build on—AOL developed the right long-term strategy and in the essential area of our business, began to grow as fast as we had in the glory days. Having fallen, AOL rose again.

The team Time Warner dispatched to follow Jon was contemptuous of AOL. They were so lacking in gratitude for what they'd been handed, they decided that the AOL name, one of the most powerful brands on the Web, should be minimized every chance they had. They believed that AOL itself—the branded online site that tens of millions of people visited every day to get their email or just to navigate the Web in a way they were familiar with—should be considered just one among many sites hosted on an advertising network. It was no longer referred to as "the AOL network"; they called it Platform A, which sounded like it was the place you'd go to catch the 5:13 train to Scarsdale. They kicked away all the momentum we had built.

They had no gratitude. They weren't happy to be there. Consequently, they were unsuccessful. See what I mean?

A Listing of Things to Be Grateful for Daily:

1. Being alive
2. Your health
3. Your family and friends
4. The talent you have
5. Your relative level of financial security
6. Memories of those who nurtured you

---

Chapter Fifteen

5. Giving Back

I derive more happiness out of giving money away than making it or spending it, and I'm not the only one. Americans have the highest standard of living in the world—and are the most generous people on Earth.

In 2006, Americans gave $300 billion to charity, which was more than the GDP of such developed nations as Denmark, Norway, Greece, or Austria. According to the World Bank, as a percentage of GDP, we give twice as much to charity as the next most charitable country (the U.K.), and 12 times as much as the French. We're not just generous with our dollars—we're generous with our time, volunteering in countless ways.

While it's axiomatic that money can't buy happiness—and I was the living proof of that—there is scientific proof that charitable giving leads to happiness. I've mentioned earlier that a Harvard study of employees at a medical supply company found that the higher the proportion of an employee's annual bonus that he contributed to charity, the happier he was.

This is certainly the case among happy people I know. No matter what their income level, the happiest people I know generously give back to society, through charity, time spent volunteering, or often both.

Cal Ripken, Jr. is in the Major League Baseball Hall of Fame. If there were a Happiness Hall of Fame, Cal would be in it, and not just because he has been blessed with talent and able to apply his phenomenal work ethic to the game he loves. Cal has dedicated his post-Oriole's career to building the Cal Ripken, Sr. Foundation—named, in an act of gratitude, after his father. Since 2003, his foundation has had an impact on more than 650,000 young people by getting them involved in baseball. His work life today revolves around charitable giving, teaching, and building participation in baseball at the grassroots level. To be sure, his company, Ripken Baseball, owns developmental league teams and runs baseball camps, and is very much a business. Yet even if his business is highly profitable, the notable thing about Cal's mission is its orientation to giving something back to his Maryland community, to the sport that made him famous and a multimillionaire, and to those less fortunate than he. Cal's work and his role in philanthropic and community activities blend seamlessly—and contribute greatly to his happiness.

Cal embodies all the tenets of happiness and success reflected in this book. He is a connector, bringing together people from baseball, business, and politics in support of the causes he believes in. He has found avenues for personal expression as a motivational speaker, author, and producer of instructional videos on the Cal Ripken Baseball Way. His higher calling is not dissimilar to Robert Redford's embrace of young filmmakers, in that Cal wants to shape a new generation of baseball players. He's dedicated to using baseball as a platform for peace. Grateful for what baseball has given him, Cal is genuinely giving back.

––––––––––––

Steve Case, in partnership with his wife Jean, created the Case Foundation in 1997. The AOL Foundation was a vehicle for the company to give back to its community and society, but this wasn't enough for Steve and Jean; they developed a philanthropic vehicle and funded it with their own money. In common with other charitable foundations created by Internet entrepreneurs, the Case Foundation has applied its resources, in part, to determining ways that the online medium and technology can improve people's lives.

Among the happiest moments I've ever spent with Steve was when he explained to me how PlayPumps International works. The PlayPump system ingeniously involves the installation of a merry-go-round for kids to play on. As they play, the motion of the merry-go-round is used to pump water for their community. To date, PlayPump International has installed more than 1200 wells in Sub-Saharan Africa in communities where lack of drinking water is a debilitating challenge. I'm pleased to say that Steve got me involved in this program, but my point in telling this to you is this: I've been with Steve at moments of great triumph, and at fun events and happy occasions. But I've never see him more excited than when he talks about PlayPumps. Steve is as committed to having the Case Foundation support PlayPumps International as it commences operations in a new nation in Southern Africa as ever he was about, say, AOL opening up in a new country in Europe. When he told me about PlayPumps, there was a audible enthusiasm in his voice. Being able to give back really makes Steve happy.

It has made my family happy, too. Two years ago, the Christmas present Lynn and I gave Zach and Elle was the donation of a PlayPump to two communities in South Africa. It was one of the greatest Christmases we've ever had.

Wealthy businesspeople, athletes, and stars have the wherewithal to endow foundations with large sums. They have tax incentives for doing so. Giving back to society with the same degree of focus that many wealthy people exhibited while building their career or fortune is not just a manifestation of Type A personalities. This kind of generosity flows from the values that a person has. It also stems from the practical realization that money doesn't buy long-term happiness when it's spent on toys, but it certainly is a tool for creating joy when employed on behalf of others.

As we know from statistics, it's not only rich people who give back to society. It's people in your church who manage the food drive. It's the friendly woman in your office who signs up everyone to sponsor her in the Race for the Cure. It's your neighbor who takes in the refugee family. It's the children down the block who collect toiletries to ship to the servicemen and women overseas.

In my own case, my work with Hoop Dreams, Best Buddies, YouthAIDS, and the D.C. Central Kitchen has enriched my life. There are a number of individuals who, frankly, I've helped get from homelessness on the streets of D.C. to having a job, or at least a chance for one. I've written big checks, and I've gotten friends to contribute their money and time, but whatever I've given these men and women, or the organizations I've supported, has been repaid ten times over. I've gotten by far the better end of the bargain. As I've said earlier, getting to know Michael Henderson or Big Ken Holden has enriched my life immeasurably. It has made me happy.

I met Ashley Judd through our participation in YouthAIDS, an incredible organization that raises money and awareness in the fight against HIV/AIDS. Ashley has been YouthAIDS' Global Ambassador since 2002, and a few years ago, I was honored to be the Chair of the organization's annual gala. Ashley is a remarkable woman, not merely because she is such a beautiful and talented actress, but because of the happiness she derives from taking on challenges a lesser person would run from. Ashley is a happy person because of way that she gives of herself to a cause that needs her. In fact, she is currently a student at the Kennedy School at Harvard University, getting a mid-career Masters Degree, as a way of improving the skill set she brings to her philanthropic activities.

Ashley describes her life as having been changed absolutely by her work for YouthAIDS, "sitting in brothels around the world, visiting with trapped, enslaved, exploited women. My life," she says, was changed by "visiting orphans, sitting in massive slums, at the bedside of the dying in hospices and clinics worldwide."

Ashley Judd perfectly illustrates several of the tenets of happiness discussed in this book. What is most remarkable to me is how she derives so much of her spirit and peace of mind from giving back to society. She has a genuine higher calling and believes that "every moment is one that I can be making a difference and helping to manifest peace."

One of the things I find so extraordinary about Ashley is the breadth and depth of the communities in which she participates, the happiness she derives from them, and frankly, how she has them rank ordered. Among the top ten different communities in which Ashley participates, she lists the film industry as only the 8th most important. Population Services International, the Washington-based nonprofit that created the YouthAIDS initiatives, ranks first. The network of fans and friends that support the University of Kentucky basketball program ranks squarely in the middle, a few notches above Hollywood.

I don't know about you, but when a successful movie star places the motion picture community several steps *below* her international network of friends and acquaintances fighting HIV/AIDS, and just below the network of Kentucky Wildcat supporters, I get a glimpse of a happy woman—and a remarkable human being.

When I see Ashley at YouthAIDS events and she tells me about what she has been up to lately, the recitation is entirely about her work on behalf of others. It's never about the movie she just filmed or some personal milestone. It's always about others.

Some people imagine they'd be happy if only they were as beautiful as Ashley Judd, or lived her glamorous life married to Dario Franchitti, a Formula 1 and Indy car driver, or made millions of dollars as a movie star. The reality is that Ashley's happiness comes from the things she does that literally any of us could do: devoting her excess time and energy to a cause larger than herself.

———

It may be obvious that a common tenet of happy people is being generous and giving back. After all, the happy respondents in The Happiness Questionnaire did not see charitable activities as a driver of happiness, which I interpret as stemming from the way charitable activities and services to others is such an innate component in their

lives. The greater question might be how giving back can make someone more successful. I can offer two real-life examples.

SnagFilms was created as an archetypal "double-bottom line" company. It is my intention to build SnagFilms into a moneymaking venture (it's not quite there yet.) The impetus behind it was also to help fix
the broken distribution system facing documentary films, while showcasing filmanthropy in action.

On the day we announced its launch, we'd lined up many, but not
all, of the most important libraries of documentary films as content
partners. One of the more important companies with a large library of
documentary films chose to pass on the opportunity to work with us.
They didn't see the benefit of having SnagFilms distribute even their
so-called long-tail properties—the films that have long ago exhausted
their ability to draw a mass audience, either through theatrical release,
television showings, or DVD sales, but which a comparatively small
audience would still seek out if able to find them. We met with a number of people in their organization, but for a variety of reasons, it just
didn't happen.

As it turns out, someone very high up in their organization is an
executive I'd never actually done business with—but on two occasions
we've both been honored together for our different charitable activities, and we've grown friendly.

Several months ago, I was raising capital for a particular business,
and our investment bankers in New York told me that this executive
had expressed an interest in working with me. They asked if it was
okay to send him the deal book they'd put together with the financial
information we were going to show potential investors. "He likes the
business, but he also really likes you personally," they told me.

Now I had never asked this executive for anything, nor had he ever asked me for anything. Our only touch point was having met at a pair of charitable events and talking passionately about our interest in different causes.

Based on those contacts, the time arrived when we started to talk about business. Along the way, naturally I told him about SnagFilms, and how we'd struck out with his company. As this is being written, his company is now in serious discussions with SnagFilms about ways we can start working together. In this case, our charitable work created the opportunity for our companies to do business together.

Philanthropy and volunteering can introduce you to new communities of interest. From a purely commercial standpoint, those community contacts can be every bit as valuable as ones derived from business "as usual."

When you are working as a volunteer on behalf of a cause, or attending a fundraising event, the distance between a CEO and anyone else is reduced. Everybody rolls up his sleeves and gets to work.

It is not a prescription for happiness to become active in charities in order to expand your business network. Having said this, it is certainly true that charitable circles can be incorporated into your business network.

———————

Sometimes philanthropic activities can mix with business, which mixes with philanthropy, and it's a win for all concerned.

Many years ago, when LIST was still in business, I got to know Mitch Kapor, the founder of Lotus Development Corporation, which produced one of the first "killer apps" for the IBM PC—the spreadsheet program known as Lotus 1-2-3.

Flash forward twenty or so years to the Spring of 2003. I saw Mitch
at Walt Mossberg and Kara Swisher's inaugural All Things D conference in southern California, and we got to talking. In this and subsequent conversations, Mitch asked me what AOL intended to do with
the Netscape browser, which we'd acquired in the mid-1990s, but
which we no longer spent money to improve.

Mitch made a case that AOL didn't have sufficient resources to
update the Netscape browser, which still had validity as a potential
competitor to Microsoft's I.E., which at that time had a market share
of about 95 percent. Mitch proposed that AOL donate the intellectual
property and source code for the Netscape browser to the Mozilla
Foundation. Mozilla would then publish the software to the Open
Source community, and the entire community could improve the
browser. There was one more request: AOL should contribute $2 mil-
lion to the Mozilla Foundation to get this off the ground.

This instantly made sense to me. Here was one of the great software developers of the PC era who was willing to give of his time and
energy to get this project off the ground. By contributing the source
code, and making a $2 million cash contribution, AOL could give
something back to the technology community. The community
would work on the browser and improve it for the good of consumers.

And thus was born the Firefox browser, which today has more than
20 percent of the browser market. It is an innovative, elegant, terrific
browser, and has had the additional effect of forcing Microsoft into
having to innovate and improve Internet Explorer.

Mitch was willing to give something back to the technology community by shepherding the Mozilla Foundation project to create
Firefox. I was able to pry the source code and the financial contribution from AOL to get this project going. Today, the browser market and

the tools consumers use to work online have been vastly improved. Win-win-win.

———————

AOL's response to the immediate aftermath of Hurricane Katrina is another example of how volunteering and giving back brings happiness and success.

Just before the Labor Day weekend, a short time after Katrina hit, I received an email from an employee who worked in our Management Information Systems department. He was pretty far down the organizational chain, and I'm pretty sure I'd never met him or emailed with him before. He was from Mississippi, and he wrote to say that perhaps his home state didn't have as good a public relations apparatus as New Orleans, because there was just as much physical and emotional damage in Mississippi as there was in Louisiana, but people from his home county weren't getting anywhere near the same level of resources or attention. He had a simple idea about how he could help.

He asked if there was an AOL truck that wasn't being used over the long weekend. My immediate answer was yes, there had to be, and it turned out there was. This was on a Thursday. He said, "I would like to ask every employee on this campus to bring a few bottles of water to work tomorrow." He planned on working with a buddy to load a truck with 10,000 bottles of water, or whatever they had, drive down to Mississippi to distribute it, and make it back in time for work on Tuesday morning.

It was so logical, and he was so organized, that I immediately said, "Go do it." We authorized the truck, as well as his sending out a campus-wide email asking for the bottled water.

He did an incredible job as it became more than a single weekend's project. For the next several weeks, our workforce got really engaged in helping him with whatever he needed: bottled water, canned goods, and clothing.

If you think about it, emailing the Vice Chairman of the company with a plan to do good works was a really great career move on his part. Yet, I'm certain that finding a way of getting on senior management's radar was probably the furthest thing from his mind when he sent me that email. He sent the email to me, because he probably knew I'd respond. All he wanted to do was to help people in need. And because of him, for weeks, wherever you went in AOL, there were collection bins for things he'd take down to Mississippi in an AOL truck each weekend.

Through his volunteerism, he proved he was reliable, had initiative and organizational skills and was passionate about getting things done. What a great employee! He did more good for himself in getting the company's management to pay attention to him than probably anything he ever could have done in his job. His heart was pure; he wasn't trying to advance his career. And yet all the skills he exhibited volunteering were the kinds of skills you would want to promote.

There's been a lot of turnover and turmoil at AOL in recent years. I'd really like to think this young man was still there and by now was practically running the place. His passion for giving back to his community showcased someone who I really hope goes far in life. He'll go far in the afterlife.

A Listing of Ways to Give Back:

1. Become a friend and mentor to a child by joining your local chapter of Big Brothers, Big Sisters.

2. Work with your ministry group or community center to organize movie nights or host food and clothing drives for the homeless.

3. Help fight the battle against cancer by participating in local Race for a Cure events.

4. Volunteer to spend time with the elderly at hospitals and nursing homes.

5. Send a little bit of home to troops overseas by writing letters and sending boxes of goodies.

6. Help provide good books and toys for disadvantaged children by placing donation kiosks in participating businesses in your community.

7. Invest in children by coaching a Little League team or tutoring in after-school programs.

8. Volunteer to feed, walk, and play with animals at the Humane Society or another local shelter.

9. Help at a local soup kitchen or homeless shelter.

10. Bring food to the hungry by becoming a driver with your local division of Meals on Wheels.

Chapter Sixteen

6. A Higher Calling

I have known highly paid CEOs who were really unhappy and underpaid schoolteachers who had the glint of happiness in their eyes. I've known miserable millionaires, but I've never met an unhappy person who truly cares for others, and who views what he or she does as having some kind of a higher calling.

Don't get me wrong. I also know a good number of highly successful and often quite wealthy people who are really happy. Think about some of the people I've described so far: Robert Redford, Ashley Judd, Bono, Cal Ripken, Steve Case, and Alex Ovechkin. I believe each one of them lives his or her life in pursuit of something greater than ego gratification or amassing wealth.

I'm not saying that a bond trader who takes home a seven-figure bonus can only be happy if she also works in a soup kitchen. (Though it would certainly help!) I am talking about finding a higher purpose to how you lead your life, whether in the office, at home, or participating in the larger community.

———————

People who have a higher calling have a purpose to their life. Their higher calling is not necessarily what they do, but it tells you a lot about who they are.

Yes, a doctor's purpose is to save lives and alleviate suffering; his higher calling likely aligns precisely with his job. A priest or a pastor is meant to live a life in literal devotion to a higher calling—Fr. Joe Durkin was a prime example of "walking the talk." Firefighters, teachers, soldiers, many politicians and activists of various stripes—all might be able to define their higher calling as their vocation.

For many of us, however, our higher calling isn't derived from the actual job we do, but the purpose we find in life either separate from, or in addition to, what we do from 9 to 5 every day.

Let's take the example of our (imaginary) bond trader. She is a really happy and successful person. She finds genuine meaning in connecting the international capital markets to fund the growth of a municipality whose bonds she's selling. By being very good at her job, she helps her municipal client save literally millions of dollars, thus reducing the burden on the taxpayers who guarantee the bonds. Even though she finds purpose in her job, and even though it may be an ingredient in her happiness, this isn't where she derives her sense of having a higher calling.

Our bond trader is actively engaged in professional and civic organizations, alumni groups, and has an active presence in her neighborhood, while keeping in close contact through Facebook with friends collected along life's pathways. She doesn't take her high level of compensation for granted; while feeling secure that she has earned her bonus, she's grateful for her advantages, and devotes not only a portion of her earnings, but also her precious free time supporting a home for unwed mothers that was started by her Roman Catholic parish. Given the full day she works, it's difficult for her to practice playing cello, but she still finds an hour on weekends to do so. After all, it has been a goal of hers for years to play Beethoven's "Serenade for String Trio in D Major."

And yet if asked what her higher calling is, she wouldn't say that it's to reduce a city's cost of funds for its school district infrastructure program. It isn't to become a millionaire ten times over.

She would tell you that her higher calling is to raise her children to be kind, happy, and well-adjusted adults.

This is a higher calling anyone could have, no matter how rich or poor, no matter what are the circumstances in their life.

The person I've just described is a composite I made up, but she isn't a fantasy of Superwoman. She is an archetype of a happy person. She is well suited for her career and derives satisfaction from a job whose meaning to her goes beyond the material benefit she receives in the form of status and income. She pursues goals she's set, which includes expressing herself as a musician. She operates within multiple work and social communities. She is grateful for what she has and is empathetic to others. She gives back to her community through her support for a vital local non-profit.

Yet it is the final element that completes her many, balanced dimensions. She has a calling higher than material benefits or ego needs: together with her husband, she's dedicated to rearing their children to be adults with good characters.

I use my invented bond trader to illustrate this point. It isn't merely clergy, doctors, politicians, or people who work in low-paying jobs in socially useful organizations who might be viewed as having a higher calling. Bono has a higher calling and so can a bond trader. In fact, anyone can find a higher calling.

I believe that those who find their higher calling often complete their journey to happiness. I know that I did.

———————

By a variety of indices, the happiest people in America are evangelical Christians. According to a 2006 Pew Research Center survey, 43 percent of evangelical Protestants described themselves as "very happy," compared to 34 percent of all Americans. They have low rates of suicide and divorce. Evangelicals live longer than the population as a whole. To me, this makes complete and logical sense.

I've mentioned evangelicals earlier, but let's look at them more closely in the context of finding one's higher calling.

If you lay out the tenets to happiness as outlined here, evangelical Christians index closely to these traits. To be a "born again" Christian is literally to have had a reckoning following which you pursue God's plan for your happiness.

Evangelicals are active members of multiple communities, beginning with their family, and certainly with their church. Their church becomes a platform for self-expression and volunteerism.

Evangelicals show gratitude for what God has given them, and empathy for others.

Evangelical Christians volunteer their service and donate their money to charities.

Importantly, many evangelicals define their religious faith as a higher calling in and of itself. Many evangelicals define their higher calling as working in service to the Lord. They show gratitude. They express themselves in terms of love for others. They testify to their higher calling in their good third place, "church."

To me, it's logical that people of faith, no matter what their faith, have a higher propensity to find purpose and meaning from life than those with no religious or spiritual grounding.

I'm not an evangelical Christian, and it has been a long time since I regularly attended the Greek Orthodox Church, the faith in which I was raised. But when that plane was circling the Atlanta airport, I knew just what to call the person I was talking to: "God."

I have many deeply spiritual friends, whether or not they are active participants in organized religion. I also have friends who are not so spiritual, or who perhaps seem more uncomfortable with the concept of a Higher Power.

No matter how I analyze it, my friends who index more strongly with spirituality or religious faith seem happiest. It's not a coincidence that they are also the ones who seem to have a calling higher than their own existential needs and gratification.

———

The happiest, most multi-dimensional people I know have found their higher calling, often through pursuing the other five secrets of happiness.

Robert Redford is a wonderful actor, and a great film director, but neither acting nor directing is his higher calling. In creating multiple communities of interest, he found his higher calling to be helping new generations of actors and directors pursue their vision as artists in an environment that will support independent filmmaking. So in that *community* (check), he's *giving back* (check), *expressing* himself (check), and has *found his higher calling* (check!). And I'd say he's definitely *grateful* (check) for meeting *the goals he set for himself* (check).

And it continues. Bono wants to sell records and play to even bigger crowds. He's not a monk, or a saint, and he has an ego. At the same time, I am convinced that Bono doesn't merely want to sell more records, or play to bigger crowds for the sake of some ego boost. Selling more records and playing to bigger crowds is a metric of success, and more practically, the greater his audience, the greater is his ability to achieve his higher calling, which is to use his position to shine the spotlight on desperate people in need.

Happy people can certainly get ego gratification from being successful at what they do. Alex Ovechkin knows he's a great player, and clearly gets pleasure from those amazing goals that end up on the ESPN highlights; it would be unusual bordering on weird if he didn't have an ego. Many of the happiest and most successful people I know are driven to be good at what they do and take pride in it. A pediatric surgeon who on a daily basis pursues his higher calling to save children's lives has a need to be recognized as a great doctor. It doesn't have to take away from his pursuit of a higher calling.

Our bond trader can and should be proud of the fact of that she's financially successfully. So long as that financial success isn't an end in itself, she has room to pursue her higher calling.

The pursuit of a higher calling was for me the last piece to the puzzle of how to become happy. I was educated by Jesuits, and taught that life must have balance, and that proper education addressed both the head and the heart.

And yet, when I graduated from Georgetown, I was a long way from understanding what my higher calling might be.

No one asked me the question at the time, so I don't have an empirical sense of how I might have answered, but it's possible that if immediately after college, I'd been asked what was my higher calling, I might have misunderstood and said that it was to pay off my student loans. Or get a good job. At that point in my life, even with the example of having been mentored by Father Joe Durkin, I might have confused the concept of "pressing need" or "immediate goal" for "higher calling."

If told that my higher calling was more like my purpose in life, I would have come up with a better answer. I probably would have said that it was to do something that made computers more useful for humans in every day life.

If I were being really honest, at that time I probably would have said that my purpose also was to be really successful and make a lot of money.

I succeeded in all those goals. I made a lot of money and saw my vision of computers and televisions converging. I have achieved a majority of the goals that I put on my list of 101 things—the material goals and the more noble ones emanating from my desire to help my family, and help others. Even in my state of relative cluelessness, sitting around the pool after that plane flight and writing up my list, I put on it an entire section entitled "Charities." Still, there was no overarching sense that my life should have purpose and meaning, no higher calling.

Unlike some people, I don't have one specific cause that can be identified as my higher calling. I'm not trying to save Africa, though I made sure AOL was involved in Bono's DATA organization and that we were actively involved in the Live8 concerts. I personally support the broader cause of helping Africa through charitable efforts such as PlayPumps International and YouthAIDS. Yet there is no way that you could say my higher calling is to help Africa.

I'm not trying to save independent filmmaking, though SnagFilms surely will help non-fiction filmmakers fulfill their dream of having their films find an audience. The concept of filmanthropy is something I really believe in, and put my money where my mouth is, but filmanthropy *per se* is not my higher calling.

There are many causes that I support. As someone with high bandwidth and broad interests, my higher calling couldn't be limited to a single thing. Discovering this along the way was an important milestone.

On my journey to happiness, the moment I felt I had really succeeded in becoming a happy person was when I finally had a clear sense of my higher calling in life.

Having been given a second chance, I have worked to live my life without regret. I made up a list of 101 goals to achieve before I died, and I have only a handful or so left to cross off.

This book has been written in partial fulfillment of that higher calling—to share the ability to pursue happiness with as many people as possible.

I've stated throughout the book that I believe certain tenets are held in common by happy people, and that by actively managing your life to adopt these traits, you will be happier, and more successful.

The exception to this formula is finding your higher calling. Oh, I absolutely believe that finding your higher calling will drive your happiness. And I certainly believe that happy people are more successful, and that happiness is the driver, not the other way around.

It's just that there is no success dividend to finding your higher calling. Finding your higher calling *is* the highest calling; it is something you do for its own sake.

Your higher calling is the answer to these questions: what service are you here to perform? On a planet with billions of people, why do you matter?

If you're a doctor, your higher calling is saving lives. Helping people. Alleviating pain. For the rest of us who play less clearly beneficial roles in society, you can find your higher calling in deep contemplation of what you most wish to be known by. Our bond trader wishes to be known by the legacy that she will leave her children: to be happy, well-adjusted adults.

To illustrate my point, let me offer the real-life example of someone I have known for more thirty years: Bill Gates. After perhaps the most successful business career in the second half of the 20th Century, I think Bill Gates has found his higher calling. It wasn't to become the richest man in the world. It wasn't to make sure that there was "a computer on every desk and in every home," though that clearly was Microsoft's mission, and certainly was the business goal Bill pursued relentlessly when he was that company's CEO. I believe Bill Gates is today a happier man because he has found his higher calling through the Gates Foundation. In giving back on an epic scale, Bill and Melinda Gates are doing more than any two people on Earth to vaccinate children against disease, and to take on other such difficult causes.

My higher calling is to leave more than I have taken . . . to be loved, not needed . . . to touch lives and be a positive force in life and business.

What today I am striving for is to ensure that when my time comes, if someone actually tallies up the column of what I've gotten out of life—a wonderful wife and two really great children, a fulfilling business career, the love and friendship of many people, more than my share of excitement and fun and, sure, genuine wealth—it will pale in comparison to what I've given back, through charity, and my time and energy, on behalf of the good things I promised God I would do, if I only I were granted a chance to get back on that tarmac in one piece.

I'm still a young man, and knock on wood, still have a long time before that accounting is due.

There is still a lot of good that I can and will do.

There still are businesses that I want to create. In the final chapter of this book I'll outline how I look at the investments I make, and the kinds of companies in which I'll be involved.

I haven't quite completed my list of 101 goals. The Washington Caps haven't won the Stanley Cup. And remember, I won't have finished my 101 goals until I've taken a ride into outer space.

Ever since I discovered my higher calling, I've been working hard on fulfilling it. I'll do so for the rest of my life. It makes me really happy.

Everything I intend to do with my life is consistent with this creed: to leave more than I have taken. To be loved, not needed.

It's the ultimate measurement in the business of happiness.

A Listing of Ways to Discover Your Higher Calling:

1. Seek it. Spend some time reflecting on your experiences. When have you felt joy or fulfilled in what you were doing? What gives you the greatest pleasure?
2. What is it that you do that you find ennobling—that lifts your spirit and makes you feel that doing this is why you were put on Earth?
3. Consider your beliefs about God. What does He want from you? What service are you supposed to perform?
4. Develop a habit of prayer to stay in touch with God.
5. What special gifts or abilities do you have? It could be as simple as the ability to make people feel at ease or as complicated as the ability to rebuild a car.
6. Ask those close to you what they appreciate about you and what they consider your higher calling.
7. What did you want to do for the world when you were a child?
8. Work hard and develop discipline so you have the freedom to discover and pursue your higher calling. Speed is your friend—by doing routine tasks quickly, you will have the leisure for better things.
9. Who do you admire? Why? Is it because you feel a similar higher calling?
10. In one phrase or sentence, how would you like to be remembered?

Chapter Seventeen

The Business of
Happiness

When I left AOL in early 2007, after it was clear that the professional managers dispatched from Time Warner really had no interest in my perspective on the business, I felt just a little bit of panic. For thirteen years, being called an "AOL executive" was the easiest shorthand to describe who I was. To some people, I was synonymous with the company. When it became clear that, rather than heading toward AOL headquarters in Dulles, Virginia, my car was going to head each morning toward D.C., I braced myself for a second reckoning. Thankfully, it didn't arrive.

On a certain level, leaving AOL at age fifty put me in a position similar to millions of American men who, for a myriad of reasons, find themselves in the prime of life but separated from the company around which their professional identity is entwined. I was primed for a so-called mid-life crisis. Obviously, I wasn't in the same boat as a laid-off worker from GM, and I really don't want to imply that I faced any kind of hardship. I'm the one who initiated the process of leaving

AOL, when I told Time Warner in June of 2006 that I wanted to retire from active management. Still, leaving AOL at that moment felt like I was being launched into the great unknown.

When Jon Miller was fired in November 2006, virtually the entire senior management of AOL chose to leave the company. Within a few weeks, the executive floor of the AOL headquarters emptied out. The new team arrived but basically hid in their offices. It was clear they had no gratitude for having been given the assignment, and they bad-mouthed the staff and everything we'd accomplished. They didn't seem to understand that by having grown the AOL Audience business to become a $2 billion annual revenue enterprise, as our revenues grew—as we reached such scale—so did our margins. We had the momentum we needed to leave behind the even higher margin, ulti-mately doomed subscription business. We had developed buzz, an esprit de corps, and a higher calling. We had a mission to serve the world's largest and most engaged audience. Time Warner didn't care about any of that, and botched their chance to keep the momentum going. They either didn't seem to understand, or were willfully igno-rant of the fact that in the competitive world of the Internet, compa-nies need to invest in content and/or functionality in order to grow their business; they must continually evolve, not just hang on in an attempt to milk profits. In the winter of 2007, the new Time Warner team seemed far more interested in squeezing that last dime out of the Access business we were winding down than investing in future growth. It was a good moment to leave, but I nonetheless feared the future.

I needn't have. A few weeks into the New Year, *Nanking* was nomi-nated for the Grand Jury Prize at Sundance, on its way to winning mul-tiple awards including a Peabody, an Emmy, and on some levels the sweetest of all: the Humanitarian Award at the Hong Kong International Film Festival.

I was quickly involved in multiple roles. I was a film producer, having some months earlier committed to *Kicking It*, an extraordinary story about redemption through sports. I was an investor in "double-bottom line" companies like Revolution Money, which I describe as "PayPal meets Mastercard without the high fees." The idea of filmanthropy was germinating within, and having built a free documentary service at AOL called True Stories, it seemed clear a business could be crafted breaking nonfiction films out of the vaults they were locked in and offered to audiences online. It also increasingly seemed possible that such a business could be launched as a means of connecting audiences to the causes that motivated documentary filmmakers to make their movies in the first place. The "Aha!" moment in which SnagFilms materialized was near.

Far from having a reckoning in which I needed to change the way I was living my life, I found myself happy and purposeful, and it wasn't an accident. For years, I'd been telling friends and audiences alike about the tenets I believed happy people had in common with one another. Interestingly to me, no longer having my daily routine, as well as my identity, wrapped around the same office building I'd entered every morning for more than a decade, it felt like I now had a better laboratory in which to test whether the happiness model I believed in so much really worked. I was the guinea pig, and the experiment was successful. While I'd left AOL with anxiety, it wasn't a surprise to pretty quickly discover that the formula I'd been telling people about really worked, even at a moment of great uncertainty in my life.

I didn't have to go into the office at AOL anymore, but I was no less organized about my life and my activities. I wrote lists and set goals.

Not being Vice Chairman of AOL enabled me to take on more speaking engagements, and frankly, gave me an opportunity I hadn't had in years to express myself without thinking about my "corporate" responsibilities. I stepped up my blogging, and my communicating with various communities of interest, from the fan base of the Washington Capitals to groups and organizations I was linked to on Facebook and Twitter. Even as reports came from friends remaining at AOL that the new team there was clueless about the power of the AOL community and seemed determined to undo many of the things we'd done to build the Audience business, I was detached and at the same grateful for all of the opportunities I had at AOL during the years I was there.

I was grateful for having had the opportunity in 1999 to form Lincoln Holdings as the vehicle for purchasing the Washington Capitals and my other sports team interests. My partners in Lincoln Holdings—Jack Davies, Raul Fernandez, Dick Patrick, Richard Fairbank, Sheila Johnson, Richard Kay, Jeong Kim, Mark Lerner, Michele Freeman, and George Stamas—are friends with whom I really enjoy seeing games, participating in charitable activities, and hanging out. They are successful people who essentially subscribe to the same tenets of happiness that I do.

I was grateful every day for my family, and the opportunity I now had to be with them. My son Zach was applying to college, and my daughter Elle was in high school. I realized how special this time was for Lynn and me, and was grateful to be able to linger at home in the morning and come home earlier at night.

***

As 2007 flowed into 2008, I realized I had never been happier. After struggling in the early part of the season, the Caps went on an incred-

ibly exciting run, winning the Southeastern Conference of the NHL
and crashing into the playoffs. We took the Philadelphia Flyers to a
Game seven in the first round of the Stanley Cup, and even though we
lost in overtime, we'd created joy and happiness for our fans. For the
first time, our fans really saw the fruits of our effort to transform the
team into a potential Stanley Cup champion. People who had doubt-
ed the strategy we'd announced of making the team worse so that we
could then make it better now began to get it.

I was living my life according to a formula that I understood from
empirical evidence was more than simply relevant for personal happiness. It could actually serve as a filter, as a way of looking at institutions—businesses in particular—and determining whether they were
"happy" or not. It could serve as a screen to determine what kinds of
businesses and institutions I should invest in with my time, money,
and energy.

The businesses that I would create, invest in, or serve on the Boards
of had to meet certain requirements. Chief Financial Officers talk
about the "hurdle rate of return" they need before they invest in a
product or a service. I had a different way of looking at the businesses
in which I'd get involved. They had to create happiness and serve
some larger purpose or have a higher calling than merely "maximizing
shareholder value." For me to be involved, there really did have to be
a double-bottom line.

Implicit in the concept of a "double-bottom line" is that the company is geared toward profitability. I'm not a socialist or a sap.
Capitalist enterprises have to be geared toward making money or they
don't survive.

In the case of, say, the Washington Capitals, maybe we could spread
more happiness if we kept our ticket prices (among the lowest in the
NHL) where they were, or better yet, lowered them. But that would

quickly lead to our lacking the financial wherewithal to put a Stanley
Cup contender on the ice. In order to create revenue sufficient to
win—which would make our fans really happy—we needed higher
ticket prices, not lower ticket prices, so we raised them. Revenue
growth is the *sine qua non* of a business able to survive and fulfill its
higher calling.

To me there also needs to be something more than profitability for
its own sake.

There are some pretty sober, serious business people who agree
with me on this. To those who believe that business is entirely about
maximizing profits, Bertie Charles Forbes—founder of *Forbes*, the
business magazine which calls itself the "capitalist tool," and scion of
the notably capitalist Forbes family—had this to say: "Business was
originated to produce happiness." I couldn't have said it better myself.
Moreover, I've developed a way of looking at businesses that I believe
is consistent with that ethos.

See if you recognize this filter.

All businesses, to some degree or another, have goals—goal setting
is a given. For me to invest in a business, it has to serve multiple communities of interest. Investors, shareholders, and financial analysts
are one community, but they're not the only one. Other communities
include customers, employees, and the physical community in which
the business operates.

The businesses in which I'll get involved have either to serve as a
means for others to express themselves, or must express themselves in
a clear and transparent way to all of the audiences they serve.

Businesses in my portfolio need to have a good rate of return, but
should exhibit a degree of empathy, and express their gratitude to
their customers, investors, and the communities in which they're

involved by being good citizens, lacking in arrogance. They should in some way give back to their community and to society, either through the product or service they create, or once they've achieved some degree of profitability, through philanthropic activities within the community in which they do business. They should have some kind of higher calling beyond simply maximizing their return on investment.

One paradigm for this kind of business is SnagFilms. SnagFilms serves multiple communities—documentary filmmakers who want their films to be seen by an audience and to be compensated for this; the nonfiction film industry, which needs a new distribution model; the audience who wants to see some of these great documentaries, but would have to travel to distant cities to attend film festivals or maybe set their TIVO for 4:00 a.m. in order to capture the movie on an obscure cable channel. Individuals that want to support a cause, but don't have the time or money, can now "donate their pixels"—literally opening a virtual movie theater on their own online real estate.

SnagFilms not only creates an outlet for filmmakers to have their documentary—their medium of personal expression—viewed by an audience, but because anyone can snag a widget with a particular film and put it on his or her own Facebook page, even the viewer can express himself, by associating with a particular movie. Filmanthropy is built upon the concept that documentary films shine a light on injustice or promote a particular cause, and by having SnagFilms exist as the living embodiment of filmanthropy in action, the continuum of empathy-gratitude-giving back is baked into the business model. It is a business that revolves around its higher calling. It isn't yet profitable, and so it's not fully actualized, but we're getting there, and when we do, I really think SnagFilms will be a model company.

While SnagFilms is the paradigm, there are strong parallels in other companies in which I play a role. I'm Chairman of Clearspring Technologies, which builds the widgets used by SnagFilms and literally hundreds of thousands of other companies. Clearspring is the leading provider of widget creation and distribution, and enables content to be shared for free across communities and networks. "Sharing," "free," "communities and networks": those words should offer a sense of why I'm so excited about Clearspring.

I'm also chairman of Revolution Money, which Steve Case and its founder Jason Hogg helped build into the fastest growing alternative payments company, dramatically lowering the cost of credit card transactions while also enabling users to transfer funds within their various communities. As the final pages in this book were being written, it was announced that American Express Company was acquiring Revolution Money for $312 million, and that I would become a special advisor on digital matters to Ken Chenault, CEO of American Express. The acquisition of Revolution Money is a tremendous validation of the business model Steve, Jason, and all of us developed beginning in 2007. Understanding that interchanges for credit card purchases were too high, and that the technology for credit card transactions was comparatively antiquated, Revolution Money set out to significantly improve the payments system around which so much commerce revolves. The business model benefited merchants and consumers alike, driving down costs and increasing efficiency. Sophisticated investors understood what we were trying to do and helped us fund development, and American Express understood how much momentum we were gathering.

Leo Durocher once famously said that "nice guys finish last." I think that's exactly wrong when it comes to happy companies and business success. The acquisition of Revolution Money, from which Steve and I, and other members of the team, have all made a significant return on our investment, shows that happy companies can finish first, or at least be very successful.

Both Clearspring and Revolution Money index across the model of empowering communities and personal expression. Both are motivated by a higher calling that has more dimensions than simply making a CFO happy by hitting his ROI target. Both are happy companies that have done very well. It isn't an accident.

As time went on, I began thinking about well-known companies that seemed to operate along the happiness tenets. After all, companies can be like people. The best companies develop and morph like individuals. They face reckonings and can change their outcomes by actively managing to new goals. All companies operate within multiple communities, but it is the mark of the great ones that they can offer happiness to their customers, investors, employees, and the physical communities in which they work. It is the mark of great companies that they don't over-index in favor of one community over another. "Maximizing shareholder value" almost by definition is voting in favor of the primacy of a single community (shareholders), possibly at the expense of other communities.

Some companies express themselves clearly and are transparent, others are misleading and opaque. Some companies are in the business of empowering others to express themselves, and are built upon the communities such expression spawns. Some companies show empathy and gratitude—for their workforce, their customers, and multiple communities. Others are arrogant and weight the scale in favor of management or their shareholders at the expense of others.

Some companies have a higher calling, and the Forbes ethos of creating happiness is embedded in their DNA. Others make no one happy, and go out of business, usually having created real damage along the way: to their workforce, their environment, their shareholders, and their customers.

I began thinking about companies I knew well and began wondering whether the happiness model might be a predictor of whether a company would succeed or fail over time. To me, placed against a screen of companies that, for one reason or another, I am interested in, I find it's actually pretty remarkable how well my happiness model holds up. There is, however, one added dimension. I have always been struck by the critical role that founders play in successful companies. Many great companies are either dependent upon, if not the founder himself, at least his or her guiding vision. At the same time, whenever I hear an analyst say, when talking about a young founder-driven company, "They have a great vision, but now professional managers need to come in and run the business," I have the urge to flee.

So in thinking about whether my happiness model works for companies or institutions, in addition to trying to determine whether they observe the same tenets held in common by happy people, I am also interested in whether a founder is still in place, or at least in whether his or her vision remains a driver of the way the institution operates (e.g. Walmart or The Walt Disney Company).

It's for this reason I track companies like Apple and Starbucks. They are founder-driven companies that faced a reckoning, and saw their original leader return with a plan. They are, to a very real extent, built upon managing multiple communities. Starbucks is in the business of creating communities around their stores, while managing relationships with thousands of coffee growers around the world. Apple assiduously manages multiple communities of interest, from applications developers to its customers. It's not an accident that there are 100,000+ apps for iPhones, a platform and product I absolutely love.

I closely follow companies like Google, Facebook, and Twitter, not just because I'm someone who's spent his adult life working in the online medium. I watch how well Firefox is doing and root for it! My interest in Google isn't only because I am friends with the Google guys, was a pre-IPO investor in the company, and helped foster both of the very big deals that AOL and Google did together. I'm not just interested in Facebook and Twitter because I see them carrying the baton that AOL dropped when it merged with Time Warner nearly a decade ago. I closely follow Google, Facebook, and Twitter because these are companies that fit my happiness model. Google's higher calling is simply expressed: to organize the world's information and make it universally accessible and useful. Googles motto is "Don't be evil." Google enables its employees to express themselves through "20 percent time"—the one day each week they can work on a project that inspires them personally. Twitter and Facebook are both built upon a platform of personal expression revolving around communities. Very early in its life as a public company, Google began to give back through the Google Foundation; Facebook empowers nonprofits to connect to others, and individuals expressing solidarity for a cause is something millions of its users do each day online.

I track how a company like Amazon taps into its community of users and enables them to express themselves as critics of products. They let the wisdom of crowds suggest what album or book you might like based on the choice you just made. I try to keep tabs on whether a company like eBay, which has seen a decline in its business, has really faced its reckoning and pivoted from it. I look to see if it is building itself back into what it once was by reconnecting to the spirit of community that was an early driver of its success.

When I see that Ford is succeeding even as GM is failing, I remember that Ford maintained a link to its founding family and founding vision, for all these years, and that the Ford family has maintained their ownership of the Detroit Lions, wrapping the company name around a community icon. Is that the whole story, the biggest difference between Ford and GM? No, of course it isn't. Nonetheless, thinking of the professional managers who have run GM for so many years, while remembering that William Clay Ford, Jr. was responsible for recruiting Alan Mulally to become Ford's CEO gives me just enough of a glimpse of the two companies to begin to understand which one is happy—and successful—and which one isn't.

I think about a company like Microsoft, and how little it has ever seemed to embrace the tenets of happiness. Perhaps I'm just fighting old wars, but it has always seemed to me that Microsoft's vision of a computer on every desk and in every home seemed less about the higher calling of empowering users than about the low road of extending its monopoly, no matter what. While unarguably successful, it's also notorious within the business community for being an unhappy company. Rather than invest in Microsoft, I'd much rather invest, like Warren Buffet did, in the Bill and Melinda Gates Foundation. The Gates Foundation will, over the long haul, succeed far more than Microsoft is likely to, because it is based entirely on the tenets of happiness: systematic plans built upon reckonings in social systems like vaccinations against disease and inner-city high school performance; empathy, gratitude, and giving back; a higher calling.

For that matter, I'd rather invest in Oprah Winfrey than the top ten performers on the New York Stock Exchange. Oprah communicates about her ongoing reckoning with her weight. She is a world-class connector among different communities. Oprah's Book Club has done more to help writers who have expressed themselves find an audience than perhaps the entire publishing industry combined. Oprah is a very real human being, but operates like a secular saint in the way she communicates her own higher calling. It, of course, makes complete sense that The Oprah Winfrey Network is affiliated with a happy company like Discovery Communications, whose founder, John Hendricks, completely understands the six secrets of happiness outlined in this book.

I find myself continually evaluating companies, institutions, and individuals by whether or not I perceive them to be "happy companies." Someday I intend to publish The Ted's Take Index, and track whether the twenty or so "happy companies" I will put on it outperform the market as a whole. I'm pretty confident they will.

In 2008, I began thinking seriously about writing this book. I evaluated the decision to do so on whether or not it would help my jouney towards happiness. From the outset, I envisioned the book as a means of building a community around the tenets of happiness I had identified. I saw this book living on in virtual form beyond its physical publication, envisioning a website, forum, and wiki in which people could share their journey of happiness with others. From the outset, I saw *The Business of Happiness* as a potential hub of a community of people interested in sharing ideas concerning happiness. This made me happy.

Writing a book, of course, is one of the ultimate acts of personal expression. Having an outlet for personal expression is a tenet of happiness, so naturally, writing this book would make me happy—notwithstanding, as all writers will tell you, the fact that writing a book can make you miserable en route to that happy moment when the torture of writing concludes.

I wanted to write this book out of a sense of gratitude for the perspective I've gained along the way. Expressing myself on the topic of happiness is a way of giving back and helps fulfill my higher calling of leaving the world with more than I have taken. Well before the book is published, merely having written the manuscript has increased my level of happiness.

As this is being written, the 2009-2010 hockey season has begun, and the Washington Capitals are off to a great start. It's still early in the season, but the Caps have pretty consistently been in first in the NHL East. It certainly appears that they're a happy team, and they'll be successful because of their happiness.

One very sad event as I was wrapping up this book was the passing of Mr. Abe Pollin, who was a friend, hero, and role model. Although his passing now sets in process an opportunity for my partners and me to acquire the portions of the Washington Wizards and the Verizon Center arena that we don't currently own, it's unknown at this moment what the future will bring. In addition to my family and Fr. Joe Durkin, I am dedicating *The Business of Happiness* to Mr. Pollin.

I've just seen an early cut of *A Fighting Chance*, the movie about Kyle Maynard's life that I'm producing, and I think it's really good. ESPN has agreed to broadcast the film to their worldwide audience in 2010. Everything's coming up roses, as they say, and I'm really grateful. I'm a happy guy.

I left AOL just under three years ago apprehensive about what the future would bring, but determined to try testing my tenets of happiness in everything I did. Three years later, an objective scorecard would indicate the approach I'm taking works. The Washington Capitals have been the Southeast Division Champions of the NHL two years in a row, sell out every game, are the fastest growing team in the league, and have the highest fan satisfaction. The Mystics are growing the size of their audience and made the playoffs. My third film will soon join the first two, which were the recipients of multiple awards. SnagFilms and filmanthropy are proving to be a highly successful concept, Clearspring Technologies is thriving, and Revolution Money just sold for a lot of money. All this is happening in the face of the worst economy in seventy years.

Humbly, when I think about my success in the 1980s with LIST, in the 1990s with Redgate and AOL, and now with Revolution Money, among other things, I have to conclude that the beliefs I hold about the correlation between happiness and success have some validity. It's one of the reasons I felt confident enough—and in fact, compelled— to write this book, the writing of which is one more important element in my post-AOL happiness resume.

And yet the thing I'm happiest about right now is not that the book is finished, though that provides me with a great sense of relief. The thing I'm happiest about this autumn is that my friend Walter Scott Lovell got a job. Knowing him makes me happy. Knowing that he's been hired for a job makes me *really* happy.

Walter Scott is a homeless ex-offender with a prosthetic leg. He became a Caps fan by watching the team's games on the big television outside the Verizon Center. While 18,000 sat in relative comfort inside the arena, Walter Scott sat through the winter months outside in his wheelchair cheering the team on.

Three or four years ago, I'd never met a homeless person, other than people in the street who maybe I helped as I walked by. But in 2007, I got involved in the issue of homelessness when two filmmakers told me about the movie they were making, and it was such a remarkable story, I agreed to produce their film. *Kicking It* is about the Homeless World Cup, which is exactly what it sounds like: a soccer competition among teams from around the world, comprising individuals who happen to be homeless. It's an extraordinary film, and making it literally opened my eyes to the people on the street—those who might sit in their wheelchairs when it's nineteen degrees Fahrenheit outside, watching the Caps on the big screen outside the Verizon Center.

After *Kicking It* came out, I got involved in a hands-on way. Lynn, Zach, Elle, and I made a significant contribution to the D.C. Central Kitchen, and rather than give Christmas presents to friends and colleagues, we let them know we'd made a contribution in their name. In 2008 and 2009, we helped bring the Street Soccer USA championship to Washington—the championship that would determine which of the teams of homeless men would represent the United States in the next Homeless World Cup. I got involved in supporting the National Law Center on Homelessness and Poverty.

So last winter, when a Capitals season ticket holder emailed me that there was a homeless man in a wheelchair who sat outside the arena watching every game, I was curious. I went outside one night, met Walter Scott Lovell, and invited him to come see the game in our box.

Walter Scott lost his leg in a car accident. He committed crimes and went to jail. When he got out of jail, his wife had left him, and as a one-legged ex-offender he found it hard to get a job, and it didn't take long for him to be living on the streets.

I got Walter some clothes and some food, and pretty soon, I started getting email from Walter. As a homeless man, the first thing he would do when the doors opened in D.C. libraries was go in and use the computers. So I got to know him, and learned his story, and I had a lot of empathy for him. One day I invited Walter to see a Washington Mystics game, and it was pretty difficult sitting next to him, because Walter Scott smelled really bad. I said to him, "Walter, you stink."

He said, "No shit. It's 100 degrees out. And then it rains. What do you expect? I'm homeless. Of course I stink."

We got to talking about his predicament. Of course he stank, and naturally no one would hire him, not just because of that. As Walter Scott explained to me, the first question on a job application is, "What is your address?" People with no fixed address don't get called back for second interviews. How can a homeless person get a job if he doesn't have an address? It's a Catch-22: can't get an apartment without a job, can't get a job without an apartment.

I got Walter an apartment and I paid his rent, so he could have a roof over his head, a shower and importantly, *an address*. I bought him some clothes, and a new prosthetic leg. I arranged for him to get training at the D.C. Central Kitchen. A few weeks ago, Walter Scott Lovell was hired for the first time since he left prison.

I have a lot to be grateful for, and I know it.

Yet, few are the days when my mind doesn't replay those lyrics from the Talking Heads: "And you may ask yourself/ How did I get here?"

I got from a pretty rough neighborhood in Brooklyn, New York to a pretty great life in Washington, D.C. I have the love of family and friends, and there are multiple communities that are important to me, and in which I'm important. I'm able to express myself, as a writer and blogger and filmmaker. I'm able to express my empathy, and gratitude, and give something back.

Finishing this book has made me happy, and I hope that reading it helps you to get on your path to happiness and success. Finishing this book is really only the second best thing that's happened to me this fall. You see, working with Walter Scott Lovell has helped make him happier—and more successful. Which makes me happier, and more successful. The model works.

So what are you waiting for? Write your list, and get going.

Acknowledgments

Writing this book was an outlet for self-expression—one of the six core tenets of happiness I've shared in the previous pages. And sure enough, it made me happy. Yet, at the same time, writing a book like this violates one of my core beliefs. A principle in business and especially in sports is that "there is no I in team." Though it's a cliché, it's also a useful reminder that all of us owe thanks to those who've made our happiness and success possible.

Every day, I'm grateful that my wife and children, Lynn, Zach, and Elle, are the central characters in my most important community. I'm grateful to my parents for their many sacrifices on my behalf, and for their profoundly positive impact on my life. And I love my mother-in-law, Maya Peterson and pay tribute to my father-in-law, Richard Peterson.

When it comes to *The Business of Happiness*, I want to thank Jeff Carneal, Harry Crocker, Marji Ross, Anneke Green, and Emily Thiessen at Eagle Publishing, who have been wonderful to work with. Laney

Becker and Jeff Kleinman at Folio Literary Management were essential partners in conceptualizing and finding a publisher for the book.

I've worked with my friend and collaborator John Buckley for more than eight years, and the book is an outgrowth of conversations John and I have had since approximately 2004, when we began writing together. John's higher calling is as a novelist, and I look forward to the day when he can write full time.

So many people have helped me get to this point in my life that I am going to organize my thanks by geography and phases of my life, and how I manage my communities of interest. Invariably there will be people to whom I owe a debt of gratitude who, for reasons owing entirely to my faulty recollection, I'll miss, and for that I apologize. I want to shout out to and thank the following people for the impact they've had on my life, and for making me happy.

From my life in Brooklyn: Joe Cucco, Kevin Fallon, the Grado family, Mark Rivera, Joanne Manos and Jimmy Manos, Jr., Agnes Varis, Bob Melendi, the DeAngelos family, the Vavas family, and my departed childhood best friend, Anthony Pisano.

From my life in Lowell before college: the entire Koumantzelis family, the Vergados family, the Mastas family, Steve Panagiotakos and family, Evan Coravos, Sam Hantzis, Senator Paul Tsongas, George Stamas, the Behrakis family, the Nikitas family, Jim Shannon, the Tatsios family, and the Demoulas family.

From Georgetown: Bill Macdonald, Michael Jacobs, Jonathon Howard, Laurence Armour, Dr. Hugh Cloke, Dr. Dorothy Brown, Jack DeGioia, John Thompson, John Thompson III, Emmett Curran, and Maria Shriver.

From my days in Lowell after college: the Hatem family, Dr. An Wang and family, John F. Cunningham, Andy Stevens, Dwight

Holmberg, Jay Battin, Harry Viens, General Costas Caraganis, Diane Staley, Michael Minigan, and Jack Connors.

From my early career before AOL: Vincent T. Pica and family, the Weibel family, the Oglethorpe family, Jeff Parsons, the Richard Franco family, Alfred Mandel, Steve Franzese, Bill Earthman, Allessandro Piol, Tom Pace, Charlie Bradshaw, Ferguson Peters, John Dobbs, Ken Puttuck, Dan Richardson, Jim Fitzsimons, Tim Draper, and everyone who worked at Redgate Communications.

From AOL: Steve Case, Jean Case, Jim Kimsey, Jan Brandt, Len Leader, Jack Davies, Audrey Weil, Bob Pittman, Barry Schuler, Mike Connors, Matt Korn, Barry Appelman, David Gang, Donn Davis, Jim Bankoff, both Mike Kellys, Kevin Conroy, Jon Miller, Lynda Clarizio, Joe Redling, Scott Ferber, Jason Calacanis, Randy Boe, John Borthwick, Adam Slutsky, Norman Koo, Neil Smit, Scott Falconer, and Andrew and Nancy Jarecki.

From the Washington community: all my partners and their families from Lincoln Holdings; the Pollin family, the Barris family, Miles Gilburne and Nina Zolt, Rick Allen, the Shriver Family.

Friends and business associates who make me happy: David Rubenstein, Donald Graham, Mario Marino, David Stern, Steve Greenberg, Terry Morris, Ken Chenault, Micah Green, Hooman Radfar, Jason Hogg, Trish Roddy, Tige Savage, David Golden, Nigel Morris, Brad Keywell, Eric Lefkofsky, Andrew Mason, Jim Hornthal, David Pottruck, Robert Redford, Ashley Judd, Suzie Kay, Mike Curtin, Jose Andres, Ellen Folts, Jim Robinson, Woody Harrelson, Bill Guttentag, Dan Sturman, Dom Salvemini, Jeff Bezos, Pete Peterson and his wonderful wife, Joan, Bob Kettler, Russ Ramsey, Tommy Gahan, Ed Mathias, Ed Quinn, John Walsh, Dan Akerson,George Bodenheimer, John Skipper, Steve Burke, Jeff Shell, Sergey Brin, Ben Bradlee, Mark Ein, the late Josh Freeman,

Bobby Friedman, Matt Wolf, Richard Hanlon, Michael Hendrickson, Big Ken Holden, Kendra Holden, Pam and Dennis Bailey, Spike Lee, John Doerr, the Maloof Brothers, Mark Cuban, Wendi Murdoch, Sheila Nevins, Chris and Lorraine Wallace, the Pedas Brothers, George Pelacanos, Frank Quattrone, Howard Schultz, Steve Jobs, the late Brandon Tartikoff, Chris Tavlirides, George Tenent, the late Jack Valenti, the Rales Brothers, Jimmy Lynn, Jason Hogg, Hooman Radfar, Tige Savage, Nigel Morris, David Golden, and Tim Armstrong.

From the Washington Capitals and Washington Mystics organizations and related parties: George McPhee, Bruce Boudreau, Gary Bettman, Bill Daly, Greg Bibb, Donna Orender, Angela Taylor, Julie Plank, the Ovechkin family, and all of the players and employees of the Washington Capitals and the Washington Mystics, and of course—our magnificent and passionate fan base.

I also want to thank Ann Nordeen, Stephen Bouairi, Trish Roddy, George Stamas, and Kit O'Connor who are dedicated on a daily basis to keeping me on track.

And finally, a profound thank you to everyone who reads this book.

Ted's Life List

I. Family Matters

1. Fall in love and get married ☑
2. Have a healthy son ☑
3. Have a healthy daughter ☑
4. Take care of mother/father ☑
5. Take care of in-laws ☑
6. Take care of extended family ☑
7. Have grandchildren ☐
8. Have great-grandchildren ☐
9. Leave trusts for family members ☑
10. Leave all financial matters in great shape for family members upon passing on ☐
11. Have children become individuals and self-actualized staying loving within the family ☑

II. Financial Matters

12. Pay off college debts ☑

13. Net worth of ten million dollars, after taxes ☑

14. Net worth of one hundred million dollars, after taxes ☑

15. Net worth of one billion dollars, after taxes ☐

16. Zero personal debt for family ☑

17. Make ten million dollars on an outside investment ☑

18. Become a partner in a venture capital fund ☑

19. Create one billion dollars in value with an outside investment ☐

20. Start a company and sell it ☑

21. Conduct an IPO on a company I founded ☑

22. Create world's largest media company ☑

III. Possessions

23. Own a beach home that stays in family ☑

24. Own a jet ☑

25. Own a yacht ☑

26. Own a convertible Porsche or Mercedes Benz ☑

27. Own a mountain home that stays in the family ☐

28. Own a great piece of art ☑

29. Own a great personal collection of watches ☑

30. Own a Ferrari ☑

31. Restore an antique auto ☑

32. Own a restaurant or club ☑

33. Support someone who makes a great breakthrough in science or art ☐

IV. Charities

34. Change someone's life via a charity ☑

35. Give one million dollars to Georgetown University/
sit on Board ☑

36. Major impact on a children's charity ☑

37. Start a family charity foundation ☑

38. Give away one hundred million dollars in lifetime ☐

39. Have a building/perpetual memorial named
after the family ☑

V. Sports

40. Own a sports franchise (basketball, hockey or football) ☑

41. Win a world championship ☐

42. Attend a Superbowl with Dolphins or Redskins ☑

43. Attend a Final Four with Georgetown ☑

44. Attend a World Series with Yankees ☑

45. Meet Mickey Mantle ☑

46. Catch a foul ball ☑

47. Go to an NBA All-Star Game ☑

48. Go to an NBA Draft ☑

49. Go to an NHL All-Star Game ☑

50. Go to a Capitals Stanley Cup game ☑

51. Go to Olympics ☑

52. Play Augusta ☑

53. Play Pebble Beach ☑

54. Play Cypress Point ☑

55. Play St. Andrews ☐
56. Go to Ryder Cup ☑
57. Go to US Open Golf Tourney ☑
58. Go to World Cup ☐
59. Get a hole-in-one ☐
60. Play in a celebrity golf tournament ☑
61. Go to a US Open Tennis Final ☑
62. Go to baseball All-Star Game ☑
63. Go to a Fantasy Camp ☑
64. Shoot baskets at Madison Square Garden or Boston Garden ☑
65. Go one-on-one with Michael Jordan ☑

VI. Travel

66. Go to Greece ☑
67. Go to Italy ☑
68. Go to Israel/Jerusalem ☑
69. Go to Hawaii ☑
70. Go on safari to Africa ☐
71. Go to London ☑
72. Go to Paris ☑
73. Go to Australia ☑
74. Sail thru Caribbean ☑
75. Sail thru Mediterranean ☑
76. Go to China ☑
77. Go to Brazil ☑
78. Go to Alaska ☑

79. Go to Egypt ☑
80. Go to Bali ☐
81. Go to Tahiti ☐

VII. Stuff

82. Be on cover of a magazine ☑
83. Produce a TV show ☑
84. Go into outerspace ☐
85. Write a book ☑
86. Invent a boardgame ☑
87. Make a movie ☑
88. Win a Grammy/Oscar/Tony/Emmy Award ☑
89. Swim with dolphins ☑
90. Swim with Great White sharks ☐
91. Get an honorary degree ☑
92. Hold elective office ☑
93. Go to White House/Meet President ☑
94. Advise a foreign government ☑
95. Live overseas for one year ☐
96. Go to Oscar ceremonies ☑
97. Go to MTV Awards Show ☑
98. See the Rolling Stones ☑
99. See the Who ☑
100. Take a year sabbatical ☐
101. Sail around the world with family ☐

Appendix B

The Happiness Questionnaire

1. Describe when or where you are most happy.

2. Would the people that know you best—family, friends, coworkers—describe you as a happy person?

3. Do you consider yourself happy...

   A. All of the time

   B. Most of the time

   C. Some of the time

   D. Never?

4. Have you ever compiled a list of your life's goals?

5. If you haven't, do you have in mind a rough list of your life's goals?

6. If you have a list in mind, please share some of your most important life's goals—those you may have already achieved or those you're still striving toward. You can list as few as 2 or as many as 10.

7. Are you on track to accomplish your goals?

8. On a scale of 0–10, with 0 being "not important," and 10 being "extremely important," how important is it that you achieve most of your life's goals?

9. Has there ever been a moment in your life—a health scare, the death of a loved one, a sudden crisis, an unexpected opportunity—when your assessment of your life's goals changed in an instant?

10. If yes, describe the event in fewer than 20 words.

11. Many people operate within multiple communities simultaneously. We have face-to-face contact with family, friends we see often, the co-workers we see every day. We are active participants in organizations, forums, churches and synagogues, teams, community associations, alumni groups, political entities. We participate within virtual communities and networks such as Facebook. Starting with family, friends, and co-workers, list some of the communities in which you are an active participant. You can list as many as 10.

12. Do you believe you participate in more communities of interest than the average person, fewer than the average person, or about the same as the average person?

13. On a 0–10 scale, with 0 being "not important," and 10 being "extremely important," how important is it to your sense of happiness that you participate in such communities?

14. Personal expression can take many forms, from writing a diary to publishing a blog; from being an artist to having unique ways of expressing your individuality. List some of your outlets for personal expression. You can list as few as 2 or as many as 10.

15. On a 0–10 scale, with 1 being "not important," and 10 being "extremely important," how important is it to your sense of happiness that you have one or more outlets for your personal expression?

16. Daily life is busy, and sometimes it is hard to reflect on things that bring us happiness—whether it is the company of our family or friends, or something as simple as a nice day, a beautiful sunset.

Do you consider yourself able to reflect on things that bring you happiness...

A. All of the time

B. Most of the time

C. Some of the time

D. Never?

17. On a 0–10 scale, with 1 being "not important," and 10 being "extremely important," how important is it to be able to step back and reflect on, or show gratitude for, things that make you happy?

18. On a 1–10 scale, with 1 being "not very much," and 10 being "a great deal," how much do you "give back to society," either through charitable contributions or through volunteering your time?

19. On a 1–10 scale, with 1 being "not important," and 10 being "extremely important," how important is it to your sense of happiness that you "give back to society"?

20. Some people believe that they have a higher calling, or that there is a higher purpose to their lives, whether it's the job they do, or the activities they participate in within their community, or in their responsibilities to others. Do you have a sense that there is a higher purpose to your life?

21. If yes, describe your higher calling, or your higher purpose in life, in fewer than 20 words.

22. On a 0–10 scale, with 0 being "not important," and 10 being "extremely important," how important is it to your sense of happiness that you feel you have some kind of higher purpose in life?

23. What makes you happy? You can list as few as 2 conditions, ingredients, or factors, or as many as 10.

24. Are you male or female?

25. What is your age?

26. Optional: Is your annual income:

    A. Under $50,000

    B. Between $50,000 and $100,000

    C. More than $100,000

Index

About the Authors

Photo: Mitchell Layton

Ted Leonsis is an Internet industry pioneer who helped build AOL into a global phenomenon. He is a serial entrepreneur who has built and sold multiple successful businesses over three decades, culminating with the recent sale of Revolution Money to American Express. His sports properties include the NHL's Washington Capitals, the WNBA's Washington Mystics, and a share of the NBA's Washington Wizards and the Verizon Center arena. As a producer of documentaries, his films *Nanking* and *Kicking It* both debuted at the Sundance film festival, and *Nanking* went on to win a Peabody Award and an Emmy. Ted is also the founder and chairman of SnagFilms. Originally from Brooklyn, New York, and later, Lowell, Massachusetts, he now lives in McLean, Virginia, and Vero Beach, Florida, with his wife and two children. Visit his website, www.BusinessOfHappiness.com

John Buckley is the author of the novels *Family Politics* and *Statute of Limitations*. He has held senior positions in three U.S. presidential campaigns, and been the top communications executive at companies including AOL, where for six years he worked closely with Ted Leonsis. He is currently managing director of The Harbour Group, a strategic communications firm, and lives in Washington, D.C., with his wife and son.